Michael Karson

Patterns of Child Abuse
How Dysfunctional Transactions Are Replicated in Individuals, Families, and the Child Welfare System

Pre-publication
REVIEWS,
COMMENTARIES,
EVALUATIONS . . .

"**P**atterns of Child Abuse presents a theoretically compelling analysis of the individual, family, and social service system bases of child abuse. It also provides innovative and convincing recommendations about critically needed revisions in the conceptualization, design, and delivery of interventions. Karson weaves together research and clinical literature and offers a uniquely integrative vision for how child welfare professionals may capitalize on current knowledge about the combined influence of family and culture on child abuse. He provides important insights about how effective preventive programs must involve sensitivity to the racial, social, and ethnic diversity of children and parents.

Karson's book is a watershed event in the understanding of the role of the child-family-culture-professional practice system both in contributing to the incidence of child abuse and, at the same time, in constituting the source of creative means to reduce or prevent it. *Patterns of Child Abuse* is a book of immeasurable value to parents, practitioners, and policymakers concerned with enhancing the life chances of the diverse youth of our nation."

Richard M. Lerner, PhD
Bergstrom Chair in Applied
Developmental Science,
Eliot-Pearson Department
of Child Development,
Tufts University,
Medford, MA

More pre-publication
REVIEWS, COMMENTARIES, EVALUATIONS . . .

"**I**n this new book, Dr. Karson establishes a very high standard for understanding and intervening in the psychological issues surrounding child abuse and presents a rich, textured theory of personality development and family functioning. He develops a sophisticated perspective that integrates a theory of individual psychodynamic functioning within a complex family systems perspective. Dr. Karson first presents a finely articulated picture of the inner landscape of individual family members, each with its unique set of characters, and then identifies the parallels between these patterns and the patterns in the family system. He shows how parental patterns are reproduced in the child and then recreated in the child's adult relationships and family and how they are reiterated not just from family to individual but from generation to generation. Dr. Karson's book brings a welcome level of sophistication, and should be an important resource to professionals working with families."

Heather E. P. Cattell, PhD
Vice President of Research,
The Institute of Personality
and Ability Testing;
Author of *16PF Questionnaire*

"**D**r. Karson has written up unique reflections on fifteen years of consultation to child protective systems. His original, and at times, defiant perspectives challenge many truisms of child welfare and therapeutic practice and thus require the reader to reexamine some central assumptions underlying protective casework and psychotherapy. Karson offers a trenchant analysis of the ways in which 'helpers' in various professions fail to either help child victims or to bring about meaningful change in family systems. Many readers, both therapists and social welfare professionals, will find this work as hard to agree with as it is hard to ignore."

Cynthia Monahon, PsyD
Author of *Children and Trauma:
A Guide for Parents
and Professionals*

"**K**arson's wit and expressiveness transform what might have resulted in merely a dry, businesslike compendium, handbook, or academic treatise into a lively, engaging, well-crafted work. His book is an inspired contribution to the professional, student, and general reader who will be intrigued and benefit from its insights and wisdom. Pulling no punches, the author tells it like it is, refreshingly direct and honest in his appraisals of the roles and responsibilities of abused children, their families, and the social welfare and court systems, as well as professional caregivers assigned to their treatment. He succeeds in being constructively critical without sacrificing the inevitable complexities involved in effective treatment and management issues. No one interested in what may well be the major public health epidemic of our time in terms of its long-term consequences for our society can afford to pass up the opportunity to read this enlightening work."

Howard Wolowitz, PhD
Professor Emeritus
Psychology Department,
University of Michigan,
Ann Arbor

Patterns of Child Abuse
How Dysfunctional Transactions
Are Replicated in Individuals, Families,
and the Child Welfare System

Patterns of Child Abuse
How Dysfunctional Transactions Are Replicated in Individuals, Families, and the Child Welfare System

Michael Karson

HMTP

The Haworth Maltreatment and Trauma Press®
An Imprint of The Haworth Press, Inc.
New York • London • Oxford

Published by

The Haworth Maltreatment and Trauma Press®, an imprint of The Haworth Press, Inc., 10 Alice Street, Binghamton, NY 13904-1580.

Cover design by Marylouise E. Doyle.

Library of Congress Cataloging-in-Publication Data

Karson, Michael.
    Patterns of child abuse : how dysfunctional transactions are replicated in individuals, families, and the child welfare system / Michael Karson.
      p. cm.
    Includes bibliographical references and index.
    ISBN 0-7890-0739-8 (hardcover : alk. paper)—ISBN 0-7890-1588-9 (softcover : alk. paper)
    1. Child abuse. 2. Abused children—Services for. I. Title.

HV6626.5 .K37 2001
362.76'8—dc21

00-049475

For Sam

Behold the child . . .
See, where 'mid work of his own hand he lies . . .
With light upon him from his father's eyes!

Wordsworth

CONTENTS

ABOUT THE AUTHOR

Michael Karson, PhD, JD, is a licensed psychologist and a Diplomate in Clinical Psychology of the American Board of Professional Psychology. He earned his PhD in clinical psychology from the University of Michigan in 1978. Since then, he has practiced in Massachusetts, largely in the child welfare system. For the Department of Social Services, he has consulted on more than 7,000 cases and conducted psychological evaluations of some 1,400 parents and children. He has trained DSS social workers on numerous topics ranging from the preservation of adoption placements to coping with belligerent clients to working with incest dynamics.

Dr. Karson has taught psychological testing in doctoral programs in Massachusetts, Florida, and New Hampshire. He is senior author of *16PF Interpretation in Clinical Practice: A Guide to the Fifth Edition,* published by the Institute of Personality and Ability Testing. Dr. Karson has written two computer programs that interpret 16PF test results, one for clinicians and one for businesses.

Dr. Karson's experience providing expert testimony in child welfare cases recently led him to obtain a law degree from the Western New England College School of Law. He is now admitted to practice in Massachusetts.

CONTRIBUTOR

Elizabeth E. Sparks is an Associate Professor in the Counseling, Developmental, and Education Psychology Department at Boston College. She earned her PhD in Counseling Psychology at Boston College in 1988. Prior to her academic career, Dr. Sparks worked for seventeen years as a practicing clinician. She has worked in a community social service agency, as a juvenile court probation officer, an adoption worker for special-needs children, a staff psychologist in a psychiatric hospital, and a practitioner/administrator in a community-based mental health clinic. Dr. Sparks currently teaches courses in multicultural issues in counseling, psychopathology, and clinical supervision. She also maintains a private psychotherapy practice. Her research interests stem from her clinical career in community mental health and focus on interpersonal, assaultive violence among African-American youth, interventions for at-risk youth, psychotherapy with women of color, and issues in multicultural training and supervision.

Preface

Every day, important decisions are made about children in the child welfare system: whether to remove them from their homes, where to place them, how to treat them, and whether to send them home again. Over the last fifteen years, I have been involved in thousands of these decisions. My role has been to expand the context in which the decision unfolds, from the immediate issue at hand to a wider network of relationships, agendas, and realistic goals. This constant attention to the bigger picture has brought certain patterns into focus that I hope will be of interest to other child welfare professionals, and to anyone concerned about the welfare of children.

Beyond that immediate purpose in writing this book, I also intend to use the starkness of child welfare dynamics as a basis for appreciating the psychological patterns that affect and inform us all. Family patterns are reproduced in individuals, and then replicated in the individual's close personal and familial relationships. Thus, I hope to use child abuse to illustrate ideas about patterns, and to use ideas about patterns to clarify the issues in child abuse.

I am not interested in ideas alone, however. My ultimate goal in learning about patterns has been to make myself more effective at intervention, and I hope this book makes others more effective as well. To intervene effectively and purposefully, I believe, it is crucial to operate from within a pattern, and not operate merely upon it. A pattern is like a living organism, in that intervention from without typically elicits a protective response from the pattern, as it tries to maintain its coherence. Intervention from within bypasses this natural defense, but it has the drawback that the clinician is required to understand the pattern and then to enter it. Understanding patterns can be difficult, and Part I of this book is devoted to the goal of cultivating fluency in the language of patterns. Entering patterns is also difficult, as it often requires the professional to adopt a role or a posture that is distasteful. Part IV of the book discusses some of the issues involved in entering

abuse patterns and also surveys some of the ways dysfunctional patterns are replicated, rather than modified, in the child welfare system
itself.

In the center of the book, in Parts II and III, are eight chapters
about specific patterns found in child abuse and neglect. In Part II,
I discuss general patterns that arise in many child welfare cases, such
as the idealization of parents, problems with personal closeness, and
pathological personality organizations. Part III covers patterns that,
in my experience, account for most of the difficult decisions in child
welfare families. I have called these patterns after the figure in each
that usually focuses attention on the difficulty of what to do about
them: the sexual abuse victim's mother, the sexually powerful adolescent girl, the disruptive boy, and the absent parent returned. All of
these patterns have less drastic versions that appear in nonabusive
families, and I hope that something relevant to the reader's personal
life will be discovered in each of them.

Any discussion of child abuse, this one included, can barely get
under way before stepping into a minefield of academic, political,
and clinical dispute. Do we blame the victim if we hold a battered
woman responsible for her children? Does it burden abused children
to apply diagnostic labels to them? Can a fifteen-year-old girl decide
to get pregnant or even just to have sex, and does the state have a right
or a duty to stop her? What does "borderline" or "dissociation"
mean? Is memory reliable? Does race matter?

I can neither avoid nor resolve these important disputes. Instead, I
intend as much as possible to contextualize them. Almost always, in
my experience and in my utilitarian way of thinking, the answer to
each of the above questions is "It depends." What it depends on, typically, is the use to which the answer is going to be put. For example, it
is one thing to call a child "borderline" to help predict that the intimacy of a particular foster family will be too difficult for him to nego-
tiate; it is quite another thing to call him "borderline" so his parents
do not have to make an effort to be patient with him, but can instead
have him medicated and institutionalized with a clear conscience. By
the same token, it is one thing to call a battered woman "borderline"
to help predict that even without the batterer, she will likely import
chaos into her children's lives; it is quite another thing to call her
"borderline" to suggest that she instigated the violence.

These concerns reflect the most complex and emotionally evocative issues facing child welfare professionals. All too often, the complexity is ignored, and people find themselves on one side or another of a disagreement that characterizes the other side as evil. In my experience, however, when two large groups of earnest, dedicated, intelligent professionals are in hot dispute, each side has a point. The problem is that usually the two groups are not on the same page in terms of their assumptions or knowledge about the situation, or in terms of their immediate agendas. The domestic violence specialist is trying to convince the poor woman that the battering is not her fault, in spite of her lifelong training to believe that it is. The DSS worker, meanwhile, is trying to find someone who can keep the children free from chaos regardless of whose fault it is. It is natural that they should butt heads occasionally, given their different agendas.

One often encounters a disparity in points of view between therapy and assessment. The therapist accepts the patient's version of events as a method of entering the patient's world, and also because the therapist is responsible to the patient, not to anyone else. If a teenage patient wants to work in therapy on recovering from abuse by his violent mother, it is not the therapist's job to ascertain if the violence actually occurred. After all, the aspects of the patient's life that he wants to change can still be changed, perhaps can best be changed, by assuming that his version of events is correct. Meanwhile, the assessment clinician may interpret the same symptom complex not as a reaction to maternal violence but as symptomatic of character pathology, or of some other origin, such as a need to idealize a father who requires that the teenager blame the mother for the teenager's problems. The evaluator may even have independent evidence that the reported violence did not occur. When the issue of visitation with the mother arises, the two clinicians may find themselves at odds. The therapist accuses the evaluator of being unempathic, and of disqualifying the reports of victims. The evaluator accuses the therapist of being naive and myopic. Instead of attacking each other, the therapist should be able to consider in the back of her mind that the violence may not have occurred, and that the reports of violence have some other meaning. The evaluator should be able to consider that even if the mother is innocent, the child's perspective may need to change before visits are recommended.

It is my hope that this book helps bridge the gaps between warring factions by encouraging people not to rush to the battlements, but instead to check the context in which the disagreement is occurring. Patterns look different depending on where you stand. In this book I try to anticipate explosions and to defuse them. For example, I acknowledge that the word "borderline" has now been thoroughly appropriated by those diagnosticians who rely on external symptoms, so that those of us still interested in internal dynamics need another term: I use "seriously disturbed." I try to explain what I mean by "seriously disturbed" and what I do not mean by it. I attempt to make clear that while most battered women and abused children do not have fragmented personality organizations, some do, and this group has to be treated differently from the majority. At least one reader, however, will jump to the conclusion that I blame the battered woman for the batterer's conduct when I provide an example of a battered woman who is also characterologically impaired.

Similarly, at least one reader will decide I am a racist if I present an example of a poor, disenfranchised black woman who is a bad mother not because of her situation but because of her psychology. These readers are not stupid or crazy. Probably, they have all too often heard white, male professionals attributing all sorts of inner-city behavior to psychology and all sorts of abuse reactivity to personality disorders. But it does not serve the children of these women to ignore the distinctions between situation and pathology; instead, it serves them to refine our ability to make these distinctions accurately.

To ensure the confidentiality of the many people I have met in the course of my work in the child welfare system, I have in every instance changed their names and other identifying features. These changes concern details that are not essential to the point I make, but preserve the anonymity of the people involved.

Acknowledgments

Robert Fusco, a former Department of Social Services administrator with whom I consulted on thousands of cases, is not only brilliant, intuitive, and empathic, he has also been an inspiration to me. He has the courage of his convictions and will stop at nothing to do his best for a child. I asked him once what keeps him in this work, at that time after twenty-five years. He immediately answered, "Jackson Pollock and the U.S. Marines." He explained that the families he meets in the child welfare system challenge him philosophically and almost artistically to make sense of chaos, and further, that there is a bold gratification from seeking out the worst depravity in human nature and not turning away. What has kept me in this field for so long is the vision of the work I gleaned from Robert.

Tom Wilkins has been my liaison with DSS offices in Holyoke and East Springfield for the last fourteen years. Our hundreds of hours together discussing cases have been central to my learning how to apply therapy principles and psychological theory to child welfare casework. What could be more gratifying than to discuss your work on a regular basis with someone who is wise?

Much of the psychology in this book emerged from long conversations over long periods of time with Lyndy Pye, Steve Bloomfield, Christine Kline, Joan Sarnat, Ira Sharkey, Ed Bordin, and Howard Wolowitz. I am also of course indebted, as are we all, to Skinner, Minuchin, Bateson, Madanes, Haley, Erickson, Klein, and, though I hate to admit it, Jung.

I have discussed cases with many people at DSS as a regular member of various consultation teams in different parts of Massachusetts. These relationships have included friendship, esprit de corps, gritty collaboration, and mutual learning. The folks include Elaine Barrus, Ed Callender, Christy Chamberlin, Joe Collins, Susan Connelly, Carmen Constable, Corinne Contarino, Carol Costanzo, Barbara

Curley, John Doherty, Peter Evers, Brian Feeney, Charlotte Finigan, Geralyn Gargiulo, Sam Gelbtuch, Margie Gilberti, Cindy Harmon, Cathy Harris, Leo Harrod, Joanne Hyland, Lee King, Maxine Krie-kamp, Julia Levitz, Anne Marie Lynch, Betsy Mauro, Ruth McDermott, Joshua Miller, Brian Mulvey, John Oteri, Myriam Pascal, Nancy Prostak, Betty Rodger, Joanne Sanderson, Al Totten, and the hope-fully charitable souls I have somehow forgotten to mention. I am also grateful to the people at DSS who have given me the opportunity to ply my trade there, including Rudy Adams, Federico Brid, William Brown, Gene Caouette, Tom Dee, Audrey Dickerson, Dan Donahue, Maria Edwards, Paul Fitzsimons, Terry Flynn, Sue Hannigan, Bruce Heller, Valerie Lovelace-Graham, Pam O'Malley, Ellen Patashnick, Olga Roche, William Warren, and again Ruth McDermott. Their leadership puts human issues ahead of financial, political, and admin-istrative concerns, making it a pleasure to provide clinical consulta-tion under their auspices.

Some people do not even know how much I owe them in writing this book. My boys Ethan and Max, my friends, my family, and Janna Goodwin have made me a happy person with loads of energy. Janna also read two drafts, and her comments have made this a better manu-script and me a better man. Liz Sparks and Christine Kline also read early drafts and made many valuable suggestions.

To name all the DSS social workers and supervisors to whom I am indebted and grateful would take too much space, but if I refer to them only en masse, then I seem to be diminishing their importance to this book. Instead, if I may, I would choose a single DSS staff per-son to represent the whole. Steve Ziperstein from the Holyoke office has always represented, to my way of thinking, the essence of the dedicated, good-natured, intelligent social worker, whose inner bounty has improved the lives of those lucky to know him, and whose spir-ited sense of vocation I can only imitate.

Introduction

Elizabeth Sparks

The purpose of this introductory chapter is to provide a theoretical context for *Patterns of Child Abuse* by presenting an overview of the child abuse literature. In the book, Karson addresses the complexities involved in the assessment of abused children and abusive families. He also highlights a number of issues that have proven difficult for child welfare professionals who must make decisions on a daily basis about the lives of children and families. The initial section of this chapter examines the social construction of child abuse and provides a historical overview of the maltreatment of children that helps us with the misunderstandings that surround the current definition. I next provide a summary of the impact of abuse on children, drawing particular attention to the developmental consequences of exposure to violence. The third section of the chapter examines the factors associated with abusive parenting. The complex interaction among these factors is highlighted, as is the diversity that exists within this population. The final section examines the sociopolitical factors that influence the child welfare system, and the way these affect which families enter the system and the responses they receive.

THE SOCIAL CONSTRUCTION OF CHILD ABUSE

The abuse of children at the hands of their caretakers has been a reality of family life since ancient times. For most of human history, children had little, if any, right to life, and infanticide was routinely practiced on children who had obvious physical deficits at birth. In most ancient societies, children were not recognized as living beings until culturally prescribed rituals had been performed (Radbill, 1987). Parents, especially fathers, had complete control over the life or death of children, who were often brutally abused (both physically and sexually), with few social sanctions imposed on their perpetrators. In general, the further back in history one goes, the lower the level of child care one finds and the more likely it is that children were physically, sexually, and emotionally abused and neglected (Hamilton, 1989). The situation began to change with the advancement of children's rights during the 1700s, and by the late 1800s there was widespread public demand for the humane treatment of children.

Our present-day concern for the welfare of children is a relatively recent phenomenon. Prior to 1964 there were no effective child abuse reporting laws (Radbill, 1987). The term "battered child syndrome" was first used approximately thirty years ago to describe physical injuries inflicted on children by parents (Kempe et al., 1962). Since then, the definition of child abuse has been expanded to include other forms of abuse and neglect. The Child Abuse Prevention and Treatment Act of 1974 (P.L. 93-247) provides a broad definition of child abuse and neglect that is used by states to frame general legislation governing the welfare and protection of children (Iverson and Segal, 1990). Child abuse covers all forms of behaviors having a negative effect on the child's sociopsychological, educational, emotional, and physical well-being (Hullings-Catalano, 1996). Child abuse and neglect has been defined as any recent act or failure to act on the part of a parent or caretaker that results in death or serious physical or emotional harm to a child under the age of eighteen (CWLA, 1999). Currently, every state has mandatory reporting laws that require professionals who work directly with children (e.g., teachers, social workers, nurses, physicians, and psychologists) to report incidents of child abuse and neglect that they encounter to child protective authorities or police.

Although society has a general consensus regarding what constitutes child abuse, there is no consistent definition of the term as it is used in the literature. This has led to subjective judgment in professional evaluations of child abuse and to problems in the generalization of results of empirical studies. It has been suggested that the definition of child abuse should reflect the norms for appropriate child-rearing practices generally held within the culture, and that it should represent an interaction between harm to the child, caretakers' behaviors, and societal assignment of culpability or responsibility for the harm (Korbin, 1987).

However, utilizing such a framework does not remove the problems associated with subjectivity that can lead to confusion and misunderstanding. For example, there are various opinions of what constitutes appropriate child-rearing practices, particularly when those making such assessments do not share the values, cultural and ethnic background, or life experiences of those who are being evaluated. In most cases, what is deemed "appropriate" tends to reflect the normative behaviors exhibited by individuals from the mainstream cultural group. Similarly, the determination of the degree of harm to the child may differ between the evaluators and those being evaluated (Trepper and Barrett, 1989). In these situations the determination of abuse is left to the institutional systems responsible for the care and protection of children (e.g., the Department of Social Services and the courts).

The context surrounding Karson's description of patterns in abused children and abusive families is one where the definition of "child abuse" and the determination of "abusive parental behavior" are often not agreed upon by all of the individuals involved in a case. Many of the families that are embroiled in conflict with the child welfare system hold very different opinions about the abusive nature of their behaviors and the degree of harm to their children as a result of this behavior. Similarly, many of the abused children that Karson describes in the prototypical cases may also disagree with the characterization of their behavior as problematic or harmful. And yet, professionals concerned with the safety and welfare of children must work within an institutional system that accepts the socially constructed definition of child abuse. This can pose challenges as they endeavor to assess and therapeutically intervene with abused children and abusive families. The patterns that Karson describes can assist child welfare professionals as they navigate these challenges. However, it is important to keep in mind that this work, and Karson's analysis of the issues involved, takes place within a sociocultural context where there is very little agreement on the definition of child abuse.

OVERVIEW OF CHILD ABUSE RESEARCH

Prevalence

Research suggests that the incidence of child physical and sexual abuse and neglect is extremely high. Data from the National Center of Child Abuse and Neglect (NCCAN, 1996) indicate that the annual incidence of child physical abuse doubled from 1986 to 1993, with the number of children known to be physically abused in 1993 totaling over 600,000. During this same period, the number of children seriously injured from all forms of child maltreatment (physical and sexual abuse and neglect) nearly quadrupled to more than 572,000 yearly. This study also documented that approximately 300,000 children were found to have been sexually abused in 1993. In 1996, more than 3 million children nationwide were reported as abused and neglected (CWLA, 1999). One million of these children were confirmed victims of maltreatment (U.S. Department of Health and Human Services, 1998). These national statistics provide a general overview of the number of children who are annually subjected to maltreatment. However, differences in the way states collect this data make it difficult to make comparisons across states. The most common categories of child maltreatment (in order of prevalence) are neglect, physical abuse, and sexual abuse. Some states also maintain data on the number of children who experience emotional abuse and medical neglect. When examining the data on child maltreatment from Massachusetts, for example, we find that 22,148 children were neglected, 6,650 were physically abused, and 1,415 were sexually abused in 1996 (CWLA, 1999). With a child population of 1,439,763, these figures reveal that approximately 2 percent of all children in Massachusetts are victims of physical and sexual abuse and/or neglect.

Clearly, child maltreatment is a serious national problem and there is an urgent need to understand the impact of these different forms of violence on the lives of children. There is also a critical need to determine the most appropriate ways to assess child maltreatment and to determine interventions that are effective in ameliorating, and possibly preventing, the adverse effects of abuse. Karson's discussion of the patterns of child abuse provides information that is useful in accomplishing this task and is therefore a timely addition to the child abuse literature.

Etiology

Four major theoretical approaches are presented in the literature that attempt to explain why parents abuse their children. These include: (1) the psychological/individual approaches, which are concerned with the psychological characteristics or traits of abusive parents; (2) the interactionist explanation, which focuses on the relationship between the parent and child; (3) the situational/contextual approaches, which examine factors outside the family (e.g., economic status and institutional racism) that can significantly affect the lives of families; and (4) the cultural-social perspective, which is concerned with the social values and social organization of the culture, community, and the family that can significantly contribute to child abuse (Leeder, 1994; Wiehe, 1989).

Most of the early theoretical work in the field of child maltreatment viewed the problem of child abuse and neglect as being largely the result of parental personality disorders (Pardeck, 1989a). Currently, explanations of the etiology of child abuse reflect more of an ecological perspective. The ecological models integrate variables from several levels (e.g., individual, familial, social, and cultural) to explain family violence (Browne, 1988a; Garbarino, 1977; Vondra and Toth, 1989). They incorporate such factors as parents' individual dynamics, the parent/child interaction, social network supports, economic issues, sociocultural milieu, and the balance between protective and vulnerable factors in both the child and the family system (Vondra and Toth, 1989).

The ecological perspective is useful because of its ability to explain such a complex social problem as the maltreatment of children; however, it is far from definitive (Pardeck, 1989b). The challenge when working with abused children and families from an ecological perspective is to maintain a clear focus on the individual. It is possible to lose sight of individual responsibility and accountability for behavior when environmental and systemic factors are incorporated into the analysis. Yet when children are abused, there is always an identified perpetrator who is responsible for the harm that results.

The challenge for those working with abusive families from an ecological perspective is to integrate individual accountability for abusive behavior with the role of environmental and sociocultural factors in the initiation and maintenance of child abuse.

Karson takes a different approach to the problem of child abuse. His thesis reflects the psychological/individual perspective. As such, the patterns that he describes explain the individual component of the problem. The value of this perspective is that it provides an in-depth analysis of the psychological functioning of abusive parents and abused children, which can assist child welfare professionals in their efforts to provide more effective clinical interventions with this population. The challenge when working with abused children and families from an individual/psychological perspective is to not lose sight of the significance of environmental and systemic factors. If we focus exclusively on the individual psychodynamics in abusive parents and abused children, the problem may be conceptualized in such a way that the resulting solutions will have limited effectiveness. Karson recognizes this challenge and cautions against it.

THE EFFECTS OF ABUSE ON CHILDREN

The literature has identified a number of psychosocial problems that result from child maltreatment. Violence (of any sort) directed toward children typically has a negative effect on development and psychosocial functioning. The specific nature of this effect, however, is determined by such factors as the type and severity of the abuse, the age of the child when the abuse began and was terminated, the nature of the child's relationship with the perpetrator, and the child's resilience. Studies have documented a high prevalence of psychological symptomatology in children who have suffered extreme physical and/or psychological trauma from such events as wars, hurricanes, kidnappings, bombings, shootings, and sexual and physical abuse. In a study of maltreated children seen in a hospital setting, Ackerman and his colleagues (1998) found that 35 percent of the children met criteria for post-traumatic stress disorder (PTSD). Exposure to violence has also been found to be associated with both short-term and long-term psychological suffering in children. Acute symptoms of stress include nightmares, enuresis, and phobias (Dawes and Tredoux, 1989; Pynoos and Eth, 1985). Longer-term effects include aggression, anxiety, depression, withdrawal, and suicidal ideation. Factors such as age, gender, temperament, coping responses, and defense mechanisms also seem to influence the effect of stress on children (Folkman, 1991). Research findings indicate that roughly twice as many young males as young females are physically abused and twice as many young girls as young boys are sexually abused. Abused boys, regardless of type of abuse, had higher rates of behavioral disorder, and abused girls had higher rates of internalizing disorders (Ackerman et al., 1998). Children who have been jointly physically and sexually abused, however, are at greatest risk for psychiatric disturbance. This risk is increased if the abuse began when the child was young and if coercion has been used to maintain secrecy.

Thus, children can respond to maltreatment in many different ways. Karson identifies two patterns: the sexually powerful adolescent girl and the disruptive boy. In both of these patterns, the abused child has found ways to transform feelings of helplessness, anger, and despair into behaviors that challenge adult control. In these patterns the "victimized child" has become the "powerful child" who is not easily controlled by adults, even when these adults are attempting to provide care and protection. Yet, within these two patterns many factors can influence the specific ways that victims respond to the environment and to the therapeutic process. The more we understand the ways in which these factors interact, the more effective we can be in intervening in children's lives.

CHARACTERISTICS OF ABUSIVE FAMILIES

Karson identifies two patterns that pose particular challenges in decision making for child welfare professionals: the sexual abuse victim's mother and the absent parent returned. He also draws attention to some of the more prevalent characteristics of abusive families, identifying such issues as the intergenerational nature of abusive parental behavior and the dysfunctional personality organizations that are sometimes found in abusive parents. These are only a few of the possible characteristics of abusive parents that have been identified in the literature. There is a substantial body of research that examines this issue (for comprehensive reviews, see Jones and Alexander, 1987; Brown et al., 1998). Studies suggest that abusive families (when compared to nonabusive families) have the following characteristics (Gillespie, Seaberg, and Berlin, 1977; Halperin, 1979; Denicola and Sandler, 1980; Browne, 1988b):

1. Poor family and parent/child relationships
2. Use severe forms of physical punishment more often
3. Have more conflict between parents
4. Experience more disruptions in relationships between children and biological parents
5. Have a higher proportion of parents who have maladaptive personality characteristics and lower self-concepts

Research has also identified trends of the dysfunctional behavior exhibited by abusive families. These include (Jones and Alexander, 1987; Hamilton, 1989):

1. Emotional unavailability to family members
2. Intrusive behavior between parents and children
3. History of intergenerational abuse
4. Indiscriminate sexuality both within the nuclear family and among extended family members
5. A lack of privacy within the context of the family unit
6. Family boundary alterations
7. Parent-child role reversals
8. Hierarchical confusion
9. Marital dysfunction
10. The presence of maladaptive family viewpoints and myths

Social isolation has also been identified as having a negative affect on abusive families (Kempe and Kempe, 1978; Hamilton et al., 1987; Miller and Whittaker, 1988). American cultural norms pertaining to the sanctity of the family and the value placed on family privacy serve to compound this variable. Although not every abusive family displays these dysfunctional trends, it is possible to find some constellation of these factors in all families that maltreat children.

SOCIAL AND ENVIRONMENTAL FACTORS ASSOCIATED WITH CHILD ABUSE

In addition to the personal and family characteristics just discussed, social and environmental factors such as parental substance abuse and poverty also heighten the risk for child abuse. The National Committee for the Prevention of Child Abuse (1989) estimates that 675,000 children annually are maltreated by a substance-abusing caretaker, while the estimates on the number of child abuse cases that involve parental substance abuse range from 20 to 90 percent (Famularo, Kinscherff, and Fenton, 1992). Poverty places children at risk for a variety of experiences that can hinder optimum development, and low-income families have been found to have the highest rate of child physical abuse (Brown et al., 1998). Children born in poverty are also at increased risk for such poor developmental outcomes as high mortality rates in infancy and childhood, prematurity, infectious diseases, and increased rates of both intentional and accidental injuries (for a more comprehensive discussion, see Lerner, Sparks, and McCubbin, 1999).

The child welfare system has been established within a sociopolitical context in which the majority of maltreating families identified for intervention are from the lowest socioeconomic groups. These families struggle with many of the factors that have been cited as threats to adequate family functioning, such as severe economic stress, hardship, and dependency (Gil, 1970; Garbarino and Gilliam, 1980). Sociological risk conditions are thought to be both a cause and an outcome of child maltreatment, in that socioeconomic status influences child-rearing practices that help shape adult psychological and sociological circumstances, which in turn contribute to the quality of parental care in the next generation (Vondra and Toth, 1989). In this sense, child maltreatment and family social and economic impoverishment go hand in hand.

The child welfare system must also contend with a sociocultural climate that frowns on public intervention in the private lives of individuals. Such macrosystem forces are filtered down to families from larger social and cultural institutions and can have a significant and pervasive contribution to the quality of parenting and of family life (Bronfenbrenner, 1977; Garbarino, 1977). It is evident from the literature that abusive families are beset with multiple problems and stressors that affect their daily lives (Belsky, 1980; Hamilton et al., 1987). As can be seen from this brief overview of the literature, many characteristics associated with child maltreatment can complicate both the evaluation of child abuse and the process of engagement with abusive families. The patterns described by Karson draw our attention to the dysfunctional behaviors and attitudes in abusive families of most concern to child welfare professionals, and can provide assistance in their work with these families.

THE CHILD WELFARE SYSTEM

The child welfare system has been charged with the responsibility of providing for the care and protection of this nation's children. In this book, Karson presents the notion that the child welfare system can sometimes inadvertently replicate abusive patterns by the way it responds to abused children and maltreating families. To gain a broader perspective of this issue, it is helpful to examine the history and current functioning of the child welfare system. The Society for the Prevention of Cruelty to Children was founded in the late 1800s and initially approached child protection in a punitive manner. Abusive parents were perceived as deviant, disturbed individuals whose children should be placed in institutional care.

Currently, child protective laws have evolved and are oriented more toward nonpunitive protection of children (Janko, 1994). The focus is on helping families in crisis to preserve good standards of parental behavior and to provide basic necessities for the optimum care of children (Radbill, 1987). The British Children Act of 1989 (c. 41) stated that the child's needs were paramount, while attempting to establish a balance between the child's needs and the rights of the parents. It mandated that parental responsibilities could only be removed by the state when a determination of sufficient cause was made after court investigation and adjudication. White, Essex, and O'Reilly (1993), in their discussion of the legal and political context surrounding the child welfare system, suggested that social workers, therapists, and other professionals are expected to forge a consultative partnership with parents, caretakers, and kin from the early stage of suspicion of abuse right through investigation, decision making, and therapy. The Act also required that issues of race, culture, and religion be taken into account in the determination of parental responsibility for child abuse.

An examination of the demographics of families involved in the child welfare system raises questions about the effectiveness of the Children Act to reduce what appears to be bias against ethnic minority and poor families. Statistics indicate that African-American children are overrepresented in the official reports of child abuse and neglect. Hampton, Gelles, and Harrop (1989) noted that 26.8 percent of the reports of abuse and neglect involved African-American children. More recent statistics from the state of Massachusetts indicate that approximately 20 percent of all maltreated children are African American, even though this ethnic group represents less than 10 percent of the state's population (CWLA, 1999). These statistics also indicate that there are differences between ethnic groups in the number of substantiated cases of child maltreatment over a six-year period (1990 to 1996). When we examine the figures, evidence suggests that there may be differential reporting and/or treatment of abusive families according to race and ethnicity. During this six-year period, the reported incidents of abuse and neglect for European-American children fell substantially, while comparable statistics for children of color either fell less dramatically or rose slightly. In 1990, 17,174 European-American children were victims of maltreatment, and in 1996 this number fell to 14,448 (a 16 percent reduction). For African-American children, 5,476 were maltreated in 1990, while in 1996 this number was 5,070 (a 7 percent reduction). For Hispanic children, the number of substantiated cases of abuse or neglect rose during this six-year period, from 4,132 in 1990 to 5,005 in 1996 (a 17 percent increase). A similar rise was noted for Native American and Asian children, although the total number of maltreated children in these two ethnic groups was substantially lower (CWLA, 1999).

Many researchers (e.g., Hampton and Newberger, 1985) suggest that factors such as race, ethnic background, and social class can determine what labels are applied to an injury or a situation, which in turn can influence the decisions made by child welfare professionals. It is possible that this bias in the decision-making process may account for the disproportionate number of reported abuse and neglect cases involving children of color. In a national study of hospital cases in which child abuse and neglect was suspected, Hampton and New-berger (1985) found that 91 percent of the Hispanic families were reported to child protection agencies; the corresponding number of black and white families were 74 percent and 61 percent respectively. Research has also found that physicians' judgments of possible child abuse are affected by socioeconomic and ethnic status, such that the determination of whether an injury to a child is "accidental" or "abuse" seems to be associated with the degree of social distance between the physician and the parents. This suggests that low-income, ethnic-minority families may be victimized by a process in which their personal characteristics, rather than their behavior, define them as abusive (O'Toole, Turbett, and Nalepka, 1983; Katz et al., 1986).

Studies that examine the way in which child abuse is handled outside the medical system have also found that class, race, and other family characteristics affect decision making. Families receiving general welfare and perceived by authorities as having a member with a mental health problem or a parent who is ineffectual were more likely to have a child removed as a result of suspected abuse and/or neglect. Katz and his colleagues (1986) found that physical injuries might more frequently be diagnosed as "abuse" in poor families and as "accidents" in more affluent families. A similar set of premises and biases that might lead professionals to identify and report certain families as abusers at an initial setting, such as a hospital, subsequently seem to influence decisions made about the fate of the family as it is channeled through the protective services and justice systems.

The conclusion that can be drawn from this research is that class, race, and ethnicity bias child abuse reporting. If this is indeed the case, then we need to question the way in which decisions are made within the child welfare system. Karson acknowledges that there are academic, political, and clinical debates surrounding the discussion of the sociopolitical and cultural factors that impinge upon abused children, abusive families, and professionals in the child welfare system. His proposed solution follows from his theoretical perspective and suggests that we find ways to improve our ability to make accurate distinctions between situation and pathology. If, however, child welfare professionals are responding to abusive families of color with the type of bias that has been identified in the literature, it will also be important to subject their decision-making process to critical review.

It is important that child welfare professionals working with abusive families recognize the diversity that exists within this population. MacKinnon (1998) suggests that child abuse is not simply the outcome of individual or family pathology but rather the inevitable outcome of an individual's position within gender and class contexts, as well as a particular genealogy of relationships (p. 233). In a similar way, Leeder (1994) maintains that child welfare professionals must develop practices that reflect an awareness of how race, social class, ethnic group membership, and cultural background influence abusive parents' lifestyle and value system. This suggests that not only must we gain skills in distinguishing pathology from circumstances, as Karson recommends, but we must also begin to develop culturally sensitive approaches to intervention. When we position *Patterns of Child Abuse* in the theoretical and empirical literature, we find that its thesis represents an in-depth view of the individual/psychological perspective. Its value lies in the application of these patterns to assessment and intervention with abusive families and abused children, and as such, it is an important and timely resource for child welfare professionals.

REFERENCES

Ackerman, P.T., Newton, J.E., McPhearson, W.B., Jones, J.G., and Dykman, R.E. (1998). Prevalence of post traumatic stress disorder and other psychiatric diagnoses in three groups of abused children (sexual, physical, and both). *Child Abuse and Neglect,* 22:8, 759-774.

Belsky, J. (1980). Child maltreatment: An ecological integration. *American Psychologist,* 35:4, 320-335.

Bronfenbrenner, U. (1977). Toward an experimental ecology of human development. *American Psychologist,* 32:7, 513-530.

Brown, J., Cohen, P., Johnson, J.G., and Salzinger, S. (1998). A longitudinal analysis of risk factors for child maltreatment: Findings of a 17-year prospective study of officially recorded and self-reported child abuse and neglect. *Child Abuse and Neglect,* 22:11, 1065-1078.

Browne, D.H. (1988a). High risk infants and child maltreatment: Conceptual and research model for determining factors predictive of child maltreatment. *Early Child Development and Care,* 31:1, 43-53.

Browne, D.H. (1988b). The role of stress in the commission of subsequent acts of child abuse and neglect. *Early Child Development and Care*, 31:1, 27-33.

CWLA (1999). Child Welfare League of America Web Site: <http://www.cwla.org>, National Data Analysis System, 11/12/99.

Dawes, A. and Tredoux, C. (1989). Emotional status of children exposed to political violence in the Crossroads squatter area during 1986/1987. *Psychology in Society*, 12, 33-47.

Denicola, J. and Sandler, J. (1980). Training abusive parents in child management and self-control skills. *Behavior Therapy*, 11:2, 263-270.

Famularo, R., Kinscherff, R., and Fenton, T. (1992). Parental substance abuse and the nature of child maltreatment. *Child Abuse and Neglect*, 16:4, 475-483.

Folkman, S. (1991). Coping across the life span: Theoretical issues. In E.M. Cummings, A.L. Greene, and K.H. Karraker (Eds.), *Lifespan developmental psychology: Perspectives on stress and coping* (pp. 3-19). Hillsdale, NJ: Lawrence Erlbaum Associates, Inc.

Garbarino, J. (1977). The human ecology of child maltreatment: A conceptual model for research. *Journal of Marriage and the Family*, 39:4, 721-735.

Garbarino, J. and Gilliam, G. (1980). *Understanding abusive families*. Lexington, MA: D.C. Heath and Co.

Gil, D. (1970). *Violence against children: Physical child abuse in the U.S.* Cambridge, MA: Harvard University Press.

Gillespie, D.F., Seaberg, J.R., and Berlin, S. (1977). Observed causes of child abuse. *Victimology*, 2:2, 342-349.

Halperin, M. (1979). *Helping maltreated children*. St. Louis, MO: C.V. Mosby Co.

Hamilton, A., Stiles, W.B., Melowsky, F., and Beal, D.G. (1987). A multilevel comparison of child abusers with non-abusers. *Journal of Family Violence*, 2:3, 215-225.

Hamilton, L.R. (1989). Variables associated with child maltreatment and implications for prevention and treatment. *Early Child Development and Care*, 42, 31-56.

Hampton, R., Gelles, R., and Harrop, J. (1989). Is violence in Black families increasing? A comparison of 1975 and 1985 National Survey Rates. *Journal of Marriage and the Family*, 51:4, 969-980.

Hampton, R.L. and Newberger, E.H. (1985). Child abuse incidence and reporting by hospitals: The significance of severity, class, and race. *American Journal of Public Health*, 75:1, 56-60.

Hullings-Catalano, V. (1996). Physical abuse of children by parents. In D.M. Busby (Ed.), *The impact of violence on the family: Treatment approaches for therapists and other professionals* (pp. 43-74). Boston: Allyn & Bacon.

Iverson, T.J. and Segal, M. (1990). *Child abuse and neglect: An information and reference guide*. New York: Guilford.

Janko, S. (1994). *Vulnerable children, vulnerable families: The social construction of child abuse*. New York: Teachers College Press.

Jones, D.P. and Alexander, H. (1987). Treating the abusive family within the family care system. In R. Helfer and R.S. Kempe (Eds.), *The battered child* (pp. 339-359). Chicago: University of Chicago Press.

Katz, M.H., Hampton, R.L., Newberger, E.H., Bowles, R.T., and Snyder, J.C. (1986). Clinical decision making in cases of child abuse and neglect. *American Journal of Orthopsychiatry,* 56:3, 253-262.

Kempe, C.H., Silverman, F.H., Steele, B.P., Droegmueller, W., and Silver, H.K. (1962). The battered children syndrome. *Journal of the American Medical Association,* 181:1, 17-24.

Kempe, R.S. and Kempe, C.H. (1978). *Child abuse.* Cambridge, MA: Harvard University Press.

Korbin, J.E. (1987). Child abuse and neglect: The cultural context. In E. Heilfer and R.S. Kempe (Eds.), *The battered child* (Fourth edition, pp. 23-41). Chicago: University of Chicago Press.

Leeder, E. (1994). *Treating abuse in families: A feminist and community approach.* New York: Springer.

Lerner, R., Sparks, E.E., and McCubbin, L.D. (1999). *Family diversity and family policy: Strengthening families for America's children.* Boston: Kluwer Academic Publishers.

MacKinnon, L.K. (1998). *Trust and betrayal in the treatment of child abuse.* New York: Guilford.

Miller, J.L. and Whittaker, J.K. (1988). Social services and social support: Blended programs for families at risk of child maltreatment. *Child Welfare,* 67:2, 161-174.

National Center of Child Abuse and Neglect (NCCAN) (1996). *Third study of national incidence and prevalence of child abuse and neglect.* Washington, DC: U.S. Department of Health and Human Services.

National Committee for the Prevention of Child Abuse (1989). *Substance abuse and child abuse fact sheet.* Washington, DC: Author.

O'Toole, R., Turbett, P., and Nalepka, C. (1983). Theories, professional knowledge, and diagnosis of child abuse. In D. Finkelhor, R.J. Gelles, G.T. Hotaling, and M.A. Straus (Eds.), *The dark side of families: Current family violence research* (pp. 349-362). Beverly Hills, CA: Sage.

Pardeck, J.T. (1989a). Child abuse and neglect: Theory, research and practice. *Early Child Development and Care,* 42, 3-10.

Pardeck, J.T. (1989b). Family therapy as a treatment approach to child maltreatment. *Early Child Development and Care,* 42, 151-157.

Pynoos, R.S. and Eth, S. (1985). Children traumatized by witnessing acts of personal violence. In S. Eth and R.S. Pynoos (Eds.), *Posttraumatic stress disorder* (pp. 17-44). Washington, DC: American Psychiatric Association Press.

Radbill, S.X. (1987). Children in a world of violence: A history of child abuse. In E. Heilfer and R.S. Kempe (Eds.), *The battered child* (Fourth edition, pp. 3-21). Chicago: University of Chicago Press.

Trepper, T.S. and Barrett, M.J. (1989). *Systemic treatment of incest: A therapeutic handbook.* New York: Brunner/Mazel.

U.S. Department of Health and Human Services (1998). *Children's Bureau.* Washington, DC: Government Printing Office.

Vondra, J.I. and Toth, S.L. (1989). Ecological perspectives on child maltreatment: Research and intervention. *Early Child Development and Care,* 42, 11-29.

White, J., Essex, S., and O'Reilly, P. (1993). Family therapy, systemic thinking and child protection. In J. Carpenter and A. Treacher (Eds.), *Using family therapy in the nineties* (pp. 57-86). Cambridge, MA: Blackwell.

Wiehe, V.R. (1989). Child abuse: An ecological perspective. *Early Child Development and Care,* 42, 141-149

PART I:
CONCEPTUAL BACKGROUND

Family patterns are reproduced in the psyches of children. For example, if parents suppress vitality in children, children will learn to suppress vitality in themselves, perhaps by becoming depressed. If children expect to be beaten when they are careless, they will learn to beat themselves when careless, by scrutinizing their mistakes with harsh and exacting criticism. When these children grow up and form families of their own, their now-internal patterns will be reproduced in their new families. Children who suppressed their own vitality, as parents, find themselves acting in a disapproving manner when their own children are vivacious. Children who were self-critical, as parents, may constantly criticize their own children.

Of course, replication of internal patterns in the person's new family is rarely so straightforward. How the existing pattern is made to fit the new situation depends on numerous factors, including the suitability of various family members to play various roles, and the availability of alternative patterns to compete with the one in question.

To place a problematic behavior such as abuse or neglect in the context of a pattern is like conceptualizing an individual's conduct in the context of a family system. The issue is not actual causality or the relative accuracy of an individual versus a systemic approach, because a number of different conceptual contexts can be true for different purposes. The issue is whether and how a particular framework lends itself to an understanding and an intervention that is helpful (Watzlawick, Weakland, and Fisch, 1974). Seeing the intrapsychic pattern behind an act of abuse or neglect can open as many possibilities for intervention as seeing the family processes behind an individual symptom. The theoretical point is that systemic interconnectivity happens not just between people, but within individuals as well, among a single person's many emotional states, impulses, and goals.

Chapter 1 presents an overview of patterns, their creation in the mind, their replication in families, and vice versa. Chapter 1 also introduces the problem of intervening in patterns without becoming either ignored by them or subsumed in them. Chapters 2 and 3 discuss the underlying theoretical issues that account for pattern formation within and between individuals. The intent is to cultivate fluency in the language of patterns by exploring the psychological structures and processes that support them. These chapters also cover ways of thinking about child abuse that are conducive to identifying patterns and intervening in them successfully.

Chapter 1

The Importance of Patterns

FAMILY PATTERNS REPRODUCED IN THE CHILD

A social worker at the state Department of Social Services (DSS) asked my opinion about a man, Mr. Avalon, who, several months earlier, had punched his two children because they would not keep quiet. When the school nurse had seen the bruises, she had reported him to DSS. Now the nurse was calling again to report further abusive treatment. The social worker was disappointed because at the time she had found Mr. Avalon to be extremely remorseful and depressed. His self-disgust had been plain; he had missed work after the incident and had been plagued with suicidal fantasies.

Mr. Avalon had been a rebellious teenager, committing minor delinquencies, dropping out of school, and drifting from job to job. Eventually, though, he settled down. He held the same position in a tool factory for several years, raised his children with his wife, and stayed out of trouble with the law. As a child, he had been beaten repeatedly by his father. These beatings were so violent that he spent most of his childhood just trying to avoid them. In the worst incident, his father used a broom handle on his back. Then, as Mr. Avalon told it, "My mother pulled a gun on my father and told him never to hit me again, or she would kill him. My father broke down and cried. He actually got on his knees and begged her to let him stay." The social worker had asked Mr. Avalon if that had ended the beatings. "No," he answered, "from then on, he just did it behind her back." The social worker had been impressed by the man's honesty and remorse, and by his resolve never to strike his children again. He was as much a victim as a perpetrator. He had been referred to a batterers' group to work on his violence and to family therapy to learn how to discipline his children. His children had continued to live with him. Now they were back in the system.

Patterns are transmitted from people's families to their psychological states and then transmitted back again from their psychologies to their close relationships. In this case, within Mr. Avalon's own head the drama of the gun was being played out. Suicide, which Mr. Avalon was considering, can be construed psychologically as a form of homicide in which the killer and the victim happen to be the same person. Mr. Avalon's suicidal impulse was tantamount to pointing a gun at the part of him that, like his father, beat children. Just as his mother threatened to kill a person who beat children (his father), he was threatening to kill a person who beat children (himself). His father's tears in the memory were like Mr. Avalon's current remorse; the person who beat children became, in either case, filled with regret and self-loathing. Mr. Avalon's resolve never to do it again predictably turned out to be similar to his father's resolve. The abuse in either case persisted, but only behind the mother's back. Here, Mr. Avalon was also in the role of the mother who did not know about it. In other words, a protective part of him threatened to shoot the violent part of him, so future violence had to take place outside of the awareness of the protective part.

How is it possible to do something behind one's own back? After the initial incident, he restrained himself when he was consciously angry, but, ostensibly in an effort to be a better father, he hurt his children for their "own good," in calmly applied punishments. He would make them kneel on raw rice to "teach them a lesson." He did this "behind the back" of the part of him that was invested in protecting his children; Mr. Avalon did not realize he was still abusing them.

Mr. Avalon was mortified to learn that he was still considered an abusive father, and he again became weepy and suicidal. He resolved, now, not to strike his children as before, but also never to make them kneel on rice, or to use any other punishment associated with physical pain. Such resolutions usually fail in my experience, because they depend on the person acting as he has never acted before. They are like a dieter's pledge not to eat sweets. In the course of a week, the dieter fulfills his pledge ten, a hundred, even a thousand times. Eventually, he feels he deserves a reward for exercising so much willpower. He manages to pass up an ice cream parlor and congratulates himself, at home, with a bag of cookies. I thought Mr. Avalon would inevitably relax his armed vigil over himself. As long as his psychological reaction to noisy children was essentially punitive, his children were in danger. I try to resist treatment plans that depend on people acting as they have never acted before. I like treatment plans that assume that people will act in character.

It turned out that Mr. Avalon would not become so upset with his children when he was supervising them, but only when he was relaxing on his own. This makes obvious sense, in that one expects children to make noise when it is officially playtime and to keep quiet when adults are relaxing. But it also makes a deeper sense in that when Mr. Avalon relaxed, when it was his own enjoyment that counted, then he was like a child again, and this in turn conjured up his abusive father. Even before his children interrupted his peace, he was already struggling with a vague sense of violence. While taking a nap, listening to music, or rebuilding his car (Mr. Avalon's main forms of relaxation), he was already anticipating a beating. He sank into a world where childhood enjoyment evoked an abusive father. In that world, his children's enjoyment could only evoke a violent response. Like many people with a disapproving parent inside them, Mr. Avalon lashed out at others to spare himself.

My idea was to address the immediate potential for violence by insisting that Mr. Avalon wear earplugs or headphones when he was relaxing. Further, I recommended that all discipline and punishment be the province of his wife, at least for the foreseeable future. For the long run, I recommended a therapy devoted not to learning to discipline, but to learning to play. I suggested he use therapy to enjoy himself, and then, with the therapist's help, to observe what happened within his psychology when he had fun. I expected he would find that he anticipated a beating. Also for the long run, I recommended that he find and pursue activities that were fun both for him and for his children together. He functioned poorly when his own pleasure counted and he functioned well when his children's pleasure counted, but neither situation affected the drama of the armed protector, the abusive father, and the gleeful child. His children's play did not change his essential relationship with them because it did not infect him with a sense of his own enjoyment; he was a tolerant father at his best, but never a loving one.

I wish I could report that my suggestions were helpful, but they were not even tried. Instead, Mr. Avalon's abusive discipline was seen by other professionals as a sign of progress since it was better than a punch in the nose, and his sincere promises not to hurt the children anymore were again taken at face value. Like the ineffective therapist who strives for change without stepping into the patient's world, I was an ineffective consultant, merely telling the social worker to be different. It was not that my wisdom fell on deaf ears; rather, I spoke in a language she could not understand. This book is part of my ongoing attempt to learn her language and to teach her mine.

As for Mr. Avalon, my guess is that the complex within him has found even more subtle ways to abuse his children behind his own back. For example, the children may mute themselves to spare him and the family further public embarrassment. When a parent does not pursue a reticent child, we do not condemn him or her as we did when the parent demanded silence overtly, but the effect on the child is similar. It is a punitive effect, whether inflicted as before by the parent or in its new form by the child. Alternatively, in the guise of compassion, Mr. Avalon may express sympathy for how immature and disruptive his children are, making them feel as though something is wrong with them when they are just being kids. Again, the effect is punitive even if the overt conduct is not. Finally, Mr. Avalon may find that "teaching them a lesson" no longer passes the scrutiny of the armed protector within him. If he is motivated unconsciously to hurt his children, he can no longer do it in the name of discipline, but many excuses are available for a punitive impulse. For example, children frequently want to do things that put their personal safety at risk; in the name of indulgence, Mr. Avalon might let them.

It is important to recognize psychological patterns so we can base predictions and treatment planning on more information. Widening the perspective from behavior to its context also allows for more options in terms of the point at which we intervene and the specificity with which an intervention can be designed. Generic solutions, based on generic labels such as "abuse" or "poor parenting," are bound to fail. They do not take into account the context of the abuse, in other words, when it occurs, how it unfolds, and which child is being hit.

By "which child," I do not mean which physical child, but which psychological child. Does the father hit the noisy, playful child, as Mr. Avalon did? The morose child? The rebellious child?

INDIVIDUAL PATTERNS
REPRODUCED IN THE FAMILY

A second example, to contrast with Mr. Avalon, involved a drunken father who struck his child when he caught her smoking pot. Mr. Barrows was a decent man, a hard-working attorney, who was proud of himself as a father. He took pride in sending his daughter, Melissa, to an expensive private school, in their having a warm, communicative relationship, and in her worldly success as a student and as a poet. He and his wife had an active social life, which revolved around dinner parties, where he invariably drank too much. Intoxication made him feel friendly and relaxed; he called it his "buzz" or his "feeling no pain." The few times his wife ever mentioned the amount he drank at parties, he rebuffed her by saying that he "earned it," and that he never drove drunk. When Mr. Barrows stumbled home after one such party, laughing at his own clumsiness, he was dismayed to find Melissa and her friends scurrying to hide the evidence of their marijuana, the smell of which pervaded the house. Besides his concern that his daughter clearly understand his views on drugs, he also was alarmed by the potential damage to his professional station if illegal drugs were found in his home. He backhanded her across the cheek. Melissa responded in the following month by skipping school frequently and staying out late. Eventually, the parents sought help from the courts, filing a CHINS (child in need of services) petition on her as truant and stubborn. Melissa defiantly swore at all the relevant authority figures, including the judge, and insisted that they had no power over her. I heard about Melissa at a planning meeting at DSS.

The thrust of my consultation about Melissa was to question the wisdom of acquiescing to the CHINS petition. The gist of a CHINS petition is that the child is at fault. Indeed, the three types of CHINS petitions—truant, stubborn, and runaway—focus exclusively on the child's misconduct. True, Melissa's mouth was vicious enough to make a reasonable adult say, as the social worker did, that even if the parents had

been wrong initially, Melissa had gone way beyond the pale in retalia-
tion. But to punctuate the story of Melissa's hostility by beginning
with her vicious mouth was to artificially exclude her father's contribution to it. Indeed, I thought she reacted so drastically to distract
people, including herself, from the fact that her father had never really apologized for hitting her. The blow inflicted by her father was
seen by the family, by the court, and even by the child as an understandable response to her flagrant pot smoking. I suggested, to coun-
ter the child-blaming aspect of the CHINS, that DSS tell the parents
that it would consider filing a C&P (care and protection) petition in
court, which claims that the parents are so unfit to raise the child that
she needs the care and protection of the state. Even to consider a
C&P, I thought, might shock the parents into recalling their participation in their daughter's drama.

It is a drastic step to go to court and allege that parents are unfit to
raise their own children. It is drastic even if the allegation is that the
unfitness is only temporary. It can be drastic even to discuss the possibility of going to court with the parents. But I felt a drastic step was
needed. The momentum of the case had built quite a head of steam in
the direction of blaming the child, and something had to deflect it.

I have nothing against blaming an adolescent for her conduct; after
all, she knew better than to smoke pot in the house or to swear at the
judge. But this was not a situation in which each family member was
struggling to accept responsibility for his or her own conduct. Instead, Melissa was being asked to take responsibility for her own conduct and for her father's as well. When one family member takes responsibility for the conduct of another, the first person is acting,
functionally, as a parent to the second. It was just too difficult for Melissa to handle the mixed message: be a parent to your father when it
comes to assigning responsibility for misdeeds; be a child to your father when it comes to obedience and deference.

The point of threatening, or at least raising the possibility of filing,
a C&P petition was to restore a structural hierarchy to a system that
was sorely lacking one, the absence of which was facilitating impulsive conduct. Instead of the DSS worker commiserating with the father about Melissa, the social worker would hold Mr. Barrows accountable for the impulsivity in his family. The social worker would,
in effect, demonstrate that she was putting her job on the line by leav-

ing the girl at home, while indicating that if anything went wrong, she would have to intervene more forcefully. The goal was for Mr. Barrows to express the same idea to Melissa: when he leaves her at home, he is putting his job on the line, and if anything else goes wrong, he may have to intervene more forcefully. The goal was to let Melissa be as independent, and only as independent, as she could prove capable of being.

However, some remedial work had to be done before Mr. Barrows would be in a position to implement this strategy because, by striking Melissa and humiliating her in front of her friends, he had already intervened too forcefully. Before he could effectively threaten to apply more force as necessary, he had to reel back the force he had already applied. The only way to do this was to apologize.

I will discuss apology at greater length later, but for now let me emphasize that an apology, a real apology, is not an excuse or an after-the-fact verbal ritual. A real apology demonstrates an understanding of why the conduct was wrong, how it hurt, what produced it, and what is different now that prevents it from happening again (Madanes, 1990). Eventually, the social worker added a task to the service plan by which Mr. Barrows would apologize for hitting Melissa, her mother would apologize for not protecting her or at least for not taking her side, and both would seek help in family therapy to learn, not how to control Melissa, but how to be better parents to a teenage girl.

Analysis of the internal patterns that Mr. Avalon and Mr. Barrows were transposing into family terms leads to ideas about therapy. The cast of characters in the drama that periodically consumed Mr. Avalon included a violent abuser (the father who punched), a violent protector (the mother with the gun), and a childlike, excited victim (the children who would not keep quiet). In Mr. Barrows' pattern, the characters included an intoxicated protector (too drunk to stop himself), a self-righteous father (who justifies hitting as deserved), and a defiant victim (who knows better than to smoke pot at home or to drink excessively). Where Mr. Avalon felt like killing himself afterward, Mr. Barrows made excuses based on his being drunk and based on his daughter's defiance. Obviously, Mr. Avalon needed help with his suicidality, and Mr. Barrows needed help with his drinking.

Less obviously, Mr. Avalon needed to learn to enjoy himself. If he could have fun without bad consequences, then when he was relaxing and his children were noisy, a different cast of characters could be constellated. Mr. Avalon needed to concentrate less on being a good father, which just made him constrained and punitive "for the children's own good," and more on being a happy child himself, so that the link between childlike happiness and abusive parents would not be so inevitable.

Mr. Barrows' internal patterns probably matched the family system. Prior to the incident, Mr. Barrows, like Melissa, had been dutiful by day and a substance abuser by night. If he caught himself using substances—if he realized he was an alcoholic—he reacted as rebelliously as Melissa did, by drinking even more. Mr. Barrows needed to alter the link between parental arrogance and adolescent rebellion, because his arrogance made him think he had the right to strike his daughter and made him scrutinize his own drinking with the kind of perfectionism that invites defiance. He could start perhaps by acknowledging that, in spite of his self-righteous assertions of parental concern, he was not as concerned about Melissa as he pretended to be, or he would not get drunk. When he justified intoxication by saying he "earned" it, he communicated the true reward for all his hard work: alcohol. Naturally, the child who had been told that he worked for her resented his duplicity and wanted to find out what was so fascinating about substance abuse.

These examples illustrate the parallels between patterns in the psyche and patterns in a family system. Again, it is important to recognize these patterns so that prediction and treatment planning can be based on more information. Also, pattern recognition, and understanding the means by which patterns are produced, facilitates the selection of an intervention strategy that takes the specific context into account. As noted, the patterns of the family system are duplicated in the psychology of the child who grows up in that system. Another kind of duplication occurs with self-replicating patterns, which are reiterated not just from family to individual, but also from generation to generation. On a simple level, it may make sense to note that sexual abuse, physical abuse, and neglect run in families. One may rely on the concept of modeling, for example, to explain these patterns, although this proves to be a frustrating concept for the clinician, as it does not help us understand why our offer of better models is virtually always rejected. The way patterns repeat themselves may be more interactive than that concept suggests.

THE CASE OF SEXUAL ABUSE

Consider a woman, familiar to anyone working in the child welfare system, who adapted to her own sexual abuse as a child by relying on dissociative defenses. Dissociation means a disruption in the normal integration of psychological functions. Most people can think and feel at the same time, for example, but some people sometimes only think and others sometimes only feel. Only-thinking people are likely to be very "rational"; they find feelings embarrassing and keep them at bay, especially when they need to think. Only-feeling people are likely to be very expressive; they are in thrall to their own emotions and do not like to diminish them. As an example, for the woman who was sexually abused as a child, the dissociation may involve thinking and remembering. When she is alert and paying attention, her memory for the abuse may be dim at best; when she is not paying attention, the memory can be vivid, in what is called a flashback. Most people integrate thinking and memory to the point where they are able to retrieve and narratively report memories. Some trauma survivors find themselves either unable to retrieve a memory or, if they do retrieve it, they are reliving it in a flashback.

As a response to trauma, dissociation seems to be a biological adaptation, since the capacity to ignore physical pain facilitates adaptive, problem-solving behavior. As one expert on political torture victims said, "In order to survive torture, you have to discard the body" (Bamber, 1999). Imagine some long-ago hunter-gatherer, injured while looking for food; if she can ignore her pain, and not only ignore it but forget it, her gathering will be that much more successful than if she hobbled along favoring the injury or gave up gathering food to seek sympathy. Of course, a survival mechanism need not be posited; dissociation may be merely a by-product of the evolutionarily advantageous ability to weed out stimuli from a confusing and rich environment. This capacity for selective attention could explain our ability to dissociate without resorting to a specific survival advantage.

In dissociation, as in hypnosis, pain can be ignored via distraction. The girl who is being sexually abused retreats psychologically from the experience while it is happening. Her mind may focus on an extraneous detail, as women in labor are taught to do in Lamaze classes; or her mind may fill with an alternative fantasy, such as riding a horse or escaping; or, most likely of all, her mind may simply shut off, disrupting the normal integration between memory and experience. During the trauma, her mind is blank; after the trauma, she avoids her emotional pain and sense of betrayal by keeping the part of her that could remember away from the part of her that went through it.

In a parallel between individual and family functioning, her mother ignores the signs of sexual abuse, and the girl does too. The mother does not retain awareness of the coy secrecy between her boyfriend and her daughter. Neither does the girl; when the girl is out playing with her friends, it is as if the sexual abuse never happened. The part of the girl that remembers, understands, and communicates has no better access to the abuse than does the mother, because neither the mother nor the daughter wants to undergo the pain of hearing about it. The mother avoids this pain by avoiding the signs that something is wrong, and by avoiding being at home. The girl avoids this pain by not thinking about it.

To maintain her avoidance of pain, the girl makes dissociation into more than a method of coping with trauma—she makes it into a way of life. She becomes something of a space cadet. Her cognitive world and her emotional world spin in different directions, so that she is rarely thinking and feeling at the same time. Genuine intimacy frightens her, because it invites her to be herself in a close personal relationship, when she is so much more comfortable keeping her mind at bay when in close encounters. If she is functional enough to work when she grows up, she spends as much time as possible on the job. She feels vaguely safe at work, because the intrusive aspects of home life (feelings, personal transactions, sexuality, and intimacy) are geographically somewhere else.

What kind of man does she find? On a purely sexual level, a man looking for a *partner* is frustrated that she is so vacant on dates, and so vacant in response to his touch. She makes him feel not like a lover, but like a child molester, because she acts not like a lover, but like an abused child. She is not mindful or present during sexual encounters.

A man may express interest in her and then be turned off by her passive response. He may feel he is approaching not a woman but a doll. Of course, another man may find her attitude quite appealing, seeing her as demure. This other man likes the way she acquiesces quietly when he tells her what time he will pick her up; the way he can criticize what she wears for the date, knowing that she will not complain; the way he can take her to the same club he would go to without her, dragging her along with his buddies. This other man wants a doll, not a woman. He wants someone who will not interfere with his need for control, and who will never act as a damper on his impulsivity. If he gets angry on the road and feels it is necessary to get ahead of the guy who cut him off, he wants a woman who sits quietly beside him and says nothing. In bed, the last thing he cares about is whether she had an orgasm. This of course suits her just fine, as the last thing she wants is to be genuinely related and conscious during sex.

Thus, the passive, dissociative woman advertises for an impulsive, controlling man as surely as if she had put a notice in the paper. If they have children together, her dissociative avoidance increases, since the presence of children make the home seem even more like her childhood home, with the introduction of toys, cribs, bedtime, and the range of parent-child interactions. She may spend as much time as possible outside the home. When she is home, she spaces out much of the time, watching TV or sleeping. She finds interactions between the man and her children threatening, because they start to remind her of her painful past, although she stops paying attention long before she is actually reminded of anything painful.

Now all the ingredients of sexual abuse are present. If she already had children before she met him, the mix is even stronger, since there is no incest taboo to overcome. The ingredients include the spaced-out mother, the impulsive, controlling father figure, and children who know they can keep their mother functional by biting their tongues when it comes to divulging things she would find upsetting. The scenario does not always produce sexual abuse (it can also lead to domestic violence, philandering, and substance abuse), but it certainly increases the chances of sexual abuse. The sexual abuse pattern is thus very powerful, because it tends to replicate itself in the next generation. Later on, I will discuss the sexual abuse mother in greater

depth, along with some other identifiable patterns in abusive and neglectful families. The point for now is that a pattern can be transmitted from one generation to the next via individuals and families.

PATTERNS CHANGED FROM WITHIN

Patterns are best changed from within, and they must be entered
before they can be influenced. Instead of basing treatment plans on an
understanding of the relevant pattern, however, treatment plans are
often based on whatever resources happen to be available. A particular therapist is chosen because she is willing to travel to the home, not
because she has the relevant skills. Once chosen, she may select a
modality with which she is comfortable and familiar, rather than a
modality that suits the particular problem. To base treatment planning on reality requires more of service providers than to "plug in"
available resources and more of therapists than to "facilitate communication" or "improve self-esteem." Therapists can be like unfit parents, struggling to avoid feeling incompetent, acting in character even
when it fails, and blaming problems on the patients.

When the only tool you have is a hammer, the saying goes, everything looks like a nail. And when the only tool you have is a batterers'
group, every instance of family violence looks like classic battering.
There is no reason to think any harder about a family whose members
hit each other than to classify the behavior as domestic violence, because any harder thought will not have discernible effects on treatment. Batterers' groups are perfectly appropriate for and highly effective with some batterers. With no alternatives, though, there is no
reason for a more refined diagnosis. Conversely, without a more refined diagnosis, all domestic violence can be managed via batterers'
groups. If some group members do not improve, then it is because
they are bad clients, not because the group was the wrong choice. Despite these drawbacks, there are advantages to having only one tool,
whether it be batterers' groups for the therapist or battering for the
parent: you always know what to do, and you have few anxieties
about incompetence.

Clinicians, like parents, feel incompetent when they do not know
what to do and when they are unable to do what they see needs to be

done. In other words, we are susceptible to feeling incompetent when we are not sure how to behave or, when we have an idea as to what would work, we cannot pull it off. We are generally much happier treating every problem the same way because it is easier and because it spares us from feeling incompetent. When everything looks like a nail, then some things are better at being nails than others. It is only when a parent or a clinician is flexible in his or her approach to children or patients that doubt arises as to whether the parent or clinician has made the right choice. When there is only one way to treat a given problem, then the only question is whether the child or patient will cooperate. When everything looks like a nail, nobody questions the hammer.

Because specific information about a family or an individual threatens the clinician's sense of complacency and also threatens the family's definition of the problem, it can be very difficult to get information from clinicians and families alike on which to base the recognition of a pattern. Conversely, merely obtaining the details can disrupt the dysfunctional response to the underlying pattern, because the details may contradict or at least expand the family's synopsis. Beyond that salutary function, getting details is like getting a local map instead of a globe when you are lost on the highway. The particular landscape of the particular family must be understood to navigate effectively. Broadly speaking, however, many families and many clinicians err by superimposing their preferences over actual information about what is going on. They are like drivers who realize how the roads *should be* laid out instead of how they *are* laid out. Children suffer as a consequence because abuse and neglect are thereby missed, because interventions are misguided, and because the empathy that fosters psychological growth is missing.

GENERIC SOLUTIONS FAIL

Empathy requires details. Parents and clinicians cannot empathically tailor their conduct to signals from the child if the image of the child is subsumed under a generic label. However, even clinicians receive powerful messages from families to behave according to expectations; because they are human, those messages have an effect. Often, the expectation is that the clinician will be unhelpful, powerless, and unconcerned. The clinician is driven by the family away from the kind of specificity that can undermine the family's point of view and create a more empathic understanding of a particular child. Thus, it can be frustrating when narrative details are sought, as in the following exchange.

> **Clinician:** We need a placement for this fourteen-year-old girl. She's out of control.
>
> **Consultant:** What do you mean, out of control?
>
> **Clinician:** Nobody can manage her.
>
> **Consultant:** Specifically, what has she done?
>
> **Clinician:** She's aggressive, impulsive, defiant.
>
> **Consultant:** Can you give me an example?
>
> **Clinician:** She does whatever she wants whenever she wants.
>
> **Consultant:** OK, what's the worst thing she has ever done?
>
> **Clinician:** She was abusive to her mother.
>
> **Consultant:** What did she do to her mother? Specifically.
>
> **Clinician:** She verbally abused her.

Superficial labeling is partly a response to a resource-driven system of service planning. By "resource-driven," I mean that decision makers stop thinking in terms of what is going on and how to help, and instead think in categories of placement alternatives (home, foster care, group home, residential) or in categories of treatment (individual, family, group). A complex, sophisticated understanding of the child is not necessary when all that is being decided is the broadest level of placement. It is like that joke about the boy who asks his mother about sex. She gives him the Big Talk, and when she is finished, he says, "So do I check the M or the F?" Rich, textured understanding is irrelevant to broad, categorical choices. The question of where to house a child should not be confused with the more subtle question of how to intervene therapeutically, and the latter requires a detailed understanding of the patterns at work.

At the end of the book, I address the roles of the various service providers, how they overlap, and how they are different from one another. Central to all service provision, however, is the desire to play the role of the benign helper. Unfortunately, many of the families in the child welfare system have no place for this particular role in any of their family patterns, and benign helpers are routinely ignored. They are like voices from another dimension that have no foothold in the family's experience from which to cross over and be heard. The problem is that the only voices that the family is able to hear may be extremely unpleasant ones, voices that the clinician, foster parent, and social worker are all unwilling to be inhabited by. An appreciation of the pattern—the drama and the cast of characters—that informs the abuse can inspire a helper to relinquish her attachment to being seen as benign, and then to adopt a role and a voice that can actually be heard by the family members. Much damage is done and many opportunities are lost when service providers cling to the role of benign helper, more concerned about their own status than about intervening effectively.

In sum, it is important to cultivate fluency in the language of patterns to ensure that intervention strategies and predictions are context specific, are detailed with respect to the psychology of the client or client system, and are realistic with respect to the manner in which intergenerational parallels are transmitted. The next two chapters attempt to enhance that fluency by examining some theoretical underpinnings of pattern analysis.

Chapter 2

Patterns in the Mind

Some background on the nature of psychological patterns should prove helpful for recognizing the ones specific to child abuse. The basic idea is that, as a result of genes and experience, the mind has a structure, a system that organizes and arranges sense impressions, memories, and behavioral alternatives. The environment informs the psychic system, which in turn makes sense of the environment. Patterns in the mind are thus both the cause and the effect of patterns perceived in the environment. This chapter and the next explore the mental structures that allow patterns to exist in an individual's psychology and to be replicated in close relationships.

The main points raised in this chapter are as follows. Imagination is constantly at work, storing, structuring, and replicating patterns. An appreciation of imaginal processes can illuminate valuable information about a person or a family. Besides being a repository for patterns, imagining itself is an important aspect of psychological health, often interrupted by abuse and neglect. The imagination is fruitfully thought of as a series of landscapes populated by independent figures. The figures of the psyche are grouped in meaningful constellations, called complexes, the patterns of which reiterate, and are reiterated in, family patterns.

The discussion that follows is largely theoretical, since in this part of the book it is the underlying theory of patterns that concerns me. As much as possible, I have tried to make this discussion practical, with examples from family interactions and psychotherapy. I am concerned, though, based on my experience, that it is not theory per se that is likely to alienate some readers, but rather my allegiances to so many different theories. How can I be a Skinnerian behaviorist *and* psychoanalytic *and* systemic, without being—ugh—eclectic? The important question for me, as with other disputes in psychology, concerns the purpose for which a theory is being used at a given moment.

In my view, a good theory is like a good map, in that it fits the geography of the relevant environment. But for one purpose, a map of political subdivisions is most useful; for another purpose, a map of roads is best; for still another, a map of elevations. An "eclectic" map, showing all the information, would be a confusing mess.

CONSTANT IMAGINATION

The human brain is complicated, capable of doing more than one thing at a time. This simple fact underlies much of psychology, from Freud's central focus on unconscious conflict to behaviorists' interest in hierarchically arranged response repertoires. Indeed, behaviorists learned a long time ago that a *pigeon's* brain is complicated enough to do more than one thing at a time. For example, a pigeon can be taught to peck a circle whenever a bell rings by rewarding it with food when it does so, and then it can be taught to lift one leg whenever a light flashes. Then, the psychologist can work with either behavior, or with both at the same time, and the results might look as if there were two separate pigeons. For example, the psychologist may stop reinforcing the leg lift (by ignoring it whenever it occurs); that response will eventually extinguish (the pigeon will eventually give up on lifting its leg whenever the light flashes after a long enough period without a reward). The leg lift will extinguish regardless of whether or not the circle pecking is concurrently being reinforced. It is common among nonbehaviorists to speak of reinforcing the individual, but actually it is behaviors that are reinforced, not people or animals. Reinforce means strengthen; a behavior is strengthened—its probability of occurrence increases—if it is followed by something that the individual finds pleasant. The pigeon can be seen as a vehicle or vessel for the separate behaviors of leg lifting and circle pecking, and each operates (almost) independently of the other.

With humans, the number of independent behaviors is larger, and the behaviors themselves are of course more interesting. For example, a woman can make dinner for her children and tell her husband about her day at work at the same time. In other words, she can be a wife and a mother and, indirectly by discussing her job, a worker all at once. For various reasons, another woman may not be able to be these different things at the same time; there may be conflict about the coexistence of the different roles. For example, if she feels guilty about work and sees it as neglectful of her children, she may manage the ensuing conflict by separating or disassociating her work repertoire from her mothering repertoire. On a small scale, she may feel comfortable talking only about the children while preparing dinner. On a large scale, she may communicate to her children her sense that she is neglectful when she goes to work, so that they come to resent her job; she may even defer working, or developing a vocational identity, until the children leave home, just to avoid this conflict. This is only one example of the possible permutations in these behavioral repertoires.

PURPOSES OF IMAGINATION

We do many things at once, and one thing we are always doing is imagining: making up stories about what is going on and about what else could be going on. This serves several important functions for the individual (Mayman, 1975). Recent theories of memory, for example, emphasize the extent to which memories are encoded in a narrative context (Loftus, 1993). Stories seem to be the flower beds in which memories are kept alive. Memory has obvious survival advantages, and imagination enhances memory. If I had shown you a picture of a man, a woman holding a gun, and a child in pain, they would not be as easy to remember as the story of Mr. Avalon's mother threatening his father. Indeed, to make it easier to remember, you would have made up your own story to explain the photo. Similarly, we encode memories all day long by making up stories. The advantages of making up stories—they organize and record information— outweigh any distorting effect that arises from the fact that, equipped to make up stories, we create those that suit our expectations and wishes.

The ubiquity of imagination also derives from another of its functions. Imagination is the setting in which long-term consequences can exert an effect on current behavior. A defining characteristic of maturity or wisdom is that remote consequences of one's actions are emphasized over immediate gratification and short-sighted goals. To the extent that individuals respond only to their immediate environments, they are kept under the influence of immediate consequences. Imagination provides a buffer zone between stimulus and response in which long-term goals can be considered.

I emphasize the advantages of having an imagination to underscore its importance in human affairs. Clinicians who want to intervene in human affairs must account for what people are imagining if they want to intervene effectively and with predictable results. Imagination is useful because it allows a person to engage in trial-and-error behavior without actually trying anything. Overt trial-and-error learning is a fine strategy when the costs associated with an error are low. When you are doing a crossword puzzle, for instance, if you jot down a few letters and they prove to be wrong, you can always erase them. But when the costs of errors are high, imagination provides a "play-space" (Mayman, 1975; Winnicott, 1960) in which alternative solutions can be attempted in fantasy without producing any actual negative effects. People who do crossword puzzles in pen, thereby making errors more costly, have to think further ahead than those who use pencils. After trying out a few alternatives in fantasy, the person selects the strategy that worked best in his or her imagination.

People are wise, intelligent, and far-sighted to the extent that the rules that govern outcomes in their imaginations are representative of the rules that govern outcomes in life. When this is so, then the way things work out in the imagination is a good guide to how things will work out in reality. Thus, we imagine saying all sorts of things to abused children when we meet them for assessments, and we choose the one to actually say that the child responded to best in our imagination. If the child in our imagination is like the child in our office, we will be fairly effective.

Imagination also provides a respite from stress (Exner, 1993). People are constantly required to adapt to new information and to unfamiliar situations. Although this can produce growth, in the short run it is stressful, partly because we are repeatedly confronted with the possibility of failure in novel situations, and partly because all this novelty robs us of the opportunity to bask in the self-esteem and pleasurable sense of mastery derived from exercising a reliable skill. Thus, many fantasies involve everything going according to plan. At the private level of imagination, one can escape the need to adapt one's behavior to novel situations, without suffering any negative consequences; the corresponding fantasy is that I do it my way and it works.

In fantasy, one can squeeze the world into preexisting patterns or paradigms that one has already mastered. Alternatively, one can use the imagination to replay frustrating events until they are so familiar that a sense of mastery over them is achieved. Of course, when the world does conform strictly to expectations, it is not pleasurable for very long; it becomes boring (Twain, 1938). At these times, imagination will introduce the unexpected, to liven things up.

The Freudian view of imagination emphasizes wish fulfillment (Freud, 1953a). People's dreams and fantasies, Freud thought, were elaborate stagings of wishes come true. Freud thought that most people wish for things they are not comfortable acknowledging even to themselves, so that the wish that the fantasy fulfills is typically disguised by symbols and metaphors. Skinner's (1953) view was identical, though worded differently, as he saw fantasy and dreams as a chance to engage in gratifying behavior in private, i.e., without outward effects that the outside world can punish by disapproving or retaliating. A man who briefly fantasizes hitting his child cannot always fairly be said to "really" want to hit his child. What he would "really" like to do is hit his child without hurting the child. He would like to express his frustration and anger without injurious consequence. The fantasy provides an opportunity to engage in the behavior, in admittedly diluted form, but without the aversive result of actually hurting one's child. An important aspect of much battering, incidentally, is the way the batterer becomes truly enraged when the initial blow produces tears or injury. He had been hoping to express his frustration without negative effect. Then the negative effects arouse further frustration and also reflect badly on the batterer, and this increases his anger.

I think of the imagination less as a stage for wish fulfillment, although certainly it can be all that, than as a place for constructing road maps that can guide the person through life. These maps are based largely on early experiences, which are investigated and stored as clues to the kind of world the person lives in (Mayman, 1968; Toth et al., 1997). Problems occur when somebody uses a map of Florida to get around Massachusetts, or a map of childhood to get around adulthood. Problems occur when the events that inscribed a particular

map were too idiosyncratic to be good guideposts to the rest of reality.

Take Ms. Dean, for example, whose three children were put into
foster care for the single reason that the housekeeping in their home
was so deplorable that the place was unfit for human habitation. The
social worker who visited the home could not stand to be there for
more than a few minutes. There were animal feces scattered about,
the stench of old grease emanating from the kitchen, and piles of re-
pulsive garbage here and there. Unlike some professionals, who seem
to think that children in the child welfare system can endure more
than they themselves could endure, this social worker took the children with her when she left.

Even in the wake of his family's disruption, Ms. Dean's husband
did not lift a finger to help around the house. Instead, he responded to
the mess, as he always had, by haranguing her with degrading comments about her incompetence. Her church, however, did step in and
cleaned the apartment from top to bottom. The pastor prevailed on the
couple to get rid of their dog and cats. The social worker celebrated
by having a visit in the home with the three children, rather than at the
office, and indicated that the children would probably be home in a
matter of weeks. Within a month, however, the odor had returned, all
the dishes in the house were dirty, and rancid garbage was again accu-
mulating in the corners.

Ms. Dean maintained that she had only two memories of childhood. In one, she was trying on her mother's new hat when her
mother found her, grabbed the hat with one hand, and smashed her
into a wall with the other. In the second memory, she had just put on
her first bra. Her father made her show it to him, and then started paw-
ing her, although she was able to escape. To me, these memories seem
to have been encoded as danger signals associated with acting like a
woman, the mother's hat and the bra being signs of womanliness to
Ms. Dean at the time. She avoided assault within her home by avoiding acting like a woman. This map had served her well, and she ran
into fewer beatings and sexual assaults than she would have gotten
without her rudimentary guidebook to life in her family.

Pathetically, the map was also a good guide to negotiating her marriage, since her husband also seemed to assault her, if only verbally,
when the issue of her womanliness came up. In other important ways,

however, her map of womanliness was outmoded. She was about to lose custody of her children because acting like *her* idea of a woman, even to the extent of keeping house, was so fraught with danger for her that she could not bring herself to do it. She either had to change her map of womanliness, change her definition of housekeeping and mothering to something besides womanly, or get someone else to perform the functions she could not.

HOW IMAGINATION IS REVEALED

Fortunately for the clinician who is trying to understand underlying patterns, people do things that reveal their fantasies and imaginal processes (Rapaport, Gill, and Schafer, 1968; Crittenden, 1992). Obviously, telling someone a dream is an example, but many unintentional behaviors from our daily lives also reveal what is going on in the imagination. These revealing responses are the ones that are not fully dictated by circumstances, in other words, that are not automatic, or the same from everybody. For example, most people do not reveal their fantasy life when answering a question about their children's dates of birth. They simply state what those dates of birth are. Typically, there are no notable aspects of their answer to this question that are not fully accounted for by the question itself and by their children's actual dates of birth.

In the same way, one has little to learn about a person from a portion of behavior that is identical or nearly identical to everyone else's. A "popular" response to the Rorschach inkblot test (an answer given by at least a third of all subjects), for example, is unrevealing because it tells us more about what the inkblot actually looks like than it tells us about the individual who is looking. (Of course, if the person gives *only* popular answers, that would mean something significant.) Similarly, if on a word association test the answer to "night" is "day," nothing about the person's imaginal processes is revealed. (Again, *why* nothing is revealed may be of separate interest.) On a larger scale, if a bride in the 1920s keeps her birth name, it reveals something about her; if a bride in the 1990s keeps her birth name, it reveals something about the times. In short, conformity masks the imagination.

Necessity also masks the imagination. When immediate circumstances are so powerful as to require a response, little can be discovered about the responder. The requirement to respond in a certain way may stem from powerful reinforcers. Buying a lottery ticket may reveal something about an individual, but cashing in a winner reveals nothing. When the individual buys the ticket, she is making a choice. When she cashes in the winning ticket, for all practical purposes, she is not. The requirement for a response may stem not from reinforcers but from threats or precursors of punishment. Showing up at court under subpoena, for example, reveals little about the witness's personality and imagination, except that he understands what happens to people who do not. The requirement for a response can also simply stem from the nature of the stimulus. The oral response "cats" reveals more about an individual's imaginal world in response to a question about her phobias than in response to a question about what kittens become. What necessity and conformity thus have in common is that the response that masks the imagination is largely or wholly dictated by circumstances. Conversely, responses generally reveal the imagination to the extent that they are not dictated by circumstances (Köhler, 1938).

Private responses are especially likely to reveal the imagination. "Private," in behavioral parlance, means not observable by anyone else, not susceptible to feedback from other people or from the physical environment (Skinner, 1953). Not all private responses tap imaginal processes, of course; the thought processes by which calculus students solve problems may be private, but they are still largely dictated by the problem and by the students' training in calculus. Still, private responses are especially unlikely to be affected by external reinforcers and punishers, and they are richly, infinitely variable, so they usually do tap imaginal processes. When private responses are made public, either accidentally as in slips of the tongue or on purpose as in relating dreams or free associating in therapy, they can be especially rich sources of imaginal processes. This is what Freud meant when he called dreams "the royal road to the unconscious." Dreams are the most private of all narrative responses, as dreams are made not only outside of the influence of other people, but outside of the influence of even the dreamer's conscious agenda.

HOW IMAGINATION IS SUPPRESSED

There are many situations in life when one's imagination is best put on hold. Any task that requires constant alertness or executing routines can be subverted by expressions of imagination (Karson and O'Dell, 1976). Unimaginative people, whose attention is typically occupied by the immediate environment, for example, make good air traffic controllers (other things being equal) (Karson and O'Dell, 1974). Imagination is also best put on hold when the situation demands accommodation of novel stimuli with energetic processing. An example might be the difference between driving to work and driving to an unfamiliar location. When driving to work, environmental stimulation is easily assimilated into expected models, and imaginal processes are unlikely to be disruptive. When driving somewhere new, imaginal processes are best relegated to the background for the sake of functioning efficiency. Thus, people daydream driving to work; they pay attention driving somewhere new.

Imaginal processes are also best put on hold when they are likely to be responded to negatively (in behavioristic terms, punished). This might occur in a situation where imaginal processes are considered inappropriate. At work or in the classroom, for example, imagination may be welcome only in the group leader, and not from anyone else. A group member's interjection of something tangential is typically considered distracting and egocentric; in the group leader or the teacher it may be considered interesting . . . or at least impossible to stop. In certain kinds of scientific writing, imaginal processes are considered violations of norms that aspire to a fantasy of objectivity. Imaginal processes are also likely to be punished in situations that are hostile to their implications. For example, their expression typically increases the intimacy in an encounter by announcing the presence of an inner life (Langs, 1977). Systems that are hostile to intimacy can be expected to punish imaginal expressions (see the discussion of seriously disturbed systems in Chapter 7).

THE EFFECTS OF PUNISHMENT

One of the basic facts of Skinner's (1953) behaviorism, which seems to be true for all organisms capable of learning, is that punished responses do not lose their motivation for expression; they merely avoid the punishing force. In other words, if a response is punished, the *tendency* to do it again is not affected, merely the *circumstances* under which the response is likely to be repeated. (Note the distinction between the behaviorist term *punish* and its lay equivalent; the former refers to any sequence in which a response is followed by an aversive outcome and has little to do with intentions or authority. In parenting, though, there is generally a good deal of overlap between the two meanings, because punitive parents arrange for unpleasant consequences to follow their children's misconduct.) This is a very important reason why corporal punishment can be ineffective in the long run, and why it can promote delinquency. The individual learns, as a result of being punished, merely to wait for the source of punishment to be absent before engaging in the behavior. If children are hit for taking things that do not belong to them, they may steal things when no one is looking or, ultimately, when they think no one will be able to catch them. (Of course, with delinquency or theft, many more factors operate than just the history of punishment.)

In many instances of avoiding punishment, of course, the source of punishment must be absent not only in the external environment, but internally as well. For example, people who are punished for speeding by police officers continue to speed if they think no police officers are present. Speeders who *imagine* the presence of police officers, however, are less likely to speed, because for them the inhibiting stimulus is frequently represented in the immediate situation, even if only in imagination. You might call this the speeding conscience. Under the right set of experiences, an individual might always be behaving in the presence of an (imagined) police officer, so that even though the tendency to speed remains strong (as expressed, say, in fantasies, or in feelings of impatience), the person never actually speeds. Eventually, the internal image of the police officer might fade, but it is strengthened by the sight of police cars (especially when they have stopped other speeders).

The tendency of punished responses not to diminish but merely to wait until the coast is clear applies to imaginal processes that are punished. A disturbed parent who is afraid of an inner life can react negatively to his or her child's efforts at imaginative self-expression. The parent's negative reaction punishes the child's tendency to be imaginative. Similarly, a neglectful parent who feels guilty when his or her child remembers instances of neglect can react negatively to the child's efforts at remembering. These parents can become internalized in their respective children in such a way that the child is put in the position of either imagining or remembering in the constant presence of a punishing force. In these examples, imagining and remembering are analogous to speeding and the parent is analogous to a police officer.

Therapy invites the patient to remember and imagine in a context that will not punish these responses. Psychoanalytic technique has developed to the point where free association—the patient's task of saying whatever comes to mind, holding nothing back—is not so much in the service of allowing the analyst uncensored access to the patient's unconscious *historical* thoughts and feelings, but more as a way of expressing the underlying imagination as it is happening, allowing access to unconscious *current* thoughts and feelings (Langs, 1977). One goal of free association is to pair the inner child with a new kind of parent, one who does not react negatively to self-expression or to remembering.

The effects of punishment on imagination include the kind of forgetting known as repression (Dollard and Miller, 1950). Repression refers to motivated forgetting; the forgotten material is not really lost, but is kept from consciousness. The act of remembering unpleasant events is punished by the aversive quality of the material that is remembered; if I see distasteful experiences whenever I look into my memory, I will stop looking into my memory. Memories become distasteful either because they were intrinsically traumatic or horrifying or because an angry, judgmental presence (an internalization of a punisher) supervises the remembering process. Repression is like trying to have a game of make-believe in front of someone who is scowling. Repression is one example of how punishment can disrupt the integration of all the psychological functions. Punishment introduces into the psyche the need to keep some things separate from others, i.e., to keep some wishes, memories, and feelings apart from the source of the punishment.

EARLY MEMORIES AS ROAD MAPS

Imaginal processes are not just the stuff of which psychological assessments are made; they are also revealed in many daily activities (Freud, 1953b). The barrier between private and public is nowhere near as opaque as most people would like to believe. Indeed, while clinicians are taught to see through this barrier, children have to be taught to observe it. This is obvious in the case of instructing children not to reveal family business, and not to do things in public that society finds aversive. Less obviously, parents train children not to be aware of other people's preferredly private processes. One girl asked her father why he was so angry and he hissed at her, "I'm not angry." This father reacted harshly to the notion that the girl could see through his social facade. Within a minute of their greeting, a different little girl asked her mother, whom she had not seen in three months, if her mother would like to take a nap. The girl recognized her mother's lack of enthusiasm for her. The mother turned to me and said, "She always makes it difficult." Both of these girls were learning not to comment on other people's supposedly private processes. Because it is difficult for children to see something important without commenting on it, both girls were also learning not even to notice other people's supposedly private processes.

On a larger scale, imaginal processes may be revealed in life choices, from vocation to sexual partners. A pervasive fantasy of sibling rivalry may underlie a person's choice of law as a profession. Of course, not all lawyers are caught in a drama of out-arguing siblings for worldly success, but some are. Similarly, a woman's series of abusive relationships with men may reflect her expectation of rage in sexual relationships. Many battered women, probably most, are caught up in a situation beyond their control, like hostages in a bank; but some are enacting a pattern from their own imaginations. As with minor disclosures of supposedly private motives, many people react negatively if these grander imaginal influences are pointed out. This is largely to protect the notion that the individual is master of his or her own house, and not merely a player in it (Skinner, 1971).

FIGURES IN A LANDSCAPE

If the imagination is the producer of a story, then much of the storytelling involves the selection of the cast of characters and the landscape in which the drama unfolds. If all we know about a movie is the cast, the director, and the setting, much of the story can be inferred (especially if the cast members always play the same kind of part). Dreammaking, relegated to the background during wakefulness, makes up stories and scenarios about events of the day, which are then expressed during sleep (Freud, 1953a; Jung, 1928).

As a relatively simple example, say that a woman is late for work as a result of unforeseen road construction. Her mind is filled with realistic concerns and ways of coping with them. Is there an alternate route? What will she tell her boss? Should she stop and call? Meanwhile, the constant imagination is at work, making a different kind of sense of things. An obsessive-compulsive individual, who takes unwarranted responsibility for misfortune, may begin to construct a dream by personifying work as an authority figure who is angry and disappointed that she is late. A histrionic individual, by contrast, may cast the part of the work obligation with a benign authority figure who sympathizes with her frustration. For the former, the theme of the dream may be a story about getting in trouble; for the latter, a story about being consoled. The tendencies and expectations that inform the dream may also operate in the present, real world. The obsessive-compulsive woman may berate herself for not having checked the traffic reports on the radio (she supplies her own angry authority); the histrionic woman may drive on the shoulder, certain that the policeman will understand.

The "landscape" in which a dream (or other narrative material) is set can be geographical or psychological. A geographical landscape might be "at work": the person may have certain kinds of ideas, feelings, or expectations at work, and these are expressed narratively in the imagination by setting the story at the place of work. Of course, every geographical landscape will have a psychological aspect, addressed in questions such as, "What is the meaning of the office for this individual?" If someone has a dream that takes place in Iowa, it would be impossible to interpret the meaning of the landscape without knowing something about the person's history with the state (or its name).

On the other hand, some landscapes are more purely psychological, although they will be represented geographically in the imagination, of course. These kinds of landscapes might be "when I'm feeling sexual," or "when I'm worried about money." The former may be represented as taking place at a cocktail party or in a bedroom, for example, and the latter at a desk or in a bank. But here the geography is more like a set design: the psyche's representation of a psychological state.

COMPLEXES

Within a landscape, numerous characters appear, called figures. Any group of figures that appear together on a regular basis can be called a constellation or a complex (Jung, 1926). I prefer to use the terms interchangeably, but some people use "complex" only if the grouping has a neurotic component, i.e., when the figures are locked together in a web of interaction that works to the individual's disadvantage.

In many people, certain figures typically accompany certain others, and some of these groupings are common enough to get their own names, for example, "inferiority complex," "Oedipus complex," or, from transactional analysis, "rescuer triad." Locating and tracking certain figures is central to certain theories. The figure of the infant is the central focus of many object relations orientations (Mahler, Pine, and Bergman, 1975), for example, while the figure of the idealized self would always attract the attention of students of Karen Horney's (1950) work.

One figure that any approach would be interested in would be the Ego. Somewhat different from the Freudian "ego," the figure of Ego, which of course means "I" in Latin, is merely whichever character in the drama is cast as the self. In other words, all the figures in the drama can be seen as aspects of the person, but it is a matter of interest which one of the roles is currently being identified with. This can vary from time to time, as when a person who usually identifies with the submissive role in a dominance complex occasionally has dreams of ruling others. A clinically interesting phenomenon occurs when the number of roles in a complex is very limited, so that to appear at all, Ego has to choose the lesser of various unappealing roles. "Identification with the aggressor" fits this problem: when the roles are reduced to perpetrator and victim, many people find it less aversive to be cast as a perpetrator (Schmolling, 1984).

Jung (1926) says that complexes are the architects of dreams. He means that the dream work is laid down onto, integrated with, or informed by preexisting narrative structures, plot lines, and lists of characters. Other theoretical languages might say that the blueprints of dreams represent not complexes but personal constructs (Kelly, 1955), wishes (Freud, 1953a), transference patterns (Langs, 1977), or learning history (Dollard and Miller, 1950).

Jungians pose the mystical question of whether figures are "ahistorical." Some Jungians think that the individual's psyche comes populated with preexisting figures, called archetypes, and that while these are pictured differently from person to person according to the specific cultural context, the underlying figures are the same in everyone. Other Jungians think that figures in the psyche are "historical," meaning that they are internalizations and representations of childhood relationships and experiences. If different people across cultures tend to have the same figures, it may be because of common environmental factors or common species practices, not because of preexisting archetypes.

AUTONOMY OF FIGURES

The interesting part of this question of historicity is what happens when figures are treated ahistorically—i.e., as if each one is an autonomous being—versus what happens when they are treated as less than autonomous, as functions of biology and personal history. In my experience, figures tend to react the way people do when they are treated as if they are not autonomous: i.e., they try to prove that they are. Thus, even the most die-hard radical behaviorist will not treat people as piles of molecules. If she does, she will not get back from them a response that makes her happy. The same is true of figures. Figures in the psyche are probably internalized images of others and of experiences with others, but it is better to treat them as independent citizens of the psyche.

What does it mean to treat a figure as if it were autonomous? A woman dreams she is eating a meal by herself in a restaurant, and she notices a man at another table looking at her. She is afraid to look at him directly, but out of the corner of her eye she sees that he seems to be glaring at her. She gets up to leave and he follows her. She begins to run down the street and he chases her. A helpful question to ask this woman would be, "What does the man want?"

To encourage her to think about the man's point of view may lead to a solution, just as it might in conflict resolution between two people. Likewise, the next time this complex manifests itself in her daily life—for example, when she feels as if the bakery clerk is disapproving of her for ordering an eclair—she may not have to be afraid to look at the disapproval, scurrying off with her dessert. To run away would only make her fear and humiliation worse, according to the dream, since in the dream he does not glare until after she is afraid to look at him directly and he does not chase her until she runs off. Instead she might ask herself, as her therapist would, what the imagined attacker is like, what he is after, and why he is so angry at her. That is, she might ask herself what the bakery clerk is up to. Once considered, the answer to this question, at least in the bakery, is likely to be that he is up to nothing at all, which may dispel her tension.

The woman is tempted to say, "I'm scared because I just indulged myself." She thereby reduces her attacks on herself to extensions of her indulgence, and treats the figure of the attacker as if he is unimportant in his own right. In my experience, this may give her an illusion of control over the attacks, but it will not bring the attacking figure into a dialogue that can lead to change. That would be fine, of course, if the attacking figure were really external, not a part of her. For example, there is no reason to wonder what a real rapist wants, to greet him, to engage him in dialogue, or to try to change him. But here, the attacker is a part of her who deserves as much respect as the part of her she identifies with. The figure is more like a husband than a stranger, in the sense that she is related to him and wants not only what is good for her but also what is good for him.

A woman may realize that her husband only gets angry at her when she ignores him, but this insight, although it may give her more control over his anger, will not change their essential mode of relating. Instead of trying to explain away the figure in the dream, she needs to know what he wants, and why her fear makes him angry, and why she considers eating to be an indulgence. (The landscape of the dream involved a restaurant, so I infer gratification as a precursor to attack.) She needs to resolve the complex in a way that does not rob her of all the energy and power embodied in the aggressive male figure.

It seems peculiar at first to treat figures in a dream as if they were real people, and I suppose it does require some imagination and a sense of play. I am not going to spell out the scientific basis for this treatment here, as it is based on behavior theory, makes dull reading, and also is as unnecessary as it would be to spell out the biochemistry of a cough before recommending a lozenge. However, I do want to note the parallel between treating the figures of a dream as real people and treating individuals in an organization as real people. There is no reason to do so when one is working with the entire organization as an organic entity. For example, imagine a new regulation covering absenteeism, which proclaims that the next most junior employee must cover for anyone who is sick, late, or on vacation. Considering the effect of this regulation on the entire organization, one can predict that problems between employees are bound to erupt under such a system. This prediction will only become muddled if one tries to consider the personal psychology of each individual worker. However, when you are resolving conflicts between two specific employees (or figures), one of whom is angry at the other for needlessly saddling her with additional work, then it is more productive to consider each individual's personal psychology, if only to keep the employees from resenting you. They will not appreciate having their feelings dismissed as a mere by-product of a confusing policy. Similarly, there are situations in which it makes good sense to consider an individual psychology as a whole, analogous to considering an organization as an integrated entity, but there are other situations, including most child welfare cases, in which it pays to consider the individual interactions among the figures in the psyche.

Once the figures that populate the psyche are accorded as much autonomy as humans are, it is natural to begin to think of each psyche as a sovereign nation, governed according to principles that vary from person to person. Personality can refer to the system of government within an individual or to the roles assigned to various figures. Who gets control over the airwaves? Who is asked to take the lead in social situations? Who, in effect, is the secretary of state? Some people, like some nations, are composed of perfectly acceptable figures, but they are assigned roles that lead to dysfunction. For example, the best fighter is put in charge of foreign relations, instead of being put in charge of a battalion. Or the best hostess is put in charge of the archives.

These individuals often need only to have their strengths aligned with their situations, rather than needing a more comprehensive change. For example, an abused girl had a baby of her own and treated her shabbily. The young mother had also been an exceptionally good big sister, protecting and caring for her little brother. The treatment consisted not of overcoming her abuse history, which would have taken far too long for her baby to benefit from it, but instead consisted of helping her be a big sister to her baby instead of being a "mother." In her mind, the most selfish figure in the system was assigned to the role of "mother," and the most competent figure in the system was assigned to the role of "big sister." It was much easier in the short run to reframe her transactions with her baby as a sibling relationship, constellating her competence, than it would have been to change her definition of "mother."

The theoretical points of view outlined in this chapter emphasize the imagination of the individual as a landscape populated by figures. This formulation facilitates the observation of parallels between family and cultural systems on one hand and psychic systems on the other. This, in turn, facilitates understanding of systems or interventions in them by, among other things, opening the way to using intervention and interpretive techniques with individuals that were developed for families and organizations, and vice versa. These applications will become clearer as the use of systems theory to understand individuals is explored in the next chapter.

Chapter 3

A Systemic View of the Psyche

If the imagination is construed as populated by figures, organized in patterns within psychological landscapes, as outlined in Chapter 2, then questions are raised regarding the manner in which these figures interact with each other. I suggested in Chapter 2 that it is productive to treat each figure as an independent entity. In this chapter, I suggest that it is also productive to interpret their interactions with each other as one might interpret the interactions between members of a family or any other interdependent organization. This leads to an interpretation of identity in terms of the typical patterns of interaction, and the typical figures that the individual recognizes and accepts. When the components of identity—the psychological figures—are viewed as being the same in everyone, certain ways of thinking about other people follow, namely, that we are all made of the same stuff but in different patterns. Dialogue among the figures of the psyche is posited as a model of psychological health. Efforts on the part of some figures to control the rest of the figures are examined as a major way in which psyches differ from each other.

CIRCULAR THINKING

Within each person's psyche, the figures interact systemically. This word has two primary meanings, and the first is that each figure responds to the situation and to the other figures that happen to be present. The idea is that each part of a system receives and transmits feedback so that it and all other parts of the system can adjust accordingly (Bateson, 1972). Since all the figures (or, in a group of people, all the people) are responding to each other, it is impossible to do justice to an interaction by stating simply that B responded to A. All families interact systemically, and it never adequately explains an interaction in a couple to say, for example, that she left him because he cheated on her. The complicated-sounding idea of ongoing, embedded mutual interaction really means that one must also look at why he cheated on her, and at least some part of that analysis will focus on it as a response to her. To say that his behavior caused her behavior is to think linearly. The fuller appreciation of their interaction is to think circularly or systemically (Bateson, 1972).

A few other examples of circularity may be useful. We find rebellious children linked with controlling, authoritarian parents. But are the children rebellious because of the parents, or are the parents controlling because of the children? Clinicians are tempted to construe the interaction according to how they first hear of it, i.e., according to whose complaint about the other family member creates the first impression. Empathy with each family member can help avoid this mistake. I like to think of the way good playwrights and good actors give even minor characters their own motives for reacting as they do, instead of considering them to be mere conveniences in the main characters' stories.

For example, in Shakespeare's play about jealousy, Othello is a noble black man who, though honored for his prowess in war, can never be certain of his social position in white society. Othello's nobility and courage win him the hand of Desdemona, who has overheard him telling her father of his adventures. When Othello selects Cassio to be his lieutenant, Iago, who felt he should have gotten the job, plots his revenge. Iago gets Cassio drunk, and then gets someone to pick a fight with him and induces a third man to intercede. Cassio injures this third man with his sword. Othello discharges Cassio, and Iago has won. Why then does Iago proceed to convince Othello that Cassio and Desdemona are having an affair?

Systemically, one might consider that Iago's conniving against the trusting Cassio is not merely a literary conceit, reflecting the main drama between Venetian society and the trusting Othello. Nor is Iago's cunning merely an attempt to get his due. Iago is also responding somewhat predictably to Othello's self-righteousness (itself an adjustment to being a stranger in a strange land). Othello's grandeur makes underlings feel small. Circularly, Othello acts even more self-righteous in response to the petty rivalries around him, and his self-righteousness makes others even more petty. Iago escalates his plot because he resents Othello's nobility, contrasted as it is with Iago's own sordid motives. Rather than stoop to learn the details of what happened in the sword fight, Othello holds to the standard of highest honor: Cassio got drunk, end of story. Othello's standards elevate Othello, but diminish others, and the more diminished they seem, the more he clings to his standards. Iago escalates his plotting because he resents the smallness thrust upon him by Othello's nobility.

Another example of circularity in *Othello* would be the systemic interchanges between a flirtatious wife, especially one who sees reassuring her husband as beneath her, and a jealous husband. Obviously, he is jealous because she is flirtatious, but it may also be the case that she is flirtatious to place him in a role with which he is familiar and comfortable. Othello, as a black man, is nervous in his elevated position, and inklings of personal security may be less soothing to him than they are disorienting and frightening inducements to relax his vigil. Desdemona may find that when she is dutiful, Othello relaxes his guard and becomes anxious and fearful, states that do not match either spouse's expectations of him. When she is flirtatious, he is jealous, but he remains on his guard. With respect to most marriages, if we were married to her we would act a lot like him, and if we were married to him we would act a lot like her.

It is probably best, for most purposes, to think systemically; it is wiser, more conducive to inviting people into a process of change, and more fair. The exception is when someone behaves unacceptably. At that point, systemic explanations must give way to protective purposes. For example, it may be wise to conceptualize a husband's jealousy systemically, but if he strikes his wife in a jealous rage, it may be foolish to examine the interrelationship between her flirting and his battery. That examination could indeed provide her with a measure of control. She might learn to avoid battery by acting submissive or cheerfully obedient, accurately realizing what part she plays in the transaction. However, that systemic view would misplace the onus of responsibility, and would disguise the degree of the husband's overreaction. For long-term effects, it may be accurate to tell the wife that she needs to be stronger and more stable, but it sounds blaming in the face of the husband's outrageous conduct.

Again, unacceptable conduct distorts a systemic explanation. A mother's neglect may be interlinked with a baby's nonresponsiveness, but to think about the neglect systemically is to invite the focus to be fixed on the baby or on the system instead of on the mother. These exceptions do not apply to thoughts about an individual's psyche. Within the psyche, it is always best to think systemically. It does not make any excuses for battering to tell the batterer that if *his* femininity were stronger and more stable, then his masculinity would be less domineering and controlling. Nor does it provide excuses for neglect to tell the woman in despair that if *her* childlike qualities were more vital and responsive, she would not be so avoidant of her inner life.

The second meaning of "systemically" is implied by the first. To say that parts of a system interact systemically is to say that it is valid to characterize the system as a whole according to its culture, norms, or expectations. Families, figures in a landscape, and other systems develop mechanisms for monitoring and controlling each other's behavior. One family may condition its members to experience isolation as aversive, as a threat. Members of this family may refuse to speak to, or at least act coolly toward, anyone who acts too independent. It is valid to characterize such a family as close-knit. Within the psyche of one of its members, an independent idea—say, a fantasy of moving across the country—may meet a very cool response. The person in whose head such a fantasy begins to occur may not listen to it, may stop the visuals from unfolding by playing instead in the mind's eye a videotape of Mom lonely and sad. It is valid to characterize this individual as dependent. For our purposes, the importance of this meaning of "systemically" is that it is okay to characterize a complex or a family as having a purpose, even as wanting something or as fearing something. We can say that a certain family wants closeness, or that another family fears secrets. We can say that a complex is designed to keep a boy from abandoning his mother, or to keep a girl from making her father angry.

Because the figures in the psyche interact systemically, most of the techniques for analyzing interactions among members of a family apply to the analysis of interactions among figures. Thus, an important motivator for each figure is the effect of its behavior on the other figures. Indeed, all psychological analyses emphasize the importance of inspecting consequences for clues to meaning. For example, in behaviorism, the meaning of a behavior is found in its effects. In family systems theory, the meaning of a behavior is found specifically in its effects on other people in the system. In one version of object relations theory, the meaning of a behavior is found in a specific effect on one person, namely, the effect on the mother's level of anxiety (Mahler, Pine, and Bergman, 1975).

PROJECTIVE IDENTIFICATION

The system of the psyche interacts with larger systems in a way that is highly reminiscent of projective identification. Projective identification is a defensive maneuver on the part of an individual who cannot tolerate the acknowledgement of a particular psychological feature within himself (Langs, 1977; Ogden, 1981). Instead, he perceives this feature as coming from outside. As an example, consider a man who cannot tolerate being seen, even by himself, as angry. When things happen that could make him angry, instead of locating the sense of anger as coming from within himself, he locates its source outside of himself. In pure projection, he merely attributes the anger to someone else. He might imagine his wife is scowling at him, or, if even less tied to reality, he might imagine that someone is trying to humiliate him or even kill him. In projective identification, he is more tied to reality, and requires some support from his perceptions that his externalizations are valid.

Thus, without realizing what he is doing, he behaves in such a way as to make other people exhibit the undesired feature, in this case anger. In projection, he imagines people are angry at him to externalize his own aggression; in projective identification, with the same end in mind, he actually makes them mad at him. He may not respond when he is addressed, or he may accidentally forget responsibilities, or he may drive slowly in the left lane. These behaviors are reinforced by their effect on others; namely, they get angry. The aversive aspect of being the object of people's anger is more than made up for by the man's ability to avoid being seen as an angry person. Another projective identification might involve the externalization of a sense of weakness. Making other people fearful allows the sociopath to avoid being seen as weak, by enabling him to attribute weakness to someone else. Intolerable psychological features are like hot potatoes that people hand off to each other by behaving in a way that puts the feature into another person.

Even features that are not intolerable to an individual can be constellated in other people, as the complement to the first person's psychological state. Some of these transactions are so natural that they hardly deserve or require psychological analysis. A person who for whatever reason finds himself feeling nurturant, sexy, or curious is likely to engender in those around him complementary feelings of being hungry, sexy, or interesting.

Many interpersonal transactions, however, are based not on a natural complementarity but on complexes. A woman who grew up under conditions of intense sibling rivalry is likely to come to expect others to resent her good fortune. Then, when something good happens to her, she may present it, or, more likely, keep it secret, in a way that in fact makes others resent it. For example, a woman who had been trying to get pregnant for a long time, and then finally did so, was fearful that her friends would envy her, so she kept the news to herself until her sixth month. When she finally told her friends, instead of being happy for her, they were upset with her for not telling them for so long. Her behavior unconsciously validated her expectations that her good news would be resented, by constellating resentment in her friends.

As another (admittedly simplified) example, a man grew up with parents who competed with each other for his affection. He came to expect that if he grew close to another man (his father), he would be attacked by a woman (his mother). In therapy, he discovered that he discusses his male friendships with his wife in a way that indeed engenders her envy. He mentioned, for example, apropos of nothing, that she would not have fit in during a trip to a casino he had taken with his buddies. She had had no interest in going with them to the casino, but the way he said it, it made her feel left out.

These patterns—sibling rivalry, parental rivalry—operated in the families of origin, then in the individual's psyche (as expectations), then in the current interpersonal system. The mechanism for their translation into the current social world is, as noted, a lot like projective identification, although the purpose is not to externalize intolerable features but to regulate and replicate the underlying pattern, or complex, and to comfort individuals with a reliable sense of how the world works and what their role is in it.

IDENTITY AND THE QUEST TO BE ONESELF

To act in character may be a fundamental human motivation. The human species is exquisitely sensitive to pleasure, and this sensitivity enables people to find pleasure in all sorts of things that most species apparently ignore. These include all aesthetic pleasures and responsivity to a wide variety of sensations. In addition, there are the basic biological pleasures of food, sex, touch, shelter, and sleep. All the pleasures that the human child experiences are mediated by the child's identity, and secondarily bolster the attachment to that identity. In other words, if I am constantly rewarded in the presence of an object or condition, I will come to associate that condition with the reward, and I will imbue it with all sorts of positive connotations. Brand loyalty in marketing depends on this very connection. I like Coke because I associate the good taste of cola with the Coke logo. Nostalgia for home is also a function of conditioning. Much good that happened to me as a child happened at home, so I am fond of home.

One constant that is present whenever I am rewarded is me. I was present during every good meal, every moment of comfort, every aesthetic experience, and every bit of pleasure. If everything good that had ever happened in my life had happened while I was writing, I would be very fond of writing. Since everything good that has happened in my life *has* happened while I was being me, I am very fond of being me. People act in character because acting in character is reinforced every time anything good happens to them.

Growing up in a family system that has cultivated a certain self is another powerful motivator for being oneself. When you act in character, you are rewarded by having things run smoothly. When you act out of character, you are dissuaded by having things run chaotically. For example, twelve-year-old Tom was supposed to be extremely insolent, an attitude that served a family function. It gave his father a good excuse for venting hostility, it gave his mother an excuse for not working outside the home as she was constantly called to school, and it made his little brother seem angelic by comparison.

When I met them, just holding the assessment session met all these agendas: Dad was exasperated about missing work because of Tom's need to be assessed, Mom was again prohibited from facing the larger world, and the brother was clearly there as the good son. Thus, Tom did not need to be insolent that day, and in fact was quite pleasant during the family session. The rest of the family proceeded to irritate him until he finally blew up. His father described him to me in insulting terms, his brother grabbed the toy Tom had picked off the shelf, and his mother made Tom let the little brother keep that toy. The family was, of course, also motivated by their desire to show me what they had to put up with, but still I think that in general they were also showing me how they condition him to be insolent. It is like that old joke in which a guy comes to a psychiatrist for help with his brother who for twenty years has lived as a chicken. The psychiatrist asks why they are coming for help now, and not twenty years ago. The guy replies, "We needed the eggs." In this case, the eggs were the secondary gains associated with Tom's insolence. The family's need for these makes Tom act in character.

Because of these different motivators, most people like to be themselves, and will take every opportunity to be the self they identify as "I." The motive to be oneself is hard to spot, in spite of the fact that it is so powerful. This is because the impulse is so ubiquitously and pervasively gratified that it is rare to see a person not acting in character, and therefore rare to see how hard the person will work to get back to the familiar. It is like the quest for oxygen. People are rarely without oxygen, so it is hard to guess from watching people under normal conditions how powerful the motive is to obtain oxygen. Analogously, people are generally acting in situations that are suited to them, because they have constructed social and physical environments made for their own identity. It is only when people are placed in novel situations that their desire to act in character becomes clear. Tavistock training, for example, teaches people about themselves by putting them in novel groups and helping them discover what roles they insist on playing. Psychological testing puts people in novel situations, and records how they manifest themselves. Psychoanalytic therapy analyzes the way the patient creates a unique relationship with the therapist that keeps the patient in character. The point for now is that one reason family complexes reproduce themselves in the individual, and then again in new situations, is that the individual has come to define herself according to a role in the complex, and manifesting that definition is a very powerful motivation.

One way to get at what it means to think systemically is to use "when-then" syntax. This can capture a relationship between figures (when I feel sexual, then my judgment disappears) or between figures and landscapes (when I am in a restaurant—when I expect to be nurtured—then an attacker appears). In families, the same syntax can be used to keep the behavior of different members tied together in the same construction. When you try to control her, then she runs away. When she exerts her freedom, then you try to control her.

When Mr. Avalon (the man whose mother threatened his father with a gun) threatens himself, he forces his abusive impulse to be expressed behind his own back. When he abuses children surreptitiously, it makes his protective feelings seem strong and effective, leading to their being expressed in a domineering, threatening manner. When Mr. Barrows (the drunken lawyer who smacked his pot-smoking daughter) is self-righteous, it leaves his anger unchecked. When his anger is unchecked, he does things that make him feel either very guilty or self-righteous.

WHEN, NOT WHETHER

To the extent that the same figures populate each psyche, differing only in how they are arranged within the psyche, we are all the same. The child molester, in whom we see nothing of ourselves, differs, in this view, in the constellation that accompanies his lust, not in the lust itself. We all have lust somewhere, we all like children sometimes, we are all blind to children's sensitivities at times, and we all have bad judgment on occasion. The child molester differs from us in that all these forces appear in the same constellation.

The pedophile's lust appears in conjunction with dominance, violation, fear, and, of course, the childlike. Notably absent from the constellation that includes his lust are mature figures capable of empathy or self-control. Presumably, his lust unfolded in a social context that did not include a benign parent, and this kept him from internalizing judgment and maturity with respect to it. Family systems that do not recognize and make space for children's lust—i.e., most family systems—produce people whose sexual psychology unfolds either on a stage dominated by parental images (with lust nearly absent) or on a stage where the appearance of lust scatters parental images. The child's sexuality cannot coexist with the parent in the family, nor with good judgment in the psyche. Most people's judgment is at its worst when it comes to sex, not only because the impulse is so strong, but also because it is an impulse not well-parented in most families.

The issue is not whether a person is lustful (or angry, or conscientious), but under what circumstances. Even when the individual has characteristics not shared by most people, such as primitive rage or auditory hallucinations, the relevant question is usually when these occur, not whether. In other words, the answer to the question for most people might be never, but that should not be taken naively to mean that the potential is not there. Instead, an absence of hallucinations in an individual's history should be taken to mean that perception has always been accompanied by a figure who can differentiate inside and outside. What separates normal people from hallucinators is not the visualization of things that are not there—we all do that— but the simultaneous presence of a figure who can tell that the seeing or hearing is going on in the absence of external stimulation. Dreams, then, are indeed hallucinatory, in the sense that most people do not know they are dreaming while they are dreaming.

Sometimes a trait is so obvious that diagnosis stops with naming it. This leads to tautologies that replace diagnosis. One psychologist wrote that a girl runs away from foster care because she is impulsive, has bad judgment, is self-destructive, and does not like the foster home. All these ideas are embedded in the presenting problem. A boy who was suspended from school for swearing at teachers was "diagnosed" as angry and oppositional. The diagnostic enterprise is far less useful when it settles for naming what it sees. Much more useful is asking when, not whether. Under what circumstances does the girl show bad judgment? When she runs, which figures accompany the running in her imagination? Is she being chased? Or is she pursuing? If she fantasizes about getting caught, which figure plays the role of her pursuer? What will this figure do if she is caught? She does not run from the foster home every minute she is there. Which foster home, psychologically speaking, did she run from? The one that failed to welcome her? The one that made her feel she was different from the biological kids in the home? Or the one that made her feel nurtured and put her in a loyalty bind with her own family? In other words, what is the psychological landscape that occasions her running away? Good diagnosis also addresses questions such as the following: How predictable are the situations that prove difficult? How quickly does the person regain composure? What occasions this recovery? How disruptive are the regressions? Which reactions by others exacerbate them?

ASSESSMENT HYGIENE

Diagnosis does not just lead to treatment; it may be salutary in itself. I call this assessment hygiene: a good diagnosis is good for its subject (Karson, Karson, and O'Dell, 1997). Depression provides a good example. Typically, the depression overshadows the systemic context in which it unfolds. If you attempt to tie the person's depression to a specific event or to a specific circumstance, you are met with glum denials. It is not just that the blues feel permanent and fundamental when they overtake a woman, for example. It is also that her depressive self-blaming makes her accept responsibility for anything bad; the depression must be her own fault, not the result of circumstances. Her narrative construction of ongoing events is colored by her depression, and then compounds it. Things seem bleak and hopeless. She is in a one-character drama; her depression makes her lose interest in other people and in the external world, so she stews in her own sad juices. A good diagnosis will not only tell us that she is depressed, but when, under what circumstances, and in what constellation of figures.

Immediately, two pathways out of depression are opened by this kind of detailed diagnosis. The first is analogous to treatment techniques that work on the individual's cognitive construction of her depression (Beck, 1989). One such technique involves her carrying a beeper that goes off at random during the day, whereupon she must write down what she is feeling at that moment in a notebook. It turns out that when she surprises herself with questions about how she is feeling (rather than approaching her feelings from within the standpoint of her depression), she is frequently not depressed at all. This confronts her with the extent to which her depressive view is only one way of construing what is happening to her. The analogy in a good diagnosis is that the question of when she is depressed also brings up the notion of when she is not. Half the battle in fighting depression is maintaining in one's imagination the possibility of not being depressed.

The second pathway from depression opened up by a good diagnosis is analogous to the cognitive-behavioral technique of identifying the sense of being trapped that generally characterizes depression, and then identifying who is doing the trapping. A good diagnosis turns a one-character drama into a multicharacter drama by specifying the other figures involved. This paves the way to dialogue with the other figures, and leads to options in relating to them. One sees the process more clearly in families than in individuals, because in families the different roles are inhabited by different people. When the depressed woman's husband is attentive and caring, yet interrupts her or does not give her a chance to speak during the session, it is obvious to the clinician that her depression is at least partly a transaction with him. But when the woman plays both roles and does not give herself a chance to speak, it is harder to see what is going on. By making the individual psychological drama into a multicharacter transaction, a good diagnosis makes the situation more like the family session.

DIALOGUE BETWEEN PSYCHIC FIGURES

If the figures in the psyche are like independent people in a system, then the figures have to coexist in some harmony. An organization develops among these figures that is analogous to government among people. The organization of the figures, like a government, has certain goals. Not everyone agrees what those goals should be, of course, but several are commonly endorsed. A good government or psychological organization will protect the minority from the will of the majority. In government, there must be a balance between the rights of individuals and the interests of the system. In the psyche, there should be a balance between a desire to satisfy a particular figure and the needs of the person on the whole. A good government and a good psychological organization should also protect the entire populace from tyranny, encourage and facilitate diversity (by recognizing that not everyone is the same, and that as many needs should be met as possible), develop a system for resolving conflicts between competing needs, and develop a feedback system between the hierarchy and the populace.

Many of these goals, at least in their application to the individual psyche, can be subsumed under the auspices of dialogue. The immediate objective of much clinical work, education, and parenting is to enhance respectful communication between figures or system members. A fundamental orientation to symptoms in Jung's writing is that when a figure is not engaged in a dialogue, it has to engage in guerrilla warfare to express itself. Symptoms are seen as communications by oppressed and ignored figures. As in politics, efforts to suppress them make them worse. Unlike politics, the guerrillas of the psyche are always central to the system; they are never outside agitators. Symptoms are said by Jungians to contain wisdom, because they are usually declarations of something that needs to happen and rudimentary attempts to make it happen. Even symptoms of suicide can be usefully construed as a sign that something needs to die. Psychosomatic symptoms often produce secondary gains that are in fact their wise purpose, such as when a man has to quit a school program that is not right for him because headaches make it impossible for him to study. If quitting were tolerated better within the psychic system, the part of him that knows he should leave would not have to resort to headaches to get him out of there.

Dialogue is hard enough to achieve when all parties are interested and capable. Within families and societies, not all parties are interested, and within psyches, not all parties are capable. Naive versions of systems theory, which construe all actions as being in the service of the system, have trouble accounting for the seriously disturbed system. Common assumptions about the goals of the system simply may not apply to disturbed systems. These might include any of the positive reframes associated with family therapy. For example, some mothers are not ultimately trying to protect their daughters by controlling them; they may instead just want to objectify and hurt them. Many men who molest their stepchildren are not playing a part in a family drama; they are just using the children as props in their own drama. Systems theory is only useful, then, when there is in fact a system, when the parts are interconnected and responding to each other.

If the child's reactions are irrelevant to the molester, then there is no feedback loop, no interconnectivity, and any attempt to understand the child's reactions in systemic terms will be misleading. Imagine an obscene phone caller dialing randomly until he hears a woman's voice. It is pointless to ask this woman what she was doing before the phone rang in an attempt to understand her connection to the call. Of course, the information would still be useful in understanding what meaning she might give to the call.

In most families, there is enough mutual concern, interdependence, and interconnection to support a systemic understanding of nearly every interchange. When a husband does something that infuriates his wife, it is nearly always accurate to say that one factor in his motivation was to infuriate her. Married as they are, he probably knows, or should know, how she will react and he probably has a stake in her reaction. In most individual psyches, the figures are also almost always sufficiently interconnected to support a systemic interpretation of their interactions. If self-restraint makes me angry, there is probably a connection between the way I restrain myself and the fact that I get angry, and there is probably a connection between the way I get angry and the fact that I restrain myself.

But in some individuals, the psychic organization may be so fragmented that the figures are not engaged in systemic interconnection (see Chapter 7 on seriously disturbed systems). In these people, dialogue between some figures may be impossible. The level of dialogue available between figures is often evident in their depiction in dreams or other clinical material. Anger that is personified as an enraged stalker may be hard to engage in dialogue, but at least a dialogue is conceivable. Anger that is portrayed as a rabid dog is extremely difficult to engage in an exchange of interests and perspectives. When the anger is a tornado, dialogue is impossible. Presumably, the humanity of the figure reflects the extent to which it was seen as human—socialized, welcomed, and included—by the individual's family of origin. Treatment usually involves humanizing the figure before dialogue can occur.

One way to look at individual therapy is to see it as a place where different figures can emerge and a dialogue between them can be facilitated by the therapist. This is very much akin to doing family therapy, but all the different family or system members are aspects of the individual patient. For example, a man who is socially bold but also reclusive has problems when his friends, of whom his boldness produces many, complain about the fact that he does not keep up with relationships. He has anxiety dreams of having to choose between going to a friend's birthday party and working on his novel. The part of him that wants to stay home needs to learn how to get along with the part of him that likes a party. Whichever impulse he gives in to becomes his oppressor, so that when he is writing, he wishes he were at the party, and when he is at a party, he wishes he were writing. A therapist can help him become a referee or mediator between the two figures instead of trying to satisfy both at once.

Individual therapy in this context examines the problems that occur when a figure only expresses itself in isolation from other figures, especially in isolation from the more rational and related figures. It is relatively rare that a person needs therapy because he is too angry, lustful, or greedy; it is much more common that his anger, lust, or greed are in and of themselves of normal proportions, but lack the brakes and the modulation that other people have. In other words, his anger, for example, may be expressed without much input from the part of him that cares about preserving relationships or social status. His anger gets out of hand because he is like a toddler expressing anger without an adult nearby to keep him from biting.

One goal of individual therapy, from this perspective, is to arrange for new or different figures to be present when anger is present. A typical scenario might have this angry man seeking treatment because of the damage his eruptions do to his relationships at home or work. The therapist ferrets out instances of anger that occur in the context of the therapy relationship. For example, the man gives the therapist a check with the therapist's name misspelled, and the therapist interprets this as an expression of anger, while the man claims it is a simple mistake. The purpose of the interpretation is to bring the man's anger into the open, and to demonstrate that it does not need to disrupt the alliance between Ego (the part of the man that the man identifies with) and the therapist. In future expressions of anger, the figure of the anger does not dominate the stage, but shares it with Ego, which is now bolstered by its alliance with the therapist. One patient, for example, repeatedly dreamed he was hiding from a monster wreaking destruction on his home. Eventually, he began to dream that I was hiding with him, and then he dreamed that, while hiding, we developed a plan together to deal with the monster.

POSSESSION BY A SINGLE FIGURE

When one figure is outside of the flow of communication with *all* other figures, serious problems can occur. If that figure is present, then it means that all the other functions of the psyche are not. We say that the person is "possessed" at such a moment by the particular figure (Jung, 1926). When other figures are present, then the figure in question is entirely absent. This helps explain why some violent people are extremely docile and submissive (Megargee, Cook, and Mendelsohn, 1967). Usually, their aggression is utterly unavailable to them; occasionally, it possesses them.

I was asked to help DSS determine whether to suspend visits between a little girl, Annie, almost two, and her mother, Ms. Stevens. The state had already decided to bring the case to trial in an effort to terminate the mother's rights, and under these conditions the parent generally retains a right to visit the child once a month, until the trial is held. In this particular case, Annie would wail and sob for the entire hour, and the social worker was concerned that the visits were harming her.

A few years earlier, Ms. Stevens had tried to kill an older child, inflicting serious injuries. This older child was permanently removed from her care at the time and adopted by someone else. Ms. Stevens was acquitted of attempted murder by reason of insanity, and was committed to a mental hospital, where she got pregnant. By the time Annie was born, the mother was out of the mental hospital, stabilized on medication, and living with her own mother. Within weeks of Annie's birth, the state successfully sued for custody of her, due to concern about the mother's mental status and her potential for homicide.

Almost two years later, Annie was in foster care, and the mother's brother had just agreed to adopt his niece in another state. Therefore, as it happened, the visit I observed was to be their last. The original purpose of the assessment was moot, but there was always a chance that the uncle would change his mind, so I met with mother and daughter anyway.

Annie indeed wailed and sobbed as soon as she saw her mother. Once I was alone in the room with the two of them, the child, who had limited verbal facility, kept crying, "Door!" and "Mommy!" The latter cry was apparently for the foster parent, although only the social worker had brought her to the visit. "Mommy" is a word to which people react very powerfully. It provides an example of how parents can misunderstand their children's capacity to mean what they say. Many parents are offended if the child refers to someone else as "Mommy" or "Daddy," while taking it as a compliment if the child calls them by one of these sounds. Typically, in my experience, the words "mommy" and "daddy" are more like ranks, or designations of functions, than they are an assertion of a primary relationship.

During the visit, Ms. Stevens kept cooing at the child in a soft voice that "everything is OK" and "Mommy is here" while holding the girl on her lap. The mother's gentleness was striking; under similar conditions, many parents, knowing they are being observed, get a little desperate and try different things to engage the child. One of the hallmarks of true empathy is that the parent will tailor her behavior to cues from the child, but this mother just kept cooing, while Annie kept wailing. After ten minutes of this, I told Ms. Stevens that the child did not need to be comforted, but instead needed to be engaged with a lot of energy. I told her that Annie's upset was filling up all the space in Annie's mind, and the parent needed to push it aside with something of her own. Ms. Stevens replied that I was wrong and that Annie needed comfort. To prove this to me, she put the child down on the floor abruptly, and as Annie more or less stumbled forward in her direction, she scooped her up into her arms again, and said, "See? She needs comfort." The toddler continued to wail.

I was on the verge of ending the visit, but I could not bear the thought that the last time this woman might ever see her baby would end like this. I spoke to her in the loudest voice I could use without actually screaming. I explained again how the baby needed something to interrupt her upset. I also told her that it was confusing to Annie when her mother kept saying, "Mommy's right here," since whoever the child meant by "Mommy" was obviously not right here. Ms. Stevens disagreed with me again, but by then I was able to point out how Annie had not made a sound since I had first spoken so loudly. "She's as glad as we are to hear something besides her own wailing," I hollered.

Ms. Stevens was never able in that visit to put out anything other than the most muted, softest, sweetest energy. This led to a few more rounds of sobbing on Annie's part. But when I had finally calmed the child down, with more yelling disguised as conversation, Annie became interested in one of the toys in the room, and Ms. Stevens played with her and the toy for almost half an hour before the visit ended. It takes aggression to engage a child, and too little aggression lets the child's emotional state spill out and pervade her experience. This mother was utterly gentle, except when she was attempting murder. Her anger existed in isolation from all other considerations, so that it either dominated her psyche or was completely unavailable.

Nietzsche once said that any person's character could be summed up in three anecdotes. It seems to me that if you can do it in only one or two, it is a bad sign that the person does not enjoy a range of experience or ways of being in the world, and that the person lives at the mercy of one or two figures.

OVERGOVERNANCE VERSUS UNDERGOVERNANCE

Many psychological problems can be construed as stemming from overgovernance or from undergovernance of the psyche. Some personalities are subject to constant and intensive efforts at control by parental or authoritative figures, or by Ego in an authoritative guise (i.e., when the person identifies with the authoritative part of the self). Ego is always an important figure in any complex, but it is only one figure; Ego does not own the psyche any more than an individual owns her family. The overgoverned person has a fantasy of being in charge of her own psyche, and values rationality, order, and rules. Figures that are not easily controlled are disowned, and projected outward, so that the person acts as if only he or she can do things right, can be counted on, and so on.

One overgoverned personality was Mort, an engineer. His stepson, John, was flunking out of high school, using marijuana daily, and staying up all night reading or listening to music only to sleep all day. At seventeen, John was too old for court involvement through a CHINS petition, but he did receive a psychological evaluation through the court clinic after he was arrested for possession of marijuana. The testing confirmed what was apparent on interview, namely, that in spite of his obvious maladjustment, John was not a disturbed person in the sense of how he related to others and how he maintained a sense of self. The psychologist recommended family therapy under the assumption that, absent a serious emotional disorder, John's conduct was likely a response to systemic issues.

The family was ridiculously stereotyped. John was challenging, rebellious, and self-righteous in his assertions of personal autonomy, and easily humiliated by Mort's jibes regarding his financial dependence. Mort was brilliant; he frequently stared at the ceiling with his fingertips together, as if he were mulling over a theoretical problem of infinite complexity, and then he would rejoin us with a pronouncement of the correct solution. John's mother, Jill, acted as if she were in a room with two hand grenades. She sat demurely, perfectly coiffed but silent, nodding at whatever either male said, occasionally mumbling reassurances that irritated both her husband and her son (the one she was agreeing with would be irritated by her solicitous attitude, the other because she was taking the opposite side).

When I asked about possible roots of John's truancy, Jill volunteered that Mort had not received a raise since his last promotion, unconsciously balancing the topic of John's failure with an example of Mort's. She wondered if his creative juices had dried up. I saw Mort's intelligence as a third world dictator, subjugating the rest of the family and even himself until they either accepted a posture of submissiveness or were driven to insurrection. I sent John from the room and pressed Mort on whether he was happy, and what would make his life better. I thought that change would follow from Mort's recognizing what his perfectionistic attitude was costing him. Svengali hypnotized the woman he loved, Trilby, and forced her to love him back, but it was unsatisfying, because he knew it was not genuine, not enthusiastic. Mort acknowledged that he would like more from Jill. In fifteen years of marriage, she had not once refused him sex, unless ill, but neither had she ever initiated it.

Mort agreed to go for a week without criticizing or correcting anyone's conduct, no matter how egregious, stupid, or even dangerous. I gave him examples, some playfully ludicrous, others mundane, to see if he could face each one and promise not to criticize. Say you come home and the toaster oven has been left on; Jill has hit the garage with her car while pulling in; and she explains the accident with bad grammar. Mort's perfectionism forced him to guarantee that he could pull this off for one week.

Jill, who had been listening intently, did not need a written prescription to know that if she wanted to improve her son's relationship with her husband, she needed to initiate sex during the week. They came to the second session ready for things to be different; even Mort managed a smile while grudgingly admitting that the sex had been great. However, as Milton Erickson has noted (Haley, 1967, 1973), clients need a graceful way out of their symptoms, and Mort would never be satisfied to think that such a simple change in his own behavior would make his family and himself so much happier. Therefore, I assured them that John was going through an adolescent phase, not because of anything related to either of them, but in response to his biological father's desertion when he was an infant. I told them that John would improve by himself, and I, with nothing else to work on, had just wanted to help them with their sex life, partly in anticipation of the day when they would be alone together after John left home. A month later, John had gotten a job, and Mort, always an early riser, was taking him out to breakfast every morning and driving him to work. Once the dictator stopped dictating, the rest of the system warmed up to him.

As noted in the discussion of projective identification as a model for transactions, other people generally fulfill the overgoverned person's expectations in their reaction to his rationality. They may take advantage of his reliability or they may resent it, but either way they are likely to act more irresponsibly and childishly around him than when they are on their own. Whether other people attack him, compete with him, or rely on him, their reactions make him all the more certain that other people are immature and unpredictable, and reinforce his rational stance. His own impulses are expressed so impetuously, without input or guidance from his rational self, which only seeks to quash, never to direct, his impulse life, that he becomes all the more convinced that impulses just mean trouble and that the best policy is constraint. This in turn makes his impulse life all the more explosive, unpredictable, and intermittent. Mort's impulsivity was contained in his vicious, incisive criticisms. A good strategy might have been to confine these to a set period every day, under the assumption that they would not just disappear. However, the family had changed so quickly that I overlooked the likely need to find an outlet for his aggression.

The undergoverned personality has a fantasy of freedom that is pursued by construing many rules of conduct as arbitrary. The person identifies with the childlike posture, and Ego, in dreams, often finds itself being judged or admonished. The parental or controlling aspects of the person are disowned, and seen as coming from outside the self. Again, the expectation is fulfilled, as the person's impulsivity and freedom constellate in others a controlling or directive response. Intrapsychically, he rarely tries to constrain himself, but when he does try, he finds himself so unruly that he imposes self-restraint in draconian terms. He may feel suicidal, or at least humiliated, because he was caught gossiping. He promises himself never again to discuss a third party in a conversation. The terms of the promise are so unreasonable that he cannot possibly fulfill them. His rare, self-imposed restraint is so harsh that he feels justified in unshackling himself from it.

MISCONSTRUING THE CHILD AS A PRECURSOR TO MALTREATMENT

A related issue on an interpersonal level is the amount, versus the stripe, of parenting that is desirable in a given situation or with a given child. Parents vary in the extent to which they are directive versus curious about their children. Many parents have fantasies about who their children will be and expect to shape the child accordingly. They imagine, in effect, scrolling their ideas on the blank slate of the child's psyche. In actuality, parenting has a lot more to do with finding out which kind of child you got than with molding her into the one you want. Of course, children do become assimilated into patterns imposed by parents, but to a large extent the family must accommodate the child. A lot of pathology stems from situations where the child has a trait that the family cannot accommodate, or the family has an expectation that the child cannot adjust to. Sex-role stereotyping provides examples familiar to most people. Much mischief ensues when the family has rigid definitions about being a girl or boy that do not fit the particular girl or boy the family happened to get.

Some families permanently define a child on the basis of behavior related to a normally transient developmental stage. They define their babies as selfish, unable to recognize that all babies are selfish, or they define their two-year-olds as oppositional. Indeed, much child maltreatment can be construed as a misunderstanding of what is age-appropriate behavior. For example, many instances of neglect make more sense when one understands that the parent treated the child as if she were much older and more able to care for herself. Thus, a seven-year-old is left in charge of a four-year-old for the evening not necessarily because the parent does not care about the children, but because the parent does not see a seven-year-old, but a "big sister," and big sisters can be left in charge of their younger siblings. Similarly, a parent is more likely to hit a child who says she hates the parent if the parent construes the words as if they were the thoughtful convictions of an adult.

Families that allow a stage the child is going through to define that child may not guide them beyond that stage. For example, an eleven-year-old boy named Jarrod was brought in for individual therapy because he was a "thief." His mother wanted to stay in the waiting room until his treatment was over, but I persuaded her to come into the office at least to provide some information. I asked her when he began stealing and she said when he was sixteen months old. This answer strengthened my inclination to view an eleven-year-old's thievery as systemic, in other words, as responsive to and designed for other family members. To construe a toddler's conduct as theft implicates the parent's motivation in arriving at that construction. Of course, the parent may be merely trying, naively, to emphasize the extent of the problem. In this case, however, Jarrod's mother described the actual incident from his infancy when he grabbed a toy while being carried through a store, conduct that does not immediately suggest to most people a criminal label.

Jarrod's mother would not hear of any alternative constructions of his behavior. My attempts to broaden the definition of Jarrod's identity were swiftly rebuffed. He was a thief, pure and simple. Neither would she hear of anything related to her recent divorce. In fact, she had left their previous therapy because the therapist kept insisting the divorce was relevant. Fortunately, I was interviewing them in front of a one-way mirror, and the team behind the mirror and I devised a plan: Every time I asked a question that could even remotely be construed as implicating the family in Jarrod's thievery or as excusing his thievery as something else, a stern voice would come on the loudspeaker reprimanding me for trying to turn this into a family therapy.

Finally, I went too far for the stern voice, and a colleague entered the room and unceremoniously removed me from the case, apologized to Jarrod's mother, and introduced the new therapist, a woman described as a specialist in stealing. She began her session with Jarrod and his mother by asking Jarrod what he would wish for if he had three wishes. Fortunately, Jarrod complied with our scheme by replying like a normal kid; he wished for a million dollars, his own video store, and a Porsche. "Just as I suspected," said the specialist. "Selfish." Jarrod's mother beamed in delight that she finally had met a therapist who understood the problem. We could not fight the family's definition of the problem, so we joined it. Mother did not complain when the specialist informed her that Jarrod was such a devious little scamp that they would require the mother's presence at all the sessions, to ensure that he was reporting factually. Also, since he spent so much time at his father's, about which he could lie without her being able to call him on it, they would need the father there as well. I left the therapy soon after, so I do not know whether the family's definition of Jarrod ever really changed, but I do think that accepting their definition got us further than challenging it had done. By the third session, for instance, Jarrod had been told to wait in the waiting room, and only the adults were meeting with the therapist, to discuss how to handle him.

Some parents hold children responsible for very little; at their worst, they view the child not as a person or an agent, but as a doll or a piece of furniture. At the other extreme are people who hold the child responsible for everything, not only for everything the child does, but for everything that does not go well for the parents. These parents "adultify" the child, and this child can become overgoverned since he grows up in a family in which his childlike qualities are disowned. Interestingly, infants are actually very much like what the first kind of parents expect. These parents construe their children as responsible for nothing, as nonagents, even as objects, and can be fairly successful at raising children, because of the similarity between what they provide and what infants need (Watson, Little, and Biderman, 1992; Manzano, Palacio Espasa, and Zilkha, 1999). This observation does not apply when the perception of the child as nonagentic stems from neglect; it only applies when it stems from seeing the child as an extension of the parent or as a prized possession. In other words, infants themselves are barely responsible for anything. These parents can be successful because of the importance of experiences in infancy for determining overall mental health. Such good groundwork is laid by these parents that by the time problems show up later because of the parents' inability to attribute an adequate amount of responsibility to the child, the child already has several good months or even years under his or her belt.

The elements of thinking psychologically thus embrace the pervasiveness of imagination, the population of the psyche with figures in a landscape, and the systemic nature of the interactions between those figures. An example of psychological thinking might help show how these operate. Take the familiar figure of the brilliant, narcissistic man, perhaps an artist or a musician but all too often a college professor, who feels that the world should bow down to his special talents. This *enfant terrible,* the adored child who becomes the center not only of his own, but of others' universes, is a figure in each of us. However, in most of us, this figure always comes to us with a nanny in tow, with someone reminding us that other people who happen not to be his parents are not as fascinated by his every self-expression as he may expect them to be, reminding the child that no matter how gifted he is, he is still expected to treat others courteously.

The nanny accompanying the wunderkind also helps him understand why he is not as accomplished as he was expected to be (Horney, 1950). When people's actual performance falls short of their grandiose fantasies, they can handle this undesirable information in several ways. One of these is, "I'm disappointed but still OK." In this scenario, the nanny is affectionate in spite of the wunderkind's failure. Another explanation might be, "I never had any grandiose fantasies to fall short of." If true, this signifies absolute freedom from neurosis; but usually it is a pretense and signifies ennui or resignation. The nanny is mute, and there is never any examination of what was and was not accomplished. A third strategy for explaining failure is, "I did accomplish my grandiose goals." Thus, to deny the validity of contradictory information requires a twisted view of reality, and distortion of reality brings with it several disadvantages for operating successfully. Usually there is a lot of rage about possibly falling short, and this rage is directed at other people who might question whether the grandiose goals were really accomplished. The nanny is intimidated, and finds herself telling the child how terrific he is. A rationalizing strategy may arise: "The other fellow cheated"; "the grader is out to get me"; "I wasn't ready." This style recognizes the reality of falling short, but blames others. The nanny connives with the child around these excuses. Finally, the wunderkind may acknowledge, "I should have done better." This style blames the self, while sustaining a secret belief that he *could* have done better, preserving the grandiose expectation. The inner nanny is disappointed in the inner child.

The arrogant artist/doctor/author is like others in being inhabited by the wunderkind and the nanny, but unlike others in the way these two figures relate to each other. The relationship between the two figures can be analyzed systemically, as can any relationship between two people. Thus, the inner child who makes excuses is responding to an inner nanny that accepts excuses to preserve her perfect image of the child; the inner nanny accepts excuses out of fear of the inner child's rage if she does not, a rage that is exacerbated by the nanny's mollycoddling.

The figures and their interplay are usually far from obvious. Often, all we are given to work with is a comment such as, "I wasn't ready." Fluency in the language of patterns can enable us to see the figures behind the comment. Appreciation of the pattern enables us to anticipate its replication in a new situation. It also enables us to locate a point of intervention, just as expansion of an individual's symptoms into a family framework does. Any response to "I wasn't ready" is likely to be perceived as a frontal attack and to invite a defensive posture. Once the underlying figures are elucidated, however, the nanny's attention can be directed to the effect of her pampering on the child.

As we survey patterns associated with child abuse in Parts II and III, we can use the systemic framework to illuminate statements and behaviors that can reveal the underlying figures and the pattern of their interaction. The goal will be to widen the focus until we can identify the relevant figures, their interconnection, and their relationship to the landscape that constellates them. This will provide better predictive power and more alternative points of intervention for conduct that is otherwise only approached frontally.

PART II:
GENERAL PATTERNS
IN ABUSE AND NEGLECT

Some of the patterns we find in abusive and neglectful families transcend any particular brand of maltreatment. Rather than relating to a particular interpersonal dynamic, these patterns derive from the disappointment and frustration that accompany all child abuse. Chapter 4 examines the tendency of the maltreated child to idealize the abusive or neglectful parent. Abused or neglected children are more dependent on their parents than are normal children. Normal children incorporate their parents into their psychologies in a manner that forms a foundation for self-esteem, confidence, and independence. When normal teenagers fight with their parents, for example, they feel supported by the internalized parent of their infancy. Maltreated children lack that internalized support, leaving them more dependent on their actual parents. This dependence makes them susceptible to idealizing the very people who have let them down. It is disturbing to take a cold hard look at someone on whom one is depending. Further, the abusive or neglectful parent reacts badly to such an honest appraisal. Finally, the normal parent can be comfortably evaluated in realistic terms because, on balance, the parent gets pretty good marks; the child needs to idealize the abusive parent to avoid being overwhelmed by the parent's faults. Conversely, the bad parent wants to be idealized because he seeks exoneration; the good parent does not seek exoneration because his transgressions are minor.

Chapter 5 briefly looks at the phenomenon of justifying one's own parenting by comparing it with one's parents' efforts. Children who resolve not to be like their own parents can end up being very much like them, as they focus not on the big picture that shows the similarities, but on the narrow differences between themselves and their parents.

Chapter 6 is devoted to the ambivalence or downright fear that maltreated children associate with close personal relationships. Most child abuse and neglect unfolds in an intimate psychological landscape, and becomes associated with intimacy in the minds of the children. This fact complicates treatment, which often is transmitted via personal relationships. Abuse reactivity to intimacy also has profound implications for placement decisions, since a major difference among placements is the degree of intimacy involved in the setting.

Chapter 7 explores the fragmented personality organization, its prevalence in the child welfare system, and its implications for service planning. I am convinced that a major focus for clinical thinking in the child welfare system should be to distinguish the traumatized, normal person or family from the seriously disturbed person or family. By seriously disturbed, I mean what Kernberg (1975) calls the borderline personality organization (which is different from what DSM-IV means by a borderline personality disorder), or what Herman (1992) calls complex post-traumatic stress disorder. By whatever name, some people and families are markedly different from the norm in ways that affect virtually every area of emotional functioning. The distinction is critical in treatment planning, prediction of recurrence, and decision making. I argue that even though misdiagnosis of severe pathology has done great harm to many groups of victims over the years, our response as a profession should be to refine our diagnostic abilities, not to act naively as if all victims are alike.

Chapter 4

Children's Idealization of Bad Parents

When parents abuse or neglect children, the children may not realize they are being abused or neglected, because they may not have anything to compare it to. One woman, an alcoholic, told me that her fourteen-year-old daughter hated her. The woman blamed herself, because of her drinking. She said the girl was constantly calling her names, ridiculing her in public, and hissing at her at home. The daughter had even threatened to kill her if she, the mother, did not stop drinking. "That's great," I said. "You should be proud of yourself." At first, she thought I was being sarcastic, but I explained to her that she must have done a pretty good job until she started drinking so heavily, or her daughter would never have gotten the idea that she had a better mother coming to her.

Some sexually abused girls think everybody knows they are being abused, or that it is happening in all their friends' families as well. The disclosures may come not from the girl herself, but from a friend or a friend's parent. The girl does not realize she has something to disclose, and mentions the abuse almost incidentally to someone else, who blows the whistle.

DENIAL OF DISAPPOINTMENT

So what kind of sense does a child make of ongoing abuse or neglect? There is intrinsic discomfort, because by definition abuse and neglect mean the child's needs are not being met. The discomfort presses on the child and insists on some kind of explanation. But the child may have no basis for concluding what the state authorities might conclude, namely, that the parent is incompetent. Unless some other rationale is offered to the child by the parent or by others, the child is very likely to conclude that abuse and neglect, like hunger, pain, and nightfall, are just part of the landscape. This explanation can be very appealing to a child because it lets the parent off the hook.

Children want to see their parents in a positive light for several reasons. One reason is that even bad parents become sources of pleasure and comfort to children when they feed and clothe them, or even when they simply ignore them. Physically abused children will feel affection for parents just for not hitting them. It is natural for children to feel gratitude to parents, whether for providing for the children or merely for not hurting them, and children express this gratitude partly by construing parents in the best possible light.

Children also view their parents positively because they are extremely dependent on their parents, and it is not a posture conducive to criticizing them. The dependency makes the child want to believe that the parent is a good person looking out for the child's best interests. That a bad person should have so much power over oneself is too terrible to contemplate. When a rock climber is testing a rope, she can afford to be skeptical; but once she has committed herself to being suspended from a particular rope, she will believe that it is strong. A child, especially an abused child, dangles from a parent, and cannot bear to perceive the parent's weakness. The abused child is also like a desperately ill patient. Surely, cancer patients are more certain of their doctor's magnificence than are patients with the sniffles. The cancer patient needs the doctor to be wise, benign, and powerful in a way that patients in for yearly physicals do not.

A third reason that children see their parents in a good light is that they telegraph their perceptions to their parents. People who abuse and neglect their children are the kind of people who do not have a robust sense of self or a deep sense of humor that can help them manage a less-than-flattering implication in the child's behavior. The parents intuit the child's vision of them as imperfect, and they do not handle it well, acting in some way that punishes any tendency to construe them negatively. (I mean, again, punishment in the behavioral sense; it is not that the parent necessarily decides to discipline the child for a perceived transgression, but that the parent is irritable or otherwise acts in a way the child finds aversive when the child has communicated that the parent is blemished.)

THE NEED FOR A PARENT
WHO TAKES RESPONSIBILITY

The essence of the child's positive view of the parent is that whatever the child lacks as a consequence of the parent's imperfection simply does not exist. The child reconciles her deprivation with her idealized image of the parent by deciding that the parent could not possibly have met her needs, because what she desires simply cannot be had. Warmth, safety, reliability, nurturance—these can all be sacrificed on the altar of parent worship. The repeatedly and unpredictably sexually abused child, for example, must choose, in effect, between holding her parent responsible for abusing her (or for not protecting her) and living in a world in which protection is impossible and safety a mere fantasy. The child will go to extraordinary lengths to prove that the latter is the case, because the impossibility of safety exonerates the parent.

An obvious example of a child proving that there is no such thing as safety—and therefore no reason to upbraid the parent for not providing it—is the child who cuts or burns herself. If there is no such thing as safety, then the parents have done their best to protect the child and cannot be faulted for failure. If there is such a thing as safety, then the child is filled with regret, disappointment, and rage. In quiet moments, the child may begin to feel safe, and this feeling stands in silent accusation that the parent has been incompetent or unloving. The child disrupts the feeling by hurting herself, by disrupting any belief in the possibility of safety. (Of course, there are other reasons for the child's hurting herself besides protecting the image of the parent, including the effort to get mastery over pain by being the agent of it; the dispelling of anxiety that occurs when she starts to feel safe because feeling safe makes her want to be emotionally vulnerable; the stimulation of the skin boundary to reassure herself that the inner world and the outer world are distinct; and the reenactment of a pattern of physical abuse, in which one part of her, the part like the abuser, is made to feel invulnerable by attacking a helpless victim, the child part of her.)

BLAMING OTHERS TO EXONERATE THE PARENT

Some children, instead of denying the very existence of the thing that the parent failed to provide, deny instead the possibility of it being provided for themselves in particular. This still exonerates the parent, but it allows a child to account for the existence of the lost experience in other families, or between the parent and other children. Thus, a child concludes not that patience is impossible, merely that no person could ever be patient with *her.* She proves this largely by being so exasperating that everyone she meets loses their patience. To prove that no parent could protect *her,* she wears provocative clothing and gets into cars with strange men. To prove that no parent could be warm with *her,* she sneers insults at adults she meets.

With such a child, service providers—therapists, teachers, social workers, and foster parents—who respond by trying extra hard to be patient, protective, or warm are barking up the wrong tree, because their efforts will only make the child strengthen her proofs. The providers are thereby put in a bind, because they are working in this field largely because they enjoy being patient, protective, and warm. This bind is discussed in the chapters on intervention. Therapeutic techniques are also discussed later, but for now I want to note that a therapist who acts impatient, unprotective, or cold is surrendering to the child's agenda. The therapist who insists on acting patient, protective, or warm is in the same bind as other adults. The therapist who maintains neutrality, who is neither patient nor impatient, warm nor cold, may be in the best position to help.

The advantage of neutrality was forcefully driven home to me when a child, Roger, age thirteen, was referred to me for therapy because he was uncontrollable. He was constantly being suspended from school, and his mother had even been evicted from her apartment because of him. She had smacked him repeatedly, but who could blame her? Roger would spit on her in public, and she would lose her temper. He was bent on proving that *nobody* could control him, not just his mother. When I brought him up to my office on the second floor of the clinic, he immediately pulled up the window screen and threw himself out, holding on to the windowsill with his fingertips as he dangled twenty feet from the ground. I said, "Roger, can't you think of a way to ruin the therapy that doesn't put yourself in danger?"

He climbed back in the window and sat down. I asked him what had been going on in his life. Roger stood up and marched downstairs to the waiting room. I strolled in, acting casual, several seconds behind him. Roger was taller than his mother, so I could see his eyes even though he stood directly behind her. I said to him, "Therapy goes better if the action stays in the office." Roger stepped forward and punched me in the stomach as hard as he could. His mother gasped. I said, obviously in pain, but trying to sound nonchalant, "Therapy also goes better if you express yourself with words." I added, "I think that's enough for today, but I'll see you next week at the same time." I tried to be neutral vis-à-vis Roger's conduct, because to disdain it would be to side with his mother against him; to condone it implicitly, by being sympathetic or understanding, would be to side with him against his mother, forcing him to defend her by demonstrating his uncontrollability. I think my neutrality made it possible for Roger to engage with me, which he did quickly and affectionately in the next session. Incidentally, his mother later mentioned that she had never hit him again after witnessing my restraint.

Examples of the child preserving a positive image of the parent abound in the child welfare system, but they are hard to spot unless the clinician links the child's behavior to the image of the parent that the child is trying to protect. Thus, Steven, an eight-year-old boy in foster care, was referred for consultation because he would masturbate publicly for days after a visit with his mother. The hospital to which Steven was taken diagnosed him as having post-traumatic stress disorder and oppositional defiant disorder. These labels may at first seem elucidating, but they are actually tautological: there is no information in the label in this particular case that was not also in Steven's behavior. The trauma to which the masturbation was a reaction was, it turned out, inferred from the behavior itself and from the fact that the child was in foster care. The oppositional label was applied because the foster mother had complained about the fact that he would not stop when she asked him to. The masturbation was linked to the visits under a hypothesis that Steven was being "retraumatized" in the visits, either by exposure to the mother or by having to leave her again at the end of the visits.

To think circularly about the masturbation is to link it not just backward in time to the visit and to Steven's early childhood, but also forward in time to its effects on the foster mother, the clinicians, the state social worker, and the mother. Looking in this direction, one could not help but notice how unwelcome the masturbation was making Steven in the foster home. Steven accounted for his mother's failure to make him feel welcome in her home by defining himself as a person whom no one would welcome. All the adults in the system were having serious doubts about whether he could be "maintained" in foster care. The mother was practically gleeful in her I-told-you-so's, while the hospital staff tut-tutted about the state's supposed desire to save money that kept Steven out of the institutional treatment he "needed."

Ultimately, a number of interventions were recommended. Steven was to be caustically and unsympathetically sent to his room if he masturbated. The idea was to switch the consequence for which the child was striving from getting kicked out of the home to getting kicked out of the living room. Steven was to be asked to pretend to masturbate on occasion, which is Cloé Madanes's (1981) idea for demonstrating to the child that the behavior is under his control, and also for letting him observe the effects of his complexes when he is not actually in them. The foster mother was to say something complimentary about Steven's mother and her child-rearing skills whenever he behaved well. The foster mother was to scrupulously avoid statements that would imply that Steven was truly or unconditionally welcome in the home, or comments that anticipated a long stay. Statements about next Christmas, for example, can make a foster child feel welcome in a way that induces him to prove that he is not. A year later, Steven was still in the home, though I think my interventions were less responsible than the fact that he had the kind of foster mother who would listen to them.

This brief case example raises a large number of issues, but the point at present is that interventions based on an accurate assessment are more likely to be effective, and accuracy requires a look at the psychology of a behavior, not just at its diagnostic category. That psychology is revealed only in a systemic analysis of its causes and effects, in other words, by looking at the pattern of which it is a part. A major feature of that pattern is often to protect the positive image of the parent.

SPLITTING

Some children preserve a positive image of the parent by splitting off from that image anything that is disappointing, frustrating, or overstimulating and attributing it to someone else. When this process occurs in its most primitive form, that is, when reality is readily sacrificed and the positive picture must be utterly pure, then it is called splitting. The child thinks, in effect, "My mother cannot have done that," and attributes either the conduct itself or responsibility for it to some other person. The purpose is to preserve, not just a positive, but a perfect image of the parent. Like many defensive operations, splitting is an exaggeration of a normal tendency to slant facts in favor of oneself and one's comrades by apportioning blame for things that go badly and credit for things that go well. When the president is a Democrat and the Congress is Republican, Republicans blame the president for the country's problems and Democrats blame the Congress. As noted, this is not real splitting, because Democrats and Republicans do not maintain a pure image of their party from which all imperfections have been expunged. But compare this party leader's sentiment: "Once our enemies persecuted us and in doing this helped us by removing the undesirable elements from our party. Today, we ourselves expel what is bad. What is bad does not belong to us" (Hitler, in 1934, in *Triumph of the Will,* 1981).

PARENTAL ACCOUNTABILITY

Abused and neglected children face a greater challenge than children who have not been mistreated. All children face frustrations and disappointments at the hands of their parents, because no parent is perfect. All children create a psychological parent who is warm and welcoming, and attribute the parent's shortcomings to other sources.

"Of course my Mom had her faults—she's only human." Even this reasonable statement implies that the mother gets credit for her accomplishments but does not have to take blame for her imperfections, which are attributed to her "humanity." The problem for abused and neglected children is that, in their effort to create a positive image of the parent, they have to ignore or rationalize so much. It is a lot easier to overlook or attribute to extrinsic forces the time your father came late to your Little League game than the time he sexually abused you. Abused and neglected children meet this burden through extreme measures that can lead to distortions in their images of the parent, other people, and themselves (Cicchetti and Toth, 1995; Willis, 1995). Subsequent behaviors based on these distortions are at a disadvantage in coping with reality (Morton and Browne, 1998).

Even within an individual parent, this rigid division of credit and blame can occur. I see this with the children of alcoholics and drug addicts. They blame the drunken parent for problems, and credit the sober parent for caregiving, almost as if they were two separate people. The addiction facilitates this division for a couple of reasons. One, addicts may behave so differently, depending on whether they are using or not, that the difference is impressive to the child and encourages the child's process of separating the two images of the parent. Two, there is a clear external marker for when the child is dealing with one parent or the other. In other words, the substance being abused, since it is a concrete thing, lends itself well to the child's task of finding some source of problems external to the parent.

But it is not just alcohol and drugs that help children divide a parent into two parts, good and bad. I have also met children who blamed a mother only when she was in love ("she goes nuts for whatever guy she's with"), a father only when he was angry ("when he wasn't beating on us, he was a pretty good dad"), and another father only when he was possessed by the devil ("he raped me, but that was before the exorcism").

These examples can also be viewed as a way of keeping a positive image of the parent by attributing their shortcomings to another, non-human figure. Thus, it's not Mom, it's love or the bottle; it's not Dad, it's anger or the devil. Division is more obvious when it involves two separate people, with one identified as good and the other as bad. The mother of a sex abuse victim is not blamed for failing to protect her daughter, even when she was in the room while it happened, because the boyfriend made her do it. A father is not blamed for abandoning his children because the mother was impossible to live with.

I am not saying that the innocent-sounding parent is "really" to blame. Obviously, the blame game has no end. If it is the parent's fault that the child was abused, and not the child's, then it was the grandparent's fault that the parent became an abuser and not the parent's. The exoneration game also has no end. If it was not the child's fault but the parent's, then it was not the parent's but the grandparent's. A sophisticated view of the world does not blame or exonerate. But I am not preaching a philosophy of causation here; I am discussing what children need to develop into healthy people. Whatever the truth about reality may be, surely the best social policy, and the best child-rearing policy, is to act as if people are responsible for their conduct. Blame follows unwanted or negligent behaviors, not because they are morally wrong, but because blaming people who misbehave or who are negligent is likely to reduce the instances of misconduct and negligence. This utilitarian view of responsibility pervades my approach to abusive and neglectful families. When the child welfare system loses its moorings, it is on the issue of blame. The root of the problem is that on one hand, the parents are often piteous and poor, while on the other hand, children need to have people they can hold accountable for life's setbacks.

When children devoted to proving there is no such thing as good parenting grow up, they may continue their proofs by becoming abusive and neglectful parents themselves. Once they have children of their own, even if they are still trying to justify their own childhoods, no one feels sympathy for them. These parents are usually treated as evil and summarily removed from families. I am thinking of a man who raped his two-year-old daughter, and a woman who murdered her five-year-old stepson. Nobody blamed the mother in the first case or the father in the second case. I think the reason the second parent was not blamed in these cases was that the offending parent seemed so evil that he or she sopped up all the blame that people could muster. When the offending parent can elicit any sympathy at all, say, by being poor, disenfranchised, organically impaired, or mentally ill, then there is usually some leftover blame for the nonoffending parent. Meanwhile, the social worker is invariably blamed for not preventing the tragedy, largely because people, or at least the press, want to feel that tragedy is preventable.

What interests the clinician is how the blame issue is seen from the child's point of view, and from the parent's. As noted, children need parents to take responsibility for things that go wrong. Most parents do this without thinking. Most parents feel vaguely guilty when their children are disappointed, even when they had nothing to do with it. If it rains on the picnic, most parents will tell the children they are sorry, and they will mean it, wishing they could have provided fair weather. Apology puts a human face on the child's disappointment, giving her an audience for her grievances and a sense of personal soothing for her frustration. Apology, of course, comes easiest when it is least needed, when the disappointment is relatively minor. I have heard parents apologize for the Super Bowl, for a bump in the road, and for the fact that it did not snow on Christmas. I have never heard a parent apologize for bringing a child molester into the family.

As noted, it is easier to take responsibility for something trivial such as a rained-out birthday party or a scraped knee than for sexual abuse, so the parent is responding as anyone would. Nonetheless, on a deeper level, it may be that the type of person who takes responsibility for what goes wrong for their children is more careful of them. Negligent hiring law, which holds employers liable for the acts of employees that they should have known not to hire, has made organizations safer. Likewise if parents are held accountable for whom they import into families, then families may become safer too. On a deeper level still, the parent is making decisions about the child without having present, in the psychological space in which decisions occur, the figure of a responsible adult. If clinicians can gently but persistently help the parent take responsibility for what has gone wrong for the child, then the parent can learn to incorporate the figure of a responsible adult into the decision-making space. In other words, a person making a decision is like an organization holding a meeting to make a decision; the key issue is who gets invited to the meeting. A goal of most kinds of treatment is to arrange for the most mature and rational figure in the person's psychology to attend most decision-making meetings.

From the child's point of view, she needs an accountable parent not just for soothing, but also for reassurance that the future will be different. The parent typically feels that if he or she acts innocent, then the child will feel better. The parent feels innocent, and believes he or she is innocent, but beyond that, thinks that the child would be relieved to know that she is living with someone innocent. In fact, the opposite is more nearly the case most of the time. Usually, the child feels that if the parent is innocent, then the child is just as susceptible to injury or disappointment in the future as she had been in the past.

For example, when a bus driver molests a child, the father is tempted to act as if the harm was entirely outside of his control. It may have indeed been outside of his control, but asserting this to the child just makes her wonder, with fear and anxiety, who will happen to be driving the next bus. Instead, the parent can step up and tell the child that he should have been more careful about whom he entrusted the child to. He can allow that he felt worn down by his responsibilities, but add that things are different now because the harm done has reminded him how important the stakes are. He can say that he was stupid to rely on someone else's judgment about whom to leave the child with, and that he will personally meet and talk to all caregivers in the future. If the parent does all this, then, even though we know the parent may not really be able to protect her from all harm, and even though the child may still be anxious about the father's vigilance and competence, at least the child's anxiety is unfolding in a transaction with someone who loves her and who may have regained the capacity to reassure her rather than in a transaction with a nameless, faceless future bus driver. In other words, if the girl is anxious about the father's competence, the father can reassure her, but if she is anxious about the character of the bus driver, than her anxiety cannot be assuaged.

SELF-BLAME TO EXONERATE THE PARENT

The unsoothed child grows up and reports memories of childhood such as the following. "I was pulling my wagon down the front steps. I tripped and the wagon got tangled up in my legs, and I broke my ankle." This memory exonerates the parent by emphasizing the child's autonomy. The memory accepts as normal the state of not being supervised, which requires no special comment in the memory. This state is linked with being injured. The memory implies that the child is responsible for her own safety, and pairs that implication with her injury. The natural course for such a child is to become adultified, to protect herself by giving up her childlike expectation that someone else will watch out for her, and giving up her childlike interest in the wagon. She can be safe at the cost of her joy and carefree pleasure.

Of course, anyone can produce a memory of an injury suffered in childhood while the parents were off duty. There are two main differences between this normal memory and an exoneration memory. The first is that normal subjects do not offer these memories during psychological evaluations organized around parenting issues. Part of the interpretation of any memory is to consider it as a communication in the context in which it is elicited (Langs, 1977). When a psychologist asks a member of a disrupting family for early memories, the family member has a myriad of recollections from which to choose, and thinks of one that is suited to the occasion. In this context, subjects who are motivated to protect their image of their parents can say, in effect, "my problems are and always have been my own fault" by selecting a memory of being injured alone.

The second main difference between normal injured-alone memories and exoneration memories is discerned by considering all the other memories and stories reported by the subject. When the injured-alone memory is offered to exonerate a parent, it will not be accompanied by other memories of parental fault or disappointment. Conversely, a well-rounded picture of a parent conveyed in the totality of early recollections, especially in response to childhood disappointments, indicates that the primary reason for reporting an injured-alone memory was not to exonerate the parent.

A third major method by which a child may preserve a positive image of the parent, besides blaming only a part of the parent and blaming another person, is blaming the self. The child justifies the parent's abuse or neglect as deserved. The father would not have hit her if she had not been so irritating. The mother would not have ignored him if he had not been so reclusive. The father would not have molested her if she had not been so provocative.

Besides keeping the image of the parent relatively benign, this strategy also enhances the child's sense of mastery over the abuse or neglect (Janoff-Bulman, 1982). The child believes she can control the situation by being less irritating, reclusive, or provocative. And she may be right. Parents do not wake up in the morning and decide to be abusive; they respond to the children (and to other stressors). Of course, we believe that it is up to the parent to control the abuse, not up to the child, but if the child can find a way to control it, it will help her feel powerful and competent, not to mention the fact that it will lead to less abuse. Thus, the abused child who becomes depressed and exhibits low self-esteem may be on a road to mastery over the abuse, literally in learning ways to avoid it, and psychologically in holding herself responsible for it and assuming the role of an agent, not a victim.

The drawbacks of feeling she deserved it are several. She does get a sense of agency, rather than passivity, meaning that she believes that things happen because of her and not just to her, but the things she makes happen are bad things. So the effect on her identity and self-esteem is quite complicated, and she still does not get a sense of making good things happen. Another drawback is that self-blaming isolates her from the parent, or from some other adult, who might otherwise engage her in a dialogue about why the bad thing happened. The parent is treated as a force of nature, like the wind or perhaps a dangerous animal, when it is up to the child to avoid the parent's wrath. This inhuman view of the parent in is not conducive to a restorative dialogue, and the child's main strategy becomes one of avoiding the parent.

The therapist can substitute for the parent in this complex. The patient comes in with depression and low self-esteem, and blames herself whenever something goes wrong. The therapist does not accept this self-blame. The easy part of questioning it is in relationship to the parent; the therapist assures the patient that the abuse or neglect was not the patient's fault. The hard part of questioning it is in its manifestations between therapist and patient. The therapist yawns and the adult patient apologizes for being boring, or the child patient loses interest in the game she is playing. The therapist takes a phone call during a session and the adult patient decides she is too sensitive, or the child patient tries not to make any noise during the call. The therapist must explore these interchanges, and reassign blame according to the structural responsibilities of the parties (almost all of which, as with a parent, fall on the therapist). The therapist must point out that it is the therapist's job, not the patient's, to remain attentive or to provide a protected environment. The therapist must demonstrate that the exposure of imperfections does not have to devastate the relationship, and does not require that the patient cover them up.

Chapter 5

"At Least I'm Not As Bad As My Mother (or Father)"

A fairly common pattern involves the abused or neglected child who has grown up and had children of his or her own. She (or he) may evaluate her own conduct as a parent by constantly comparing it to her mother's, which was worse. She uses the difference between her own conduct as a parent and her mother's conduct to justify and excuse her own shortcomings. A parallel pattern occurs with her boyfriend. She thinks, in essence, at least he is not as bad to her children as her father was to her.

FOCUS ON THE PARENT AT THE EXPENSE OF THE CHILD

There is nothing wrong, of course, with learning from your parents' mistakes, and many good parents resolve not to repeat on their own children what was done to them. The child of an alcoholic, for example, may decide to be a teetotaler; or a physically abused child will resolve never to strike her own children. But in this particular pattern, the difference between the parent's behavior and the grandparent's becomes the focus of attention, to the exclusion of an objective evaluation of the parent's. The parent does not look to the child for feedback on how to behave, but to her own mother. Instead of letting the child's reactions guide her conduct, she is focused almost exclusively on her similarity to or difference from her mother. Thus, a woman screams at her children in an arbitrary and frightening manner, and gets drunk three or four nights a week, but she defends herself to the state authorities, and to herself, by noting that her mother got drunk every single day, and not only screamed at the children but hit them as well. One woman insisted that she was not an alcoholic, in spite of irrefutable evidence, but admitted readily to having a "serious drinking problem." Apparently, the label of alcoholism was the last barrier between her self-appraisal and her assessment of her mother.

The pattern is created when the child in an abusive home focuses on the parent at the expense of focusing on her own needs. Abused children ask not what their families can do for them, but what they can do for their families. Their imaginations do not turn to treats and toys, but become preoccupied with the parent's mood. They become experts at assessing the state of the parent, while remaining clueless about their own needs. They may become obsessed with the question of whether and under what circumstances Dad will drink, or on the question of what cheers Mom up. In these families, focus on the child is sacrificed in favor of focus on the parent. The mother who is not as bad as her own mother repeats this pattern in her new family. She focuses on the parental behavior (which by now is her own behavior) and not on the needs of the children (which by now are her children). Her evaluation of her own behavior is almost entirely relative, and this evaluation considers only information about parental conduct, hers and her mother's. Ignored are signs from the children, first herself and then her own children, about whether their needs are being met.

When parents judge their own behavior independently of its effect on the children, harm to the children is almost inevitable. It is like people who trust a map more than their own eyes, but here the map was drawn by a child abuser, so it is even more concerning. The problem with relying on a map, or with tailoring one's parental conduct to a standard as opposed to the children's reactions, is that no prescription or formula for how one should behave can be comprehensive enough or flexible enough to rival an approach based on feedback (Chuang-tzu, 1981). It is like trying to learn how to bowl only by studying technique, and never looking down the alley to see how many pins were knocked down. In parenting, the relevant feedback is the effect on the child. How can a parent make even a simple decision, such as whether the child can stay up late, without considering how this particular child will react one way or the other?

Parenthetically, one may note an analogy to many social service and educational programs implemented with an eye, not to their actual effect on children, but to how they look to other adults. Thus, we retain antidrug programs that are utterly ineffective (Dukes, Ullman, and Stein, 1996; Zagumny and Thompson, 1997; Rosenbaum and Hanson, 1998) largely because those in charge of paying for them are not primarily concerned about whether children use or do not use drugs. Their first concern, in my experience, is political: how self-righteously can they assert that drugs are bad? We have therapists whose reputations depend on how they act at meetings and not on how their patients do. Good intentions, even in a righteous cause, should not be celebrated, or funded, if ineffective.

Ironically, the parent who looks not to the effect on the child but instead to a comparison with her own mother can become very much like her own mother. The big picture—the similarity between them—is missed because the focus is on the differences. The increasingly narrow gap between the parent and the grandparent is attended to with such fervor and hope that the parent does not notice that it is becoming narrower. Any discernible difference gives the parent great satisfaction and is emphasized; similarities dishearten the parent and are ignored. A man may think not about how much time his son needs to spend with him, but instead may focus on whether he is spending more time with his son than his own father spent with him as a boy. Since the relevant issue for this man is to be better than his father, any detectable difference between them will suffice, and the amount of time he spends with his son will almost inevitably dwindle to the point where it is just a bit more, in the father's eyes, than his own father spent. This alone makes the two parents so similar as to be almost indistinguishable to anyone but the man himself. On top of this, he is evaluating their time together as a father now, not as a son, and fathers always think they have spent more time with their sons than their sons do. And mothers always think they drink less than their daughters think they do. Children may accurately remember a childhood filled with beatings, while the parents, equally accurately, recall their rarity. The difference in perspective culminates in the father-who-was-not-as-bad-as-his-own-father being even worse than his own father except in his own mind.

Chapter 6

The Avoidance of Personal Closeness

FEARS AND JOYS OF INTIMACY

Everybody is ambivalent about personal closeness. Genuine intimacy offers an opportunity for some of life's greatest rewards, but it also creates powerful vulnerabilities and the potential for extreme psychological pain. For most people, it seems to be better to have loved and lost than never to have loved at all, meaning, if I may break down the poetry into the cold hard calculation of behaviorism, that the rewards of personal closeness generally outweigh the risks, even though things go badly at the end. However, for some people, especially those who have been abused or neglected, the balance shifts, and it is better never to love at all.

For most people, even when mentors betray or ignore them, even when lovers dump them, even when friends forsake them, the ensuing pain is absorbed into a network of positive relationships, easing the sting. Most people will feel, in effect, "So-and-so may have hurt me, but at least my other friends like me." In extreme crisis, they may be reduced to feeling, "Life is bare and bleak, but at least my mother loved me." This method of coping—by accessing internalized supports—is not available to many victims of abuse and neglect. It is especially unavailable during childhood itself, when the array of potential internalized resources is constricted, and the abusive or neglectful parent is one of the few figures to whom the child can turn for soothing and for a compensatory sense of self-worth in the face of disappointment.

The sense of hurt and betrayal that people feel when they are disappointed in their intimate relationships is soothed, intrapsychically, by

embedding it in a context of supportive, internalized warm relationships just as surely as the whole person is soothed, interpersonally, by
the warmth and support of close friends. Abuse victims, who must
have serious questions about whether or not a parent loved them, will
hesitate before risking genuine intimacy with others, because there is
no safety net.

A seventeen-year-old girl, Jade, was removed from her parents'
home when she was ten, along with her four younger siblings. Even at
that age, she was already the primary parent in the family, responsible
for virtually all housekeeping and child-rearing duties while her parents spent their time looking for drugs. Eventually, seeing that the
parents would never change, and recognizing that "the children" (an
appellation that did not include herself) were not doing that well,
Jade called DSS. At the time I saw her, the younger kids had all been
adopted, two by one couple and two by another. Jade had been in foster care for seven years, blowing out of each of the other children's
two adoptive homes after intense arguments with the parents, as she
held tightly to her role of primary parent. She had been the only child
in her current foster home for almost two years. Her relationship with
the foster parents ran hot and cold, ranging from the brink of eviction
to promises of lifelong connection. She held a job while going to high
school, which earned her the foster parents' respect and emotional
support, and now she was planning to continue working while heading
to community college. She was looking for DSS permission to move
into her own apartment, even though she was not yet eighteen. She
had been in therapy briefly, right after removal from her parents at
age ten, but not since.

Jade reported only two early memories when I asked her. In the
first, she was living with her grandmother on the first day of kindergarten, her parents being off on their own at the time. Excited about
school, she woke up early and dressed herself and did her hair. Her
grandmother intervened gently, approving of her choice of clothes
but helping to fix her hair so it looked good. Grandmother walked her
to school, and when the day ended and Jade emerged from the building, Grandmother was standing there waiting for her.

Jade's second memory was from the following winter. She was
living with her parents again, and her mother had just had a new baby.
Jade woke up in the middle of the night and wandered into the warm

kitchen, where her mother was caressing the baby and heating up formula. Suddenly, Jade's pajamas caught fire, as she had lingered too long beside the space heater. Jade got the fire out quickly but was burned. When the police came, Jade had to convince them that it had really been an accident.

These memories represent two complexes, one that governs Jade's public life, and one that governs her personal life. The first memory is organized around school, which, like work for adults, constellates a public persona. The memory says that when she is operating from her public persona—when intimacy issues are not tapped—Jade can function quite well, feeling supported by parent figures. In a public geography, she can even be parented, allowing, as she did, her grandmother to do her hair. In Jade's current life, this pattern allowed her to receive emotional support from her foster parents related to work and school. Presumably this pattern originated in Jade's family, where she was undoubtedly rewarded and supported when she acted responsible and intelligent, in other words, when she took care of business at home.

The second memory is organized around images of a warm kitchen and a mother feeding an infant, the essence of the intimate and personal. In these surroundings, Jade is in danger. Presumably, things did not go well for Jade as a child when she tried to get her own needs met, and did go well only when she met the needs of others. Yearning to experience the closeness between mother and infant, Jade suddenly found herself on fire. Turning to others is dangerous, in this complex, because others are not reliable: they do not protect you and they do not put out the fire. When she is independent, parent figures are reliable, but when she depends on them, they are not even strong enough to explain what happened to the police. Jade had to do this herself. In Jade's current life, this pattern plays itself out in her avoidance of personal closeness (no confidantes and no boyfriend), and in the emotional fires that erupt when she gets too close to her foster parents.

The second memory is another exoneration memory of autonomy (see Chapter 4). The abused or neglected child reports a memory of something bad happening to her without any hint of accusation against the parent. Usually, it is not so drastic as catching on fire, but more like falling down or getting an electric shock. Here, Jade implicitly exculpates the parent for not preventing the injury. Instead, she emphasizes her own autonomy as a child, and is almost proud of the fact that, even though she was injured, she did not depend on anyone else for help. Some people leave neglect out of the memory because they do not have in their imagination even the idea that parents can prevent injuries to children. Others leave out the neglect to exonerate the parent for reasons discussed in Chapter 4, as an effort to protect a positive view of the parents. For Jade, recognizing her mother's inability to protect her would have highlighted the fact that the mother *should* have protected her. This, in turn, would lead to her depending on the mother, which is exactly what puts her in a dangerous posture. Dealing with problems on her own, on the other hand, constellates helpful parents, as in the first memory.

Jade's memories show how separate a neglected or abused child's personal world can become from her public world, and how inadvertently destructive it can be to leap over the garden wall and attempt an intimate encounter with such a child. I recommended that Jade try individual therapy in exchange for getting her own apartment. My hope was that by the time she turned eighteen, when she could avoid all services if she chose, the individual therapist would have engaged her in the therapy process. It would take a talented and lucky therapist to sidestep Jade's aversion to personal closeness, not to mention the generic aversion to dependency of any late adolescent working on developmental issues of establishing social independence. Still, a therapist who did not encourage dependency, but who used the sessions as a relatively safe crucible in which to gently approach intimacy issues, could help Jade learn to approach intimacy with different expectations. The goal would be for the therapy to become the container for Jade's intimacy issues, so she could go about her daily life without having to worry about their erupting unexpectedly.

Thus, the abused or neglected individual avoids personal closeness for several reasons. The potentially close relationship can easily become too important to the abuse victim, and there is a dearth of compensatory supportive relationships if things go bad. In addition, personal closeness is avoided because it is the arena in which abused and neglected individuals have been previously hurt. If you were beaten or molested, for example, in an elevator, or even given very bad news there, you might develop an aversion to elevators. If something terrible happened to you in a theater, you might stop going to the movies. The psychological landscape in which most abuse and neglect transpires is the terrain of intimacy. Much of what hurts about abuse and neglect is the fact that they occurred in a close relationship, thereby eliciting, beyond whatever immediate physical and emotional pain is associated with the experience, a sense of betrayal (Madanes, 1990). This is one reason that children who are sexually abused by their fathers typically suffer greater trauma than those abused by strangers. (Other reasons they suffer more include the fact that the child of a molester may be less robust in many ways than the child of a normal person.) It hurts more to be betrayed, even through gossip, by a close friend than by a mere acquaintance.

When abused or neglected children find themselves becoming intimate, whether with a friend, teacher, therapist, or parent figure, their alarm bells go off, because they are becoming vulnerable again to reinjury. These children will go to extraordinary lengths to disrupt the development of intimacy, so as to reduce their vulnerability. This makes them difficult to engage. One way to manage their problems with closeness seems rather obvious but is difficult to implement. The solution is to avoid constellating intimacy with these children, except in highly regulated situations such as a therapist's office where relative guarantees of safety are offered to overcome and assuage the child's anxiety. It is difficult to restrict the intimacy to which these children are exposed for two main reasons. One is that prolonged contact between children and nice people constellates intimacy whether one wants it to or not. The other major problem is that the people to whom the children are exposed by the child welfare system can be relentlessly nice. People do not go into the business of foster parenting, social work, or teaching because they want to remain distant from children (generally speaking), but because they want to get close to children.

EXCESSIVE KINDNESS IN SERVICE PROVIDERS

Although the intentions of kind service providers are laudable, and although the behaviors they express are nothing to complain about in and of themselves, in a larger sense we see a vague replication of the abusive or neglectful experience in the way that the adult figures put their own needs and agendas (to be nice) ahead of the child's need (to regulate intimacy). In other words, the adult becomes more attached to the role he is playing than to its effect on the child. An abusive parent clings to the role of, say, kingly control at the expense of the children; the foster parent may cling to the role of kindly tolerance, also at the expense of the child.

When a child is suffering, there is a very powerful impulse on the part of the adult to put his arm around the child's shoulders. Standing beside the child, it is a nice gesture because it involves comforting contact that has no intrinsic sexual connotations. Unfortunately, once a child has been abused by parent figures, and has become hypersensitive to the dangers of intimacy, even this natural and unintrusive gesture becomes fraught with potential danger. Sensitive adults will not caress or hug, even sideways, a child who has been sexually abused any more than they would hug someone in pain after a severe sunburn. Ironically, the more severe the abuse or neglect, the more powerful the impulse to comfort, and the more it is incumbent on the adult to restrict the comforting to a manageable level. If a person has been starving in the desert for weeks, subsisting on whatever edible material she can eke out of that environment, when she finally returns to civilization, hungry and desperate, you do not give her a chocolate cream pie. By the same token, when a child emerges from an abusive or neglectful experience, it is a mistake to fill up her plate with warmth and affection.

ADVANTAGES OF CROSS-CULTURAL FOSTER PLACEMENTS

Because of the need to regulate intimacy, I think the impulse to put black kids in black homes and Hispanic kids in Hispanic homes and white kids in white homes is often wrongheaded. Sometimes, it is a case of putting a political agenda ahead of the needs of the child. When a particular child does not need warmth, which she finds disorienting and frightening, but instead needs a period of stability and recuperation, a cross-cultural placement can be very useful to the child. The fact that the parents in the home look and sound so little like the people who abused and neglected her can facilitate her ability to differentiate between the two situations, making the available support less frightening. Indeed, cultural differences between foster parents and children can be seen as exaggerations of one of the main purposes of foster care itself, which is to provide the child with a home that is not as intimate, and therefore not as complicated and frightening, as the child's own home. Also, obvious cultural evidence that the foster family is not directly competing with the child's commitment to his parent can help relax any loyalty binds.

I assume it hardly needs saying that many situations exist in which it is advisable to place children in foster homes that seem familiar to them. These situations primarily involve children who do not react badly to intimacy, and children who may not be returning to their families of origin. In the latter case, the potential length of stay in foster (or adoptive) care changes the cost-benefit analysis of deferring intimacy issues to their therapies versus confronting these issues in foster care. An extended stay in foster care means that it will not just be a period of stability and recuperation, but a new place to live.

If abused and neglected children cannot always handle intimacy, then we may need a whole new way to think about foster care for some children. When foster care provides orphans with new families, then it makes sense to emphasize its familial qualities. When foster care is used, as it is primarily in the child welfare system, to provide a place for the child to live while the parents are getting their acts together, then it is possible that the familial qualities of foster care only get in the way. This issue is sometimes managed with older children by treating the foster home as a boarding house. It can even be arranged that mature children should receive their own foster care payments directly from the state, from which they pay rent and board to the foster parents. This financial gesture can be reinforced by making sure that the rules of the placement correspond to those of a boarding home, rather than to those of a family. Many things that foster parents require, such as curfew, quiet, chores, and respect, are as valid among roommates as they are between parent and child. When the adults assert these requirements as parents ("under my roof, you'll follow my rules"), they invite an adolescent response at best, and at worst a response imbued with the child's fears of intimacy. When the adults assert these requirements as roommates ("let's figure out how to do the food"), they invite a more mature response, and are not as likely to constellate the child's fears of closeness.

A good model comes from a clever woman who had just moved into her divorced boyfriend's home with him and his twelve-year-old son. One evening, her boyfriend had to work late, and the child asked her if it would be okay for him to make a milk shake. She inquired of the boy in what respect he was asking her. He did not know what she meant, so she elaborated: "Are you asking me permission, like I'm a substitute parent? Are you asking me as a roommate? Or are you asking me as an adult friend?" "What's the difference?" asked the child. "If you're asking me as a parent, well, I'm not your parent; you have parents. If you're asking me as a roommate, then go right ahead; a little noise won't bother me. And if you're asking me as an adult friend, then I can tell you that this project will go a lot better if you have the kitchen cleaned up before your father gets home from work." It is astonishing how a little role clarity can take much of the tension out of a relationship, but foster parents rarely differentiate between children who are joining their families (however briefly) and children who are guests, roommates, and boarders. And when they do differentiate, they may be criticized for not treating every child the same.

This perspective of emphasizing the child's fear of intimacy can also raise questions about the wisdom of kinship care. Kinship care is the placement of children with relatives or friends outside the nuclear family. Obviously kinship care has some distinct advantages, in that it may be less disruptive for the child, and the relationships formed in kinship care can usually become or remain permanent. For some children, though, kinship care can evoke fears of intimacy and loyalty binds even more strongly than regular foster care. A child may have generalized his fears to the entire extended family, making the kinship home seem anything but a sanctuary. Also, the particular kinship foster parents may have either a preexisting loyalty to or a preexisting ax to grind with the child's natural parents. In the former case, they may view the child as the source of the family's problems and validate that belief by facilitating the child's misconduct. In the latter case, they may induce the child to defend the parent by misbehaving. Blood may be thicker than water, but it is also a better carrier of disease.

I was involved in service planning for one twelve-year-old boy, Juan, with an unusually traumatic history. He had grown up in war-torn El Salvador and had witnessed the execution of most of his adult relatives. In addition, he had been sexually abused while a displaced person. In America, he was cast upon the foster care system to which I was consulting. The first several weeks in any home would go very well, but after a few months, Juan would settle in and stop acting as if he were about to be thrown to the wolves at any moment. Once he got comfortable, he would celebrate his sense of freedom by relaxing and expressing himself sexually and aggressively. In one home, he sneaked into the parents' bedroom at night to molest the foster mother through the sheets. In another home, he eventually urinated only in the corners, never in the bathroom, much less the toilet. The consensus was to place him in an institutional setting and outside of the foster care system.

I suggested an alternative plan, which might be called "honeymoons only." I thought we could capitalize on Juan's initial good conduct by moving him every three months to a new home, even if things were still going well when it was time to move. My hypothesis was that the strangers stopped seeming like strangers after a few months, constellating his issues around intimacy, loss, and loyalty. He disrupted and mocked the intimacy available in these families to avoid being engulfed by fears that he would again be abandoned while vulnerable and passive. I thought his psychological problems could be addressed in individual therapy, and avoided in foster care.

My suggestion that he be moved from home to home was met by a few professionals with nothing short of horror, as if I were dooming this child to a life of trauma and disruption, as if I were not recognizing his status but creating it. Actually, my intent was to try to help change his self-experience from someone who cannot live in a family to someone who could, and to give him a history of familial successes (though limited) rather than a history of familial failures. Also, I pointed out that the disruption of moving from home to home is really no different, on the level of personal intimacy and loss, from living in an institution where the staff turnover approaches 50 percent a year. It is just that the disruption is more noticeable in the home because the child moves from place to place rather than the staff. I argued that multiple foster placements may be traumatic in the abstract, but fortunate is the child for whom this is actually a trauma; for this particular boy, I did not think multiple foster placements would even show up on his radar, compared to what he had been through.

My advice was not taken, and the child was institutionalized. People, even trained clinicians, do not like to accommodate the reality of a child's limitations, but instead prefer the hopeful role of optimists, regardless of how unrealistic it may be. I cannot say, of course, that Juan would be better adjusted if my idea had been pursued. I do wish the child welfare system were less concerned about how recommendations sound and more concerned about their effects.

The last time I saw Juan, after a year in a residential facility, I took him out for breakfast. He was clearly very hungry, but refused to order off the menu. He would rather not eat than have to decide what to ask for. I ordered for him, eggs, sausage, hash browns, pancakes, and a muffin. Then he still would not eat unless I told him in which order he should do so. It seemed to me that he was trying to figure out how to have no self at all, the better to fit in with an institutional agenda.

DISADVANTAGES OF IDEAL FOSTER PLACEMENTS

In another variation on the theme of avoiding personal closeness in foster care, some children require homes that are not as "good" as the best homes can be. The "better" a home is, in other words, the more it looks like Cosby's Huxtables or, from my generation, the Cleavers or Donna Reed, the more frightening it is to a child who is afraid of intimacy. As is obvious from my discussion of cross-cultural placements, I do not have much sympathy with the policy of always trying to place the child in an "ideal" home (ideal for some hypothetical child) and then wringing one's hands in sympathy and concern when what could not possibly have worked out because of intimacy and loyalty issues did not work out. I would rather place a child in a home that is not as "good," but which accommodates the child's pessimistic self-image, commitment to his or her parents, and fear of intimacy. You can take the child out of the family, I feel, but you cannot take the family out of the child.

There are two main ways in which a home can be less than "ideal" and thereby better at meeting the child's actual needs. One way is to structure the home in a manner notably different from the traditional family, similar to a boarding house instead of a surrogate family. The less the home resembles the child's notion of a family, the less likely it will be to evoke loyalty and intimacy binds. Thus, single-parent homes (where the parent is of the other sex than the child's single parent), homes of gay couples, and homes with such a large number of children that they are run more like camps than families all fill this bill.

An equally controversial, but equally psychologically valid, method of avoiding the overly challenging "ideal" home is to use foster parents who are not as loving, organized, or patient as the ideal foster parent. The foster parent who has all these wonderful qualities poses a great threat to the child's image of the natural parent. The child is made to wonder why his or her own parents are not so endowed. These qualities also cultivate intimacy, because the child perceives that the organized, patient, affectionate foster parent is genuinely trustworthy. Intimacy, as noted, may be too much for the foster child to handle. If only kind and generous foster parents are available, perhaps they can pretend not to be once in a while. One brilliant foster mother, presented with a teenage girl who had run from her last several placements after only a day or two in each, simply asked the girl to let her know before she ran, so she would not waste time looking for her or worry that the girl was still her responsibility (Broga, 1999). The girl stayed for three years.

Some kids have been physically abused so often that they have no sense of identity independent of abuse. To put them in a nice home is like trying to deal with a tree that has grown up around barbed wire by ripping the wire out of the tree. I recommend that children who have been severely and repeatedly physically abused be placed with foster parents who act assertive, emotionally reserved, bossy, or practical, who are, in short, not particularly nice. These children know how to relate to brusque, matter-of-fact treatment, to sarcasm, and even to disdain a lot better than they know how to relate to kindness and concern. When people, including children, do not know what to do, they get anxious. Chronically abused children can relate to tough homes, and can even appreciate the absence of physical abuse in them, as long as the home is not so kind as to disorient them. When disoriented and anxious, these children will try to reinstitute a landscape with which they are more familiar, by misbehaving until people treat them badly.

One foster home was almost closed down because the social workers disapproved so strenuously of the foster mother's demeaning, militaristic attitude toward the children. She ran the home like a boot camp, hazing the kids verbally, suspicious of their motives, and yielding no warmth whatever. I wanted to keep the home open because I thought there were some abused kids who would be able to function only in her home. Also, I felt that her overt aggression meant that she could be trusted not to express her negative feelings for the kids as covert or corrosive hostility.

The foster home in poor economic condition also reduces loyalty binds and disperses intimacy issues. One of the great problems for the foster care system is the fact that children, like everybody else, dislike any movement downward on the socioeconomic ladder. People can be happy with very little, and people can be happy with a lot, but what tends to make people unhappy is to go from more to less. If a family's income drops from $200,000 a year to $100,000 a year, they will mope and groan as much as a family that has gone from $40,000 to $20,000.

The problem in foster care is that most foster children come from poor families. Poverty may be a better predictor of foster placement than any other factor, even child abuse (Jenkins and Diamond, 1985; Zuravin and DePanfilis, 1997). Presumably, middle-class people who abuse their children have financial resources for avoiding the foster care system. Their solutions can range from hiring child care workers to buying the children distractions such as video games to sending the kids off to camp. The point is that a return home from foster care may mean a loss of luxury for poor children, making it difficult for them to readjust to their own homes. Further, the creature comforts of middle-class foster homes (relative to the natural homes) can exacerbate loyalty binds, because the superficial hedonism of children prefers those comforts. Intimacy issues can be exacerbated as well, since the relative comfort of foster homes can make poor kids feel warm and cozy.

Abused and neglected children often have problems with personal closeness. Whether in therapy, school, or in foster care, sympathetic adults naturally want to embrace and comfort these children. This impulse, understandable, even laudable, does not take the specific child into account and often leads to conflicts and disruptions. In any setting, a creative approach to the actual pattern presented is more likely to be successful than a generic approach that puts the adult in a desirable role but leaves the child out in the cold.

Chapter 7

Seriously Disturbed Patterns

If the psyche, as suggested previously, is a community of independent figures appearing in different groupings in different landscapes, then an individual's personality can be described according to which figures tend to appear in which roles and which figures are ignored by the system as a whole (are never assigned a role). For example, the obsessive-compulsive almost always casts the rational scientist figure in the role of spokesperson, and may not even acknowledge the existence of certain emotional figures, including those associated with exuberance, grief, and anger (leaving them to their guerrilla warfare). The hysteric puts the diva in charge of communicating with the outside world, and the system as a whole may not acknowledge figures associated with responsibility and autonomy.

THE USE AND MISUSE
OF THE BORDERLINE LABEL

But what of a psyche in which there is no organized assignment of roles; what of a psyche in which there is no system as a whole? These are the kinds of psychologies denoted by the label "seriously disturbed." The kinds of personality organizations (or *dis*organizations) associated with them have been called borderline or primitive (Kernberg, 1975; Klein, 1948) (primitive because they are like the personalities of infants). These labels, these days, are more confusing and distracting than communicative, for reasons that are not really relevant here. Our concern is with the crucial difference between essentially normal people who are reeling from trauma or otherwise coming to grips with it, and people whose personalities are organized in a way fundamentally different from ours.

To avoid all the pitfalls and land mines associated with the label "borderline personality organization," I use the term "seriously disturbed." By this I mean what most psychoanalysts mean by "borderline," but not what DSM-IV (the American Psychiatric Association's official lexicon of diagnoses) means by "borderline personality disorder." The latter would be merely one kind of serious disturbance. In DSM-IV terms, my meaning of serious disturbance would equate, roughly speaking, to "personality disordered." There is not an exact correspondence, since the original borderline concept I call "seriously disturbed" was based on features underlying behavior, while almost all DSM diagnoses are based on the external features of behavior. The main problem with my use of "seriously disturbed" is that it can produce a situation in which a man works his whole life, never does anything wrong to anyone, and shows no overt symptoms, but is "seriously disturbed" because his reality contact is fragile, his relationships are shallow, and his sense of self is diffuse and fragmented, while another man can break the law, continually lose jobs, blow up all his relationships, and be a veritable encyclopedia of psychiatric symptoms, but not be "seriously disturbed." So please keep in mind that "seriously disturbed" refers to the inner life, as described here, and not the superficial adjustment (Deutsch, 1942).

This chapter explores the patterns associated with seriously disturbed personality organizations as they unfold in the child welfare system. First, however, let me introduce you to Mr. Parker.

Mr. Parker was referred to me by his DSS worker for advice on how to relate to him. She was concerned that her gender had become an obstacle to assisting him to regain custody of his children. His children were in foster care because his ex-wife had lost custody of them to the state when she was jailed for drug use and petty thefts. He had met his wife in prerelease, where she was getting out of jail for possession of cocaine, and he was finishing up a sentence for statutory rape. He told me he was innocent of this charge, that he had never had sex with the girl, and that even if he had, it was not as if she were a little girl; she was sixteen (he claimed) and he was twenty. "I find this is a woman's state," he told me. First, they believed the girl's story

over his, and then they believed his wife's story when she told authorities that he beat her.

Mr. Parker's wife had already had a child, and had given custody of
her daughter to her own sister when she was put in jail the first time
around. At their wedding, he was accused of threatening his new
sister-in-law's life. He was reincarcerated until trial, but was eventually acquitted of threatening murder. Also on the wedding night, his
wife went to a hospital and received twelve stitches in her head. She
said at the time that she had fallen down the stairs, which he maintains is the truth; now she says he beat her that night.

Eventually they had two children of their own, now a five-year-old
boy and a three-year-old girl. His wife had divorced him, alleging
battering, and had gotten custody of the children. After the children
went into foster care, DSS found Mr. Parker to be employed, involved
with a new girlfriend, and without a recent criminal record. The
department instituted a plan to return the children to his care, but he
kept getting into squabbles with the social worker, which delayed
things. Then his ex-wife's older daughter said she had witnessed him
beating up her mother. However, her statements were discounted
somewhat because she may have been induced to make them by the
aunt she lived with, the same woman who accused him of threatening
to kill her.

Mr. Parker had not been diagnosed as seriously disturbed by his
own therapist, because at the time I met him, his therapist thought the
treatment was going well. Their sessions had become planning meetings on how to defeat the Department of Social Services. She had
agreed to testify for him in court if need be. If what they were doing
was therapy, it was not a kind of therapy that involved any need on the
part of the patient to change something about himself. A few months
later, when the therapist wondered aloud why he had not paid her yet,
and why the DSS workers found him so irritating, Mr. Parker responded by quitting therapy abruptly. The therapist then reported that
maybe he had some seriously disturbed traits after all.

Diagnoses of psychological disorders come not only in types but
also in levels (Kernberg, 1975, 1984). A diagnostic scheme that emphasizes levels, rather than types, has only a few important distinctions (three, four, or five, depending on how you count). Each level of
diagnosis embraces all the different ways of being troubled. Kernberg

likes the example of hysterical traits (flightiness, repression, and re-activity) in normals, hysterical personality in "high-level" serious disturbances, infantile personality in "low-level" serious disturbances, and hebephrenia in psychotic adjustments. At each level the same traits are expressed, but the overall level of adjustment influences whether they look like a breezy attitude toward unpleasant facts or an adult's delusional belief that she has become a happy little girl. Similarly, Jacobson's (1971) discussion of depression traces its forms across different levels of psychopathology (I am simplifying) from normal downheartedness to characterological hopelessness to seriously disturbed despair to psychotic command hallucinations.

Take a trait such as Mr. Parker's aggressive machismo. Its expression in a personality depends a great deal on how disturbed the person is. In a relatively healthy person, it is expressed within a constellation that also includes a mature figure that ensures that the aggression is polished and controlled. The classic image of the bullfighter provides a high-level version of aggressive machismo. Presumably, psychological bullfighting in a healthy individual is only one of several modes of operation and is constellated by the psychological stadium and the psychological bull. A mid-level version of the same image would be the bullfighter without the bull and without the stadium. This is a person who construes every encounter as a bullfight, whether it is or not. He is still controlled and polished, but the personality lacks the flexibility not to be a bullfighter when the situation calls for some other attitude. A seriously disturbed version would be Mr. Parker himself, someone who expresses aggressive machismo without rules and without any higher purpose than to demonstrate his power over others. The corresponding image would be the bull.

One clear advantage of diagnosing by level, as opposed to type, is that agreement among clinicians becomes respectable. The inadequate levels of agreement about diagnoses documented in DSM-III (and not even reported in DSM-IV) would be much better if categories were lumped together into broad levels. Thus, the agreement between psychiatrists on whether an individual is personality disordered is more reliable than the agreement as to which particular personality disorder an individual has (American Psychiatric Association, 1987).

FRAGMENTATION

Although people operating on different levels may have similar personality traits, they are not the same in some very important ways. This is what is so important and, admittedly, so difficult to understand about seriously disturbed people. They (to me, by definition) are *not* reacting as the rest of us would if we were in their shoes (unless, of course, we had been in their shoes from the start). Most important, what is soothing and healing for someone whose identity has developed to a point of integration but who was then traumatized is not at all soothing to someone whose identity is fragmented. Gentle pursuit, for example, can be soothing to most people, as evidence that the pursuer is truly interested, and can slowly overcome the aversion to intimacy that many traumatized people feel; for seriously disturbed people, however, gentle pursuit can be frightening, and the ensuing emotional closeness can be overwhelming. This is what happened to Mr. Parker in his therapy, where the therapist eventually, just by spending time with him, came to assume that they had a warm relationship, an assumption that frightened Mr. Parker. It is also what happened in his romantic relationships. Eventually, his new girlfriend too would come to fear his capacity for rage, but not until their relationship had developed to the point that emotional closeness became an issue.

The goal of therapy with the seriously disturbed is to accept their limitations and to learn to work around them. One seriously disturbed boy, for example, learned in therapy to tell other people, when he was furious, "get out of my face." He even learned to tell people, while still calm, that if he ever told them to get out of his face, they had to leave him alone, because he had discovered that if he were pursued while angry, he could become violent. He explained all this to the staff of the residential facility where he was to spend a few weeks. The first time he got angry, he said, "get out of my face," went to his room, and slammed the door. Unfortunately, a staff member thought that this would be a good time to explain to him that slamming doors was not allowed, and opened the boy's door, whereupon the boy threw a chair through the window. (Turning a simple mistake into a major one, this made the boy even harder to place again. The boy was kicked out of the program; the staff person was consoled by others.)

The term "borderline" was first applied to people who were more disturbed than they appeared to be. The "border" involved was that between normal psychological functioning and psychosis. These people, far from insane, were able to hold down jobs, maintain social functioning (at least superficially), and relate reasonably to clinicians. On closer scrutiny, and especially in emotionally evocative situations that tapped intimacy issues, their functioning would deteriorate.

A great deal of clinical writing has been devoted to describing the seriously disturbed condition, partly because of the huge amount of clinical resources that this group consumes. The prevalence rates in the general population are estimated to be about 4 to 7 percent, but in many clinical populations, including those involved in the child welfare system for extended periods, the prevalence ranges as high as 50 percent. At first, this may seem stunning, but the whole idea is that these people function at their worst in close personal relationships. Therefore, it should not be too surprising to find them heavily represented among people who have chaotic, abusive, or neglectful families.

IDENTITY DIFFUSION

So much of the clinical literature is devoted to describing seriously disturbed conditions because there is really no analogy in normal psychology that would enable clinicians to grasp the disturbed world through introspection or intuition. Many clinical conditions have normal counterparts, which the imaginative clinician can use as a purchase on the psychopathology involved. For example, the obsessive-compulsive's repetitive checking of locks or washing his hands is very similar to any superstition, just more so. The chronically depressed person feels very much what normal people feel after a huge letdown or a blow to the self-esteem. The key elements of seriously disturbed pathology, however, including identity diffusion and poor boundaries, have no counterpart in normal functioning. When you try to imagine what it is like to have an amorphous identity, the part of you doing the imagining is not itself amorphous. (It is rather like imagining you are dead.)

Similarly, everyone has had experience treating other people two-dimensionally, and not as whole human beings. For example, when you go into a movie theater, you tend to view other people merely as occupiers of seats, or as potential obstacles between you and the screen. For most people, it is easy enough to make the transition from two dimensions to three, when you see someone you know or if one of the other patrons interacts with you in some way. The relevant point here is that even though you can imagine what it is like to treat other people as two-dimensional, as the seriously disturbed do, you cannot really imagine what it is like to treat yourself that way, as the seriously disturbed also do.

These qualities were evident in Mr. Parker's memories of early childhood, which, in his case, were generic and subjunctive. By generic, I mean that by and large they lacked the details or specifics that would distinguish them from someone else's memories. "I didn't want to go to school the first day of kindergarten. My mother walked me down there. The teacher came over." I asked for more, but he could not or would not provide more. By subjunctive, I mean that specificity is absent even as to occasion: "Going up to the mountains all the time to visit." I asked for a specific incident. "We did a lot of fishing." Even subjects who have good reason to be cagey, say, pilots trying to keep their licenses or prospective employees looking for work, can usually come up with a few specific, positive memories. Mr. Parker was building a self on generic memories, and such a self has a weak foundation. Further, to treat a person three-dimensionally, even if the person being treated is oneself, one needs to know something about his story, his life in anecdotes. Mr. Parker was in no better position to treat himself as a whole person than was a complete stranger, because he seemed not to have any better backlog of psychological information about himself than a stranger would have.

Thus, understanding the seriously disturbed is very difficult to do, both intellectually and emotionally. However, the difficulty of the task is not a good excuse for ignoring the distinctions between the seriously disturbed and the normal. Later chapters will comment on how service providers inadvertently reproduce patterns of child abuse and neglect in their dealings with clients of the child welfare system. Here, I just want to mention one crucial way in which this occurs. As noted previously, much child abuse and neglect can be construed as a misestimation on the part of the parent of the developmental status of the child. Abuse ensues after the parent treats the infant's crying, for example, as defiance, and hits the infant as if the child was much older. Analogously, much mistreatment by service providers ensues after the clinician misestimates the client's level of pathology, such as mistaking seriously disturbed rage for posttraumatic panic, and the clinician responds with warmth that threatens, rather than reassures, the client.

The golden rule informs much child welfare work. In general, social workers and clinicians treat clients as they would like to be treated were they in the clients' shoes. They try to be essentially friendly and good-natured, clear about their expectations, prompt and courteous, and they try to be sensitive to the fact that they are either wholly unwelcome in the clients' lives or are involved because of serious problems. In return, social workers and clinicians would like to be treated pleasantly and respectfully or, at worst, like a cop who pulls you over for speeding, i.e., with some resentment but still with recognition that the cop is only doing her job. When the reciprocity of the golden rule is not found, there may be an abuse of power on the side of the professionals or seriously disturbed pathology on the side of the clients. (Of course, there may be an abusive reaction to diminished power on the side of the clients or serious pathology on the side of the professionals, but that is not the topic at present.)

Mr. Parker simply did not treat the social workers reasonably. He was derisive, mocking, and volatile. When he finished taking the written personality test I gave him, his social worker told him that the visit that day would have to be cancelled. A torrential downpour had flooded many roads, including, as it happened, those around the foster home. Mr. Parker immediately assumed he was being lied to, folded up the answer sheet from the personality test, and stuffed it into his pocket. The social worker left us alone for a moment to call the foster home for an update on the roads. I wanted that answer sheet, but I did not want to ask for it directly and turn it into a power struggle. So I tried to get it by playing on his tendency to see people as all good or all bad, figuring that maybe the enemy of his enemy was his friend. I leaned over toward him and said, "These bureaucrats." He dug into his pocket and handed me the answer sheet without comment.

BOUNDARY PROBLEMS

It is hard to understand much about the seriously disturbed without understanding something about object relations theory, which I will cover rapidly and simply. It is admittedly an unusual name for a theory. The idea is that psychological forces (libido and aggression) are projected from a person like beams of light, and that these beams hit other people, which became their objects. The word "object" is used as in the phrase "object of my affection." These subject-object connections become the building blocks of the individual's psychology.

In object relations terms, there are three main tasks of psychological development. These include the differentiation of oneself from others, the development of an integrated, cohesive picture of oneself, and finally, the development of an integrated, cohesive picture of others. The newborn infant learns fairly quickly that the skin is the boundary between the self and the outside world for many purposes. The skin is an especially clear boundary for tactile and motoric experiences. In other words, the baby feels only things that happen to and within the skin, and feels nothing that happens outside it. Motorically, the baby learns soon enough that she can move through intention alone only things within the skin, and cannot move things outside of it except through contact. These simple truths are learned experientially. Babies imagine moving all sorts of things, no doubt, but only when they imagine moving their hands or legs or mouths is there any discernible effect. This is the earliest form of differentiation of self from the rest of the world. However, it is not complete. It is much more difficult for the baby to learn to differentiate the source of sounds, for example, than to learn the boundary of the skin with respect to tactile sensations. Eventually, most people do learn which sounds come from within and which come from without, but not everybody does so on a reliable basis. Auditory hallucinations can be construed as confusion about the source of sounds, in other words, as a boundary problem.

The differentiation of self from the rest of the world is probably never complete. Even healthy people will occasionally display mild boundary ambiguities. For example, a young girl tells her dad, who is watching a football game on television, that she is hungry. He replies, "You just ate." Perhaps he is really saying, "You're trying to get me away from my football game and I'm not budging." Perhaps he is saying that he has independent access to knowledge about her internal states. Perhaps he would rather make his daughter question her judgment about her own body than take the trouble to get off the couch or admit that he does not feel like feeding her right away. Either way one can see how boundaries are never complete, since other people can tell how you are really feeling by observing your recent circumstances. (Indeed, psychoanalytic therapy depends on the analyst's independent access to knowledge of the patient's internal state.) The form of the father's speech—a comment about her rather than about himself—maintains a blurring of distinctions between self and other. This blurring is of course trivial in the example given, but can be very important in trying to manage a relationship with a seriously disturbed individual, who finds clarity about boundaries offensive and ambiguity about boundaries confusing.

On a larger level, few people ever completely get over the feeling that the great narratives of history, not to mention the evening news, are meaningful primarily in the contexts of our own lives. I wish I had a dime for every citizen of Boston who explains the Red Sox drought as a consequence or corollary of his or her own drama. (They'll probably win this year because I wrote that.) These minor boundary diffusions notwithstanding, most people have a stable and reliable ability to differentiate self from other, especially relative to key psychological forces. Seriously disturbed people lack this ability, other things being equal.

Like so many disturbed people, Mr. Parker's difficulty separating his inner world from the environment showed up most clearly on psychological testing. The idea behind psychological testing is that it puts subjects on roughly equal footing in basically novel situations that are standardized from subject to subject. The idea is to know beforehand how different kinds of people tend to respond to the standardized stimuli. Testing also puts subjects in a situation where they cannot avoid responding. Thus, for example, one could converse with

Mr. Parker for a very long time without realizing that his vision of himself was amorphous and diffuse, not tied to specific narrative memories. In a social conversation, even if he did refer to his childhood in his oblique and generic way, one would assume that he was being discreet or coy, not that he was incapable of producing textured memories. The standardized process of requesting detailed memories in testing, however, highlighted this inability, because in the context of the evaluation, vague responding was not a satisfactory way to manage the demand made on him.

The best single test for self-other ambiguity is the Rorschach, the famous inkblot test. The subject is asked, in essence, to name things that the inkblots resemble. When he names something the inkblot simply does not look like, he is demonstrating some confusion about the relative weights to place on his preferences and on reality. For example, where most subjects see two girls, perhaps dancing together, Mr. Parker also saw two girls. But where most people see their buttocks, he saw their mouths. This is an extremely distorted response that indicated that once he gets something in his mind, he does not let reality stop him.

The seriously disturbed person's problem distinguishing interior reality from exterior reality makes it difficult for him to impart to his children a well-differentiated sense of self. That sense of self normally grows out of a comfortable feeling of being separate from others. When the others from whom the child is trying to be separate get confused about what is separate and what is not, then it is hard for the child to know what is hers and what is the parent's. Mr. Parker, for example, told me how he explained to his son how electricity works so that the boy would not put things in the electric outlets—when the child was eleven months old. This conduct can be seen as an invitation by the parent to the child to ignore his full personhood and to become a combination of intellect and precociousness, an invitation that the child perforce declined at that age, but which will become more inviting as the years go by.

A reliable differentiation of self from the rest of world is considered a good thing, but it does have its burdens. The most notable of these is that all the unpleasant things that happen inside you cannot be easily dispensed with. When you are feeling angry or disappointed or rejected, you cannot simply act as if those feelings are coming from someplace else. Thus, there is a high cost to being seriously disturbed in its likely interference with close personal relationships and with reliable functioning in other important life spheres, but one of its advantages is that unpleasant feelings can be farmed out.

When a seriously disturbed person is placed in a situation with good interpersonal boundaries, he can feel quite oppressed. Clarity about roles can have the unintended effect of driving back into his selfhood all the unpleasant feelings and memories that he has been attributing to others. Thus the seriously disturbed person typically will be antagonistic to good interpersonal boundaries. Mr. Parker, for example, constantly came late to visits with his children, sometimes as much as an hour, breaching his children's sense of the boundaries around the visits. He would also bring up professionals' personal lives when talking to them, presumably because the boundaries of a professional relationship were anathema to him. His therapist misconstrued this at first as a comfort with intimacy, but later it became obvious that he only talked about personal issues when he was not supposed to, and did not take advantage of the safety of a therapy relationship to discuss his inner life, only the therapist's.

RAGE AND ABANDONMENT FEARS

The disturbance in self-object relating makes seriously disturbed people extremely fearful of abandonment. When such a person becomes attached to someone, he lacks a reliable sense of the other person's agenda. Therefore, when the other person is not immediately and entirely available, the seriously disturbed person has no way to assure himself that she will return. Other people have no more reality in his mind than would an apparition or, say, a dream of a lost loved one. If a deceased loved one appears in your dream, you have no way of knowing if she will ever be back in a future dream. Further exacerbating the seriously disturbed person's abandonment fears is his incapacity to self-soothe. The aching part of him does not have a reliably internalized parent figure to comfort him. Thus, when he misses someone, he does so inconsolably.

Seriously disturbed people are so afraid of being abandoned that they feel compelled to test the durability of relationships. They are like Laurence Olivier's character in that scene from *Marathon Man* where, as the Nazi dentist, he tortures Dustin Hoffman's character, asking over and over again, "Is it safe?" Olivier worries is it safe to go to the bank and get his diamonds; the seriously disturbed person wants to know if it is safe to count on the other person. No amount of reassurance can satisfy him on this score, because every bit of reassurance induces him to feel warm and close, which only makes him more anxious that he will be abandoned. Mr. Parker sought guarantees of never being abandoned by his wife by beating her up. If she really loved him, she would endure any rage he expressed, and once endured, that degree of rage became the baseline against which he would measure further acceptance.

There are a number of interesting theories about the causes of serious pathology. One is that excessive anger at an early age disrupts the formation of a cohesive sense of self (Kernberg, 1975). The anger may be related to a biological predilection toward aggression, or to unfortunate frustrating or traumatic events that elicit a degree of rage that is too much for that individual's ability to integrate. The rage may be construed as a figure that is too difficult for the other figures to get along with. Trying to coalesce a sense of identity in the presence of such rage would be as difficult as trying to hold a family dinner with an armed gunman in the room. Along these lines, I testified at his children's adoption trial that if Mr. Parker's rage were not expressed every now and then, then life would begin to seem to him shallow and unreal. I said he could act appropriately for extended periods, but eventually his conventional facade would crumble and give way to anger. Mr. Parker, sitting next to his lawyer, growled in a loud voice, "This is shit." The judge kept his poker face, but the DSS lawyer later assured me that such outbursts do not go unnoticed in a courtroom.

THE MATERNAL HOLD

Another set of ideas that puts serious disturbance in perspective conceptualizes the infant's relationship with the parents as an analogue to the "maternal hold" (Mahler, Pine, and Bergman, 1975). In this scenario, the image of a mother holding a child is seen as the fundamental interchange between an individual and her world. This version of child development is quite compatible with the psychology of figures- in-landscapes described previously. In the maternal hold, the child passes through various states of mind, or roles (or figures), to which the parents have various responses. These roles and responses create expectations and role relationships, which become internalized and form the building blocks of the self. For example, when the child is hungry, the parents may be nurturant or, say, annoyed; when the child is angry, the parents may be hurt or perhaps withdrawn; when the child is cranky, the parents may be soothing or, say, rejecting.

Obviously, some parental responses are better for children than are others. For example, it is probably better for children if their parents are soothing in response to crankiness than rejecting. However, even a rejecting parent can facilitate the development of a reliable role relationship, which can serve as a building block for a self.

What creates real problems in this version of child development is a parental response of anxiety. Whether the parental response to the child's state of mind is positive or negative, as long as it is firm, the child will continue to feel held, and the firmness of the hold is considered essential for integrating the ensuing role relationship. When the parental response is one of anxiety, however, the child experiences the role relationship as she would experience a loose, insecure, and fragile set of arms holding her. It is parental anxiety, then, that makes the child's particular state of mind truly toxic and difficult to integrate into a coherent structure. It is as if the firm parent has *some* response to each of the child's psychic figures, so that each figure finds a place in the parent's world. The figure that elicits parental anxiety, however, does so because the parent has no set response to it, and the figure thenceforth operates outside of the parent-child system and therefore outside the integrated features of the child's selfhood.

When too many of the role relationships, or a few but crucial role relationships, that make up a self are not integrated into a cohesive sense of self, then seriously disturbed fragmentation occurs. The child's psychology becomes like that of a country in civil war, or like that of a totalitarian state in which the various functions of society are so restricted and independent of each other that distrust and disharmony between systems impedes their functioning.

Seriously disturbed people are unwise. I mean to imply that wisdom is reflected in behavior that stems from multiple perspectives and that is responsive to remote or deferred consequences. Multiple perspectives are facilitated by a well-integrated psyche, where all of the figures know about all of the other figures, where they align in hierarchies of organization according to the demands of the environment, and where each figure is assigned to the tasks that he or she does best. This dialogue and role clarity among figures is missing in the disorganized psyches of seriously disturbed people.

Responsivity to remote consequences is also difficult for the seriously disturbed person, since it requires that concern about long-term effects be present even when the individual is presented with short-term gratifications. This in turn requires a level of integration and organization that the seriously disturbed psyche lacks. Wise behavior is governed by an assessment of costs and benefits (*U.S. v. Carroll Towing Co.,* 1947, in which Learned Hand first formulated risky utility balancing). Included in the costs is the cost of the behavior itself (the ends do justify the means as long as the cost of the means is included in an assessment of the ends). Included in an assessment of the benefits are remote or deferred benefits (reduced by their improbability of coming to fruition). Far from considering deferred benefits, the seriously disturbed person tends to act under a constricted time horizon. His sense of identity is defined largely by things that have happened in the last several minutes, and his objectives are confined to things that can happen in the next several minutes.

IMPULSIVITY

Identity diffusion produces impulsivity partly because planful behavior requires knowledge of the person for whom the behavior is being planned. If I plan to make you dinner, I want to know something about you, including your dietary restrictions and your culinary preferences. If all I know about you is that you have severe restrictions and strong preferences, but I do not know their specific nature, then I will not bother to plan. Instead, we can a pick a restaurant at the last minute. The seriously disturbed person does not have a solid sense of the person, himself, for whom he would be planning behavior. He responds to this condition by not making plans.

When something disappointing happens to most of us, we absorb that disappointment into the larger sense of who we are. As noted previously, this process is facilitated by the presence of soothing parental figures. The point for now is that when the larger sense of who we are is missing, i.e., when the identity is diffuse, then recent events do more than affect the individual, they define him. When Mr. Parker's wife would disobey him, he would not merely feel impotent and enraged, which implies a separate part of him doing the feeling. He would *become* enraged impotence.

A clinician with a good imagination can put herself into the place of just about anybody doing just about anything. It may be hard to imagine hitting your son, but if you are healthy enough to feel that such an impulse does not define you, then it is possible to construct a scenario in which you can imagine, if not an uppercut, then a swat on the butt. You can begin by imagining a string of defeats at work, severe economic frustrations, and a child who has just decided to see whether honey makes good shoe polish. I met a woman who left her one-year-old in the bathtub just long enough to run out of the bathroom and answer the phone. It seems to me just a matter of foolish pride to announce to the world that I have never done such a thing and that I never would, true though these may be. But it is another matter entirely to assert that I never could, which would be untrue. When someone engages in behavior that you cannot imagine ever, under any reasonable circumstance, being able to do, then you may be looking at seriously disturbed conduct. For example, I can imagine a horrible series of events over the course of several years driving me to such distraction and despair, to such a sense of futility and ineffectiveness, that I began to hurt myself as a way of focusing the pain and precipitating the oppressive sense of dread. I cannot imagine any set of circumstances, however, that would lead me to burn a baby with a cigarette. I am suggesting that certain behaviors are in and of themselves indicative of a serious disturbance.

IMPLICATIONS FOR SERVICE PLANNING

Diagnosis of a serious disturbance, with its implications of rage reactions to intimacy, dissatisfaction with the durability of relationships, and identity diffusion leading to a lack of wisdom, has numerous implications for child welfare work. Children with serious pathology should be placed in relatively permanent settings, but not challenged with the intimacy and familial meanings of adoption. Professionals in the child welfare system know that many children will live comfortably in a foster home for months or even years, only to disrupt just after either the decision to adopt or the finalization of adoption. This disruption may stem from some of the factors I discussed in Chapter 4, regarding the child's investment in the image of the parent; in other words, the child may be proving that nobody could have loved him.

Beyond those motives, the child may be taking the notion of adoption seriously and taking the opportunity to introduce into his new family, now that he has been told he will be loved permanently, all the emotion and impulse that has been deferred. Or the child may feel that adoption is going to cause a loss of self. It is as if he thinks, "It cannot be I who has been adopted. Where am I? How can I get myself back? I know—by creating chaos." My point here is that one can predict which children will react disruptively to adoption. These are the children with serious pathology, as evidenced by poor reality contact and identity diffusion on psychological testing, dynamics of rage and abandonment, and a history of boundary problems.

The child welfare system operates on a modified Peter Principle. The Peter Principle, you will recall, suggests that people are promoted as long as they are doing a good job, the result being that people keep getting promoted until they are no longer competent to do the job they have attained. In the child welfare system, goals are increased until the child fails. If a child is so aggressive that he cannot go to school with other children without hurting them, then his sarcastic, disrespectful speech will be overlooked. If the child then achieves an extended period of time without attacking others, and is even able to collaborate with them, then rare is the system that declares success and becomes satisfied with his adjustment. Instead, most systems will take now for granted his ability not to be violent and will start "treating" him (or hounding him) for speaking disrespectfully.

Similarly, a child unable to manage family life will be placed in an institution. If at some point she seems ready to risk a more normal placement, she will be put into foster care. If she then succeeds as a foster child, people will start talking about guardianship and adoption. When the adoptive placement disrupts, and she finds herself back in an institution, only then will clinicians wonder if they should have settled for foster care.

The antidote for this Peter Principle, where children's goals are promoted until they fail, is to look at the children's current adjustment. If this adjustment, as reasonably and realistically described, would have been considered at an earlier stage to be a major success, then it is probably a good idea to settle for this current adjustment as the goal. The diagnosis of serious disturbance in a child, or even an adult, is seen as a condemnation to a life without adoption, family, and the normal gratifications of personal closeness. Instead, the diagnosis should be seen as a warning to settle for less than grandiose goals.

The diagnosis of serious disturbance in children also has profound implications for the choice of placement. These choices generally boil down to one of the following. Restricted foster care refers to families that have been recruited and approved for the specific child. A restricted foster parent might be anyone from a favorite teacher to the parent of a friend to a relative. Unrestricted foster care refers to families that are basically in the business of taking in child welfare children who need a place to live. In Massachusetts, they can take up to four foster children, as long as they do not have more than six children in the home including their own. Specialized foster care refers to unrestricted homes that receive more money than typical homes, special training, extra supports, and fewer children. Typically, only one child is placed in a specialized foster home, and there is regular consultation with support staff. Group homes are residential facilities with staff, as opposed to parents living in their own house. They are run pretty much like dormitories, although the level of control over the residents varies from program to program. The residents are educated in the local public school, whether mainstreamed or in special education. Residential treatment centers combine group homes with their own school, the theory being that the integration of all services will provide better treatment. The upside of this integration is that all the clinicians and teachers can communicate with one another about the child. The downside is that the facility is much more separate from the community and it has a much greater financial stake in keeping the child in the institution than does a facility that is paid for only part of the day. In addition to these primary placement options, there are time-outs, shelters, diagnostic placements, hospital diversion programs, and mental hospitals.

Usually the key elements in selecting a placement alternative are the child's ability to tolerate normality and the meaning of the placement to the child and the family. Some families view residential treatment and group homes as implying that their child is defective, and resist such placements. More common, unfortunately, is the family that already views the child as defective and sees these institutional placements as confirming that view. Many families balk at the idea of placing their children in foster care, as if any potential success on the part of the foster parents would reflect badly on the natural parents. Many natural parents doom the foster placement by making it clear to the child that their self-esteem is on the line, inducing the child to defend them as outlined in Chapter 4.

In one case, a girl was abandoned by her mother at a young age, and left in the care of her grandmother. After several years, her grandmother kicked her out for being too much trouble. The state placed her in a nice foster home, where she quickly endeared herself to the family, and talk of adoption soon followed. The location of the foster home was kept secret from the grandmother, for fear that she would undermine the placement. The grandmother phoned every middle school in that part of the state until she found out where the child had been enrolled. Then she sent a card to the child at school, which was passed on to the girl. The card said simply, "Nobody will ever love you as much as I do— Grandma." The child ran away from the foster home that night, eventually destroyed her relationships with everyone in the foster family, and never adjusted to another foster home.

One way to improve the foster care system would be to make as clear as possible what is not at all clear now, namely, that the foster parents are working for the natural parents, not competing with them. However, even this perspective would not help a child whose parent insists that the child is too wicked to live in a family, or who interprets the child's success in foster care as a personal affront.

The diagnosis of children as seriously disturbed has profound implications for their ability to tolerate normality. These children should not be pushed into intimacies they cannot handle. Often, as noted in Chapter 6, less-than-ideal foster homes can hold seriously disturbed children, whereas more doting foster parents may threaten their adjustment. Affection can inadvertently challenge these children's defenses against personal closeness and provoke abandonment fears.

One reason seriously disturbed people act differently from other people is that they do not connote affection, attention, and approval as rewards. In most people, these three important reinforcers acquire great power because in most families, they precede biological reinforcers (caresses, food, warmth, etc.) and become associated with them. When extremely aversive experiences have been transmitted by caregivers, then affection, attention, and approval can become warning signs of bad things to come, provoking escape or attack responses in caregiving situations.

The seriously disturbed child, like the normal child, acts in a way that validates her sense of who she is, but the sense of who she is can be so twisted by fragmentation of the identity that the ensuing behaviors seem strange to us. One seriously disturbed adolescent succinctly described himself as a "burning outhouse." He would act in such a manner as to validate this self-perception, by making people avoid him in fear and disgust. For example, he would go for weeks without washing his hair, and then he would go to a salon for a haircut. The hairdressers would react to him as they would to a burning outhouse, looking repelled, keeping their distance, and sending him away. Rather than feeling humiliated, he reported feeling "strangely relieved."

The implication is that seriously disturbed children should not, as much as possible, be placed in familial situations, which are likely to be too much for them to handle. Of course, it is not always possible to tell which children are seriously disturbed and which are not, especially since many of the surface symptoms are alike when comparing trauma reactions with serious disturbance. But when it does become clear, then it does an injustice to the child to hold out optimism while creating a series of failures.

When it is the parent who exhibits serious pathology, then, in my opinion, this more than any other factor contraindicates reunification. In general, the evaluation of a parent with respect to reunification consists of determining whether the parent has done anything wrong in the area of child rearing, and whether what they did was in character. (I also assess the child's potential for growth without the parent, the child's realistic alternatives, the parent's ability to remediate past harm, and the availability of resources to compensate for parental deficits.) The assumption is that misconduct that was in character is likely to recur. If the misconduct is not in character, it is more likely to reflect situational or transitional forces. With seriously disturbed parents, any child abuse or neglect is likely to be repeated. This is because some of the key psychological aspects of abuse and neglect are by definition in character for seriously disturbed parents. These include intimacy violations, poor boundary management, and treating others as props.

One problem in assessing seriously disturbed parents is that they function much better once the children are removed from the home. Beyond the fact that anyone's functioning is likely to improve with fewer demands, seriously disturbed parents, once the children are removed, are no longer confronted with the intimacy of child rearing. These people may then look good when their cases are reviewed in court, since without the children they attend services regularly, maintain employment, and generally behave themselves.

The conditions under which the parents function well or badly must be considered in light of their relevance to raising children. Social workers must develop more subtle expectations of parents' behavior than merely to refrain from overt abuse and to attend visits and sessions, and then the clinicians must evaluate the parents according to the more subtle criteria. For example, a parent may promise never to hit her children again, and a series of visits in which there is no hitting will be presented in court as a compliance that argues for reunification. Instead, the service plan should say that the parent will be good-natured and playful when the child is insolent. This response would indicate real change in the parent's role relationship with the child's insolence, rather than a mere refraining that is not likely to last beyond the period of time in which the parent is under the department's scrutiny.

Many of the key reinforcers that make parents behave well are missing with the seriously disturbed parent. Powerful reinforcers for most parents include the quiet joy they feel when their children are having fun or feeling secure, and their chance to satisfy their curiosity about their children when the children express themselves. These two powerful motivators of parents, joy and curiosity, do not operate effectively on seriously disturbed parents. Their children's happiness tends to evoke resentment or fear rather than joy.

For example, I observed Mr. Parker visiting his children at the DSS office. (Unlike some psychologists, I prefer to observe visits in an office setting, where the focus is on the parent's responsivity to the child. Frequently, in my experience, home visits tell us more about the home than about the parent, as the children organize around the refrigerator, the television, and anyone who happens to drop by.) His son was not really hungry and did not eat the food Mr. Parker had brought. He did toy with the foil topping of the yogurt container, trying to peel it off in one piece. Mr. Parker, not noticing the game the boy had made of it, grabbed the yogurt from him and tore the foil off it. His daughter had been watching the son's efforts with interest, and asked her father specifically just to get the foil started, so she could peel it off herself. Mr. Parker peeled off her foil entirely as well. Here, I think he was blind to their potential pleasure in peeling off the foil because he took no joy in their pleasure. If their pleasure made him happy, he would have been more attentive to it.

When the children of seriously disturbed people express themselves, instead of satisfying their parents' curiosity about them, it tends to make the parents irrationally angry. This is because it casts the parents into a crucible of personal closeness. For example, Mr. Parker's children went about building themselves a fort in the DSS playroom out of chairs, a table, and an old blanket. Mr. Parker had brought coloring books, and when the children expressed no interest in them, he sat and colored them himself. The children began verbalizing their fantasy play, discussing the security of the fort, the bad guy who was after them, and what weapons they could use to defend the fort. They asked Mr. Parker if he wanted to play, too. He looked up from his coloring book, saw what they had done, and immediately dismantled their fort. He claimed later that he had been trying to make sure they were safe, but, in my opinion, what he was trying to keep them safe from was not a physical mishap but the dangers associated with fantasy play: childish exuberance and inevitable disappointment.

If the seriously disturbed individual's children are young enough, or detached enough, to be able to grow without him or her, it is prudent to consider having them adopted into new families or by extended family members. This is what I recommended for Mr. Parker's children. With older children, the focus should change from reunification to an exploration of how much parenting the parent can actually and competently accomplish without deteriorating. The parent is charged with doing an amount he or she can handle, and the state then does the rest. For example, many parents who would be incapable of raising their own children without becoming emotionally overwhelmed are still capable of providing care, say, a couple of afternoons a week and every other weekend. The parent is then no more distant from his or her children than is the traditional divorced father, except that the primary parent for the remainder of the week is not the mother but a foster parent.

Here, too, it is best not to look for perfect solutions, but for good, realistic solutions, ones that can be implemented and sustained. The seriously disturbed parent may be capable of raising her children only a couple of days a week, but the children may be so tied to her psychologically that they cannot be transplanted into a brand-new family. If the fantasy of a permanent, cohesive family structure is not relinquished, the Peter Principle will again operate on what would otherwise be a good compromise. When the parent functions well on her one or two days a week, the parent or the social worker or the lawyer may press for an increase in the amount of time—until the parent fails. Under the approach that seeks the ideal of a permanent, cohesive family, the parent succeeds or fails. Under the recommended approach, in which foster care supplements whatever the parent is capable of providing, the parent succeeds to a greater or lesser degree. Again, when the child is young enough to be able to pull up stakes and begin again with a new family—when a permanent, cohesive family is not merely a fantasy—then the child's need for permanency can dictate a make-or-break approach (Bowlby, 1969). But when the child is too old or too attached for this, it makes sense to consider keeping the natural parent involved to whatever degree she can handle.

Parents and clinicians resist this approach, on behalf of asserting the parent's self-esteem issues: he feels bad about himself if he does not get full custody of his children. But this is a knife that cuts both ways, since his self-esteem will be better if he is succeeding at what he is assigned to do, rather than being assigned more than he can do and failing. It may help to remind the parent that he will be the child's parent forever, not just until the child is eighteen. This opens the possibility of planning not just for the next several years of childhood but for the entire life of the child. The child's relationship with the parent will be better in its last forty years if the parent was operating within his competence in its first eighteen.

PART III:
SOME SPECIFIC MALTREATMENT
PATTERNS

The four patterns presented in Part III are frequently encountered in child welfare work. Each includes a figure that the child welfare system cannot easily accommodate. The sexual abuse victim's mother is described in Chapter 8. Like the battered woman, she is at the same time innocent of the abuse but also required by professionals and by her children to act as a responsible parent. It is difficult for her to take responsibility for the care and protection of her children when the violations were not her fault. For the professionals, it is hard to hold her accountable without blaming her. Chapters 9 and 10 present the sexually powerful adolescent girl and the disruptive boy, both of whom create placement problems when they cannot live at home. They are not disturbed enough to warrant institutional care, but they are too difficult for foster homes to manage. The absent parent returned is discussed in Chapter 11. He or she has been out of the child's picture for an extended period, but has recently resurfaced, asking for custody. Legal problems are created, since he or she is not currently unfit, but the child has developed permanent bonds elsewhere.

I selected these patterns because a disproportionate amount of decision-making difficulties are associated with them. There are many recognizable patterns and figures that I do not discuss. Adolescent sex offenders, alcoholic or addicted parents, and batterers, for example, are also very common, but they do not give decision makers fits about what to do, partly because a great deal has already been written about them, and partly because the choices are few. Gay teenagers and the barely adequate parent are also figures of interest, but each of these groups is too varied to cover as a specific pattern. One gay teen may be operating in a context very different from the next, whereas most sexually reactive teenage girls and most disruptive boys are of a stripe. Perhaps subtypes of gay teens will someday be identified, and a lexicon of such patterns eventually described, but I am not at that point. That is not to say, of course, that each specific gay teen (or barely adequate parent) is not operating within clinically identifiable patterns. It is just to say that the patterns in the psyche of one are not customarily found in the next. The similarity of the patterns I do discuss between one instance and the next suggests that familiarizing ourselves with their features will provide us with useful road maps for future cases.

Chapter 8

The Sexual Abuse Victim's Mother

THE PERPETRATOR,
THE VICTIM, AND THE MOTHER

In Chapter 1, the cyclical nature of sexual abuse was explored, wherein sexually abused girls grow up to pair with impulsive, narcissistic men who, if they have any predilection toward child molesting, will find this impulse facilitated by the mother's dissociative tendencies. The roles in sexual abuse often boil down to the child victim, the male perpetrator, and the mother asleep in the other room. In reality, of course, the mother may be at work; it is shocking how often sex abuse occurs in families in which the mother works from three to eleven. Or the psychological equivalent of being asleep in the other room can be manifested in other ways. Mother might be physically in the house while the abuse is occurring, but not know what is going on. It is natural to ignore upsetting information, and the sexual abuse mother may, because of her own abuse history, already be expert at ignoring things, so it is not surprising how often the mother misses the warning signs.

Because sexual abuse is so terrible to contemplate, it is natural for nonparticipants within these families to avoid its complexity. Simplification facilitates emotional distance. Sexual abuse is so repugnant to most people that even experienced clinicians, social workers, lawyers, and judges will define various members of the family as either wholly guilty or wholly innocent. This stark division of blame can do more harm than good, because it keeps the roles in the drama distinct and unintegrated. It is good for the child to get the sense that the sexual abuse was not her fault. On the other hand, exculpating the child can inadvertently trap her in the position of passivity and ineffectiveness that she is trying to escape.

Thus, one theory of self-blame is that it is one way for the victim to try to get some mastery over the experience: it did not just happen to me, it happened because of me (Janoff-Bulman, 1982). Also, in actual fact, there are indeed sometimes ways for victims, without being assigned blame, to learn different behaviors that can keep them safer. Blame of the perpetrator is always appropriate in the sense that he should take responsibility for his conduct. But sometimes it backfires and keeps clinicians from achieving the desired end. Members of the family always have a more differentiated and textured view of the perpetrator than the child welfare system does. Characterizing him as evil can induce these families to balance that image by recalling their contradicting positive memories of the man. The family winds up defending the perpetrator to rebut the professionals' condemnation. If the system were slower to condemn, the family would have nothing to counterbalance. This dynamic does not operate with strangers, in other words, with men whose image in the family is no more complex than their image in the larger system.

The mother tends to fall on the guilty or innocent side, depending on the blamers' assessment of the state of her knowledge as the abuse was occurring. Some people will consider her guilty if they think she knew what was happening, others if they even think she should have known. Here, too, the system's efforts to categorize her as guilty or innocent interferes with the integrative efforts of the clinical work. The issue for the clinician is rarely what happened in the past and is instead a concern for the future. The relevant question is whether the mother can rehabilitate herself in the children's eyes. Naturally, the more she knew or should have known, the harder it will be for her to achieve this goal. But the emphasis should be on rehabilitation, not on guilt or innocence.

Sometimes the mother was so involved with the abuse that her participation must raise questions about her fitness to be around children. One woman not only stood by and observed her boyfriend molesting her daughter, she also watched him stand her son up against a wall and shoot bullets around his head, handing him the bullets one at a time for his single-shot rifle. In a case such as this, the boyfriend's psychology is almost incidental to the relationship between the mother and the children. In such cases, I am reminded of the huntsman in "Snow White," leading the child into the forest to cut her heart out. His conduct would be clearly criminal, but it is also clear that he is working for the queen, not for himself.

THE FUTILITY OF BLAME

The issue of blame has other practical consequences, as well. Therapy may be forestalled by the fact that progress would require exposure of information that would lead to further criminal charges and incarceration. Therapeutic support is useful from the outset when sexual abuse has been discovered, but real psychotherapeutic work, in the sense of changes in the constellations of figures and reworking identity definitions, often has to wait until all the criminal implications have been settled.

As noted, the horror of sexual abuse and the intensity of blame associated with it keep the three roles in the sexual abuse triad distinct and unintegrated. The victim, the perpetrator, and the mother asleep in the other room need to get to know one another, metaphorically, and to realize that they have much in common. One does not like to admit that the victim was also "asleep in the other room" in the sense that she quickly forgot or ignored the full ramifications of what happened. One also does not like to admit that the perpetrator was like the mother in the sense that sexual abuse crept up on him as well. One day he was changing the girl's diaper, and the next he was massaging her vulva, while the part of him that should be protecting the girl was asleep at the switch.

One does not like to look at the fact that the mother may be getting something out of the abuse, and may therefore share some of the motivation and some of the perpetrator's role. She may be relieved that sex is being enacted between her boyfriend and her daughter so she can be left out of it. She may resent the daughter's playfulness and enjoyment of her own body, when she herself never felt that way, and she may be glad that her daughter's bubble of innocence is being burst. To put it more sympathetically, she may be relieved of anxiety over anticipating what she believes to be inevitable when her daughter is abused and stops being blithe and carefree. When the girl is girlish, the mother waits for the other shoe to drop. When she is depressed and victimized, the mother is upset, but the situation is not nerve-wracking.

The daughter, meanwhile, may have powerful sexual fantasies about the perpetrator, and may seek the molestation. It is legally and politically accurate to say that the daughter is morally and criminally innocent, but in many cases this formulation does not encompass the girl's feelings. We are presumably stunned by the judge who, apocryphally, acquitted a child molester, noting that the victim was "an unusually seductive four-year-old girl," as if the responsibility for engaging in the conduct can in any way be distributed between an adult and a child. Indeed, a different perpetrator in Massachusetts recently took the stand and asserted as his defense that the six-year-old girl had initiated oral sex. The judge found this theory so repugnant that this first offender was sentenced to eighteen years in prison. Within the psychology of the victim, the stark segregation of roles via moral blaming can disrupt the child's opportunity to come to terms with the interaction between the abuse and her own lust. One of the reasons sexual abuse is bad is that it poisons the child's sexuality by making it seem as though feelings of lust lead to violation and betrayal. The child welfare system does not need to compound that injury by treating the child's lust as unwelcome, ghostly, or dangerous—in other words, as something not to be discussed.

Finally, to continue this brief exploration of the way the roles in sexual abuse are more ambiguous than they first seem, treatment of the perpetrator involves understanding his role as a victim. He is as helpless in the face of his lust for the child as the child is. I am not trying to arouse any sympathy for perpetrators; in fact, I do not even work with them individually because I keep thinking about capital punishment. What I am trying to say is that to be effective with them clinically, it helps to understand their psychology. Much of what perpetrators need to learn to do to keep sexual abuse from happening is what mothers and victims need to learn to do to keep sexual abuse from happening.

Sexual abuse can be an identity-defining event. One insightful therapeutic technique in working with a victim is to add up the number of minutes in her entire life that she was being sexually abused and to divide this sum by the number of minutes she has been alive

(Madanes, 1990). The quotient is always quite small. The idea is to communicate that the victim does not have to be defined by the experience. One often hears sexual abuse therapists distinguishing between a "sexually abused child" and "a child who has been sexually abused." The admittedly trivial semantic difference can indicate a profound clinical difference. Other adults, however, can let a few incidents of sexual abuse define the child.

One Hispanic family I met refused to use the word *niña* (girl) in reference to the seven-year-old victim, instead calling her a *mujer* (woman) because she was no longer a virgin. In another family, a two-year-old girl had been forced to fellate a neighbor. There was no indication that the family had contributed to this traumatic event, negligently or otherwise. Nonetheless, it was learned over a year later that since the time of the assault, the mother had refused to kiss the girl on the lips. I am sure that forcible fellatio has a tremendous impact on a two-year-old girl, but in terms of defining her identity as a victim of sexual abuse, I doubt it is any more powerful than the mother's refusal to kiss her on the lips. Every time the mother declined to kiss her, the child was made to feel stained and branded.

In a complex as rigid as the sexual abuse triad, no figure can be considered independent of the others. The dissociative, passive woman has no independent meaning apart from the impulsive, narcissistic perpetrator or the violated child. For the perpetrator and victim, there is always a mother asleep in the other room; for the mother and child, there is always a child molester lurking nearby; for the man and woman, there is always a child whose violation is suggested in their exchanges.

One sometimes sees the complex in early memories or in psychological testing. For example, the earliest memory of one sexual abuse mother, Ms. Franklin, involved the heat failing to work in her room when she was a young child. She recalled lying awake, unable to get warm, her lips turning blue with cold, shivering, alone. She decided not to bother her parents, who were asleep in their own room. Her case had come in when her son asked at day care if the provider changing his diaper wanted to rub his penis, as his father did. The investigation turned up the fact that a year prior to the boy's disclosure, Ms. Franklin had found her husband molesting their son while giving him a bath. She reported having spoken to him sharply at that time, satisfied with his promise never to do it again.

In Ms. Franklin's early memory, there is a suffering child. Protection would be available and easily implemented, but the parental figures who could solve the problem are not informed about it, presumably to spare them the relatively minor inconvenience of fixing the radiator or changing the sleeping arrangements for that night. In the memory, the parents' sleep is more important than the child's rescue. In the bathtub scene, the mother's inadequate response may be understandable in our eyes, as we recognize that no parent wants to face the terror and upheaval of realizing that one's spouse is a pedophile. In the child's eyes, however, Ms. Franklin's response communicated that her complacency was more valuable than his protection. In subsequent molestations, he found himself in precisely the same position as his mother in her early memory, suffering a preventable ill but disinclined to bother the parent who could solve his problem.

In a case such as this, incidentally, to show how a complex can act as a road map to treatment, and not just to replication, one wants to find examples of it in the therapy sessions. For instance, the child is making a castle and looks longingly at some blocks, but does not ask his mother to fetch them. The therapist can highlight the child's glance, train the mother to notice and respond to such things, or train the child to put his needs into words. Similarly, the mother may come to an individual session even though she feels ill. Her therapist can emphasize the fact that she, the therapist, does not require the mother to sacrifice her well-being for the therapist's sake. In other words, the therapist does not accept the mother's attempt to ignore her own suffering so as not to inconvenience the therapist.

REPEAT INVOLVEMENT WITH SEX OFFENDERS

One pattern to be aware of in dealing with sexual abuse mothers involves the woman who has been involved with more than one child molester. This is the single best, though still not definitive, indicator that her involvement with child molesters is motivated and not accidental. I have already mentioned some possibilities for what this motivation may be, including the desire to be left out of sexual transactions by arranging for them to occur between two other people and resentment of or anxiety about her daughter's enjoyment of safety and innocence.

A few other potential motivations occur to me. One can generally be subsumed under the heading of desensitization, in which mastery over a bad experience can be achieved by arranging for it to be repeated often enough that it loses its bite. This is analogous to the jury in the Rodney King case being exposed to the videotape of his beating so many times that it lost its impact.

Another motivation based on repetition would be "making passive into active," wherein the victim repeats the trauma but in an active role (Weiss, 1993). This provides a sense of mastery and control. Her imagination may be devoid of alternative scenarios that are entirely free of sexual abuse dynamics—she cannot see herself in a family in which there is no sexual abuse at all. Instead, given her resignation to the idea that sexual abuse must occur in a family, she chooses one of the less aversive roles. Almost anyone, given the choice between being a victim and a perpetrator—and the choices available to abused children can easily boil down to these two—will choose to be a perpetrator. This is what was meant by the concept of "identification with the aggressor" when applied to Jews in concentration camps (Freud, 1936; Schmolling, 1984). If life boils down to being either a Nazi or a Jew, it seems natural to prefer to be a Nazi. Presumably, the people who did not identify with Nazis in concentration camps were those with the most robust alternative roles available, in other words, those for whom life did not boil down to only two roles. They could still be friends, workers, historians, and so on, rather than having to choose between Nazi and inmate. The third role in sexual abuse is more appealing still, namely, the role of the parent asleep in the other room.

It is not a sign of true therapeutic progress for people merely to switch roles within the configuration. If the perpetrator discusses his own victimization, for example, it may be a step toward progress in that it adds dimensionality to his perpetrator role, but it does not in itself constitute a reshuffling of the available role alternatives within the drama. It may only be a response to new contingencies under which the perpetrator role is now even more aversive than the victim role, since the perpetrator is subject to scorn, isolation, and imprisonment. It may leave the different roles as limited and constricted as before, and locked in the same configuration.

A different kind of repetition occurs when the sexual abuse mother has spent her entire life unnoticed, in a kind of fog, with little to reflect back on with pride or self-assurance. Perhaps, in her whole life she has performed a single noble act that garnered her great social rewards from the child welfare system and from her children and relatives. This act was to kick out the perpetrator when she discovered the abuse. When her life settles back to normal, and she is no more tuned in to her surroundings than before, and her children are struggling with the sequelae of the abuse, it seems natural for her to hark back to her finest hour and to arrange, unconsciously, for it to happen again.

The seriously disturbed (see Chapter 7) motive to externalize chaos can also produce repeat involvement with offenders. This dynamic also operates in some battered women. In my experience, the vast majority of battered women, like the population at large, are not seriously disturbed. They can generally best be understood in the terms of so-called battered woman's syndrome, in other words, as women whose helplessness is learned, and whose depressive, dependent stance, including their return to the batterer, is an adaptation to the battering itself (Walker, 1979). However, some women, especially those who end up in a series of violent relationships, are expressing an identity concept that requires the battering for fulfillment of their perceived role. Obviously, one must be careful in discussing this motivation not to blame the woman. Apart from any moral or political concerns, blaming the woman (as with finding motivation in any victim) tends to have unfortunate clinical consequences. It makes other providers defend the woman, and it makes the woman defend herself, rather than eliciting exploration and change. Incidentally, this is the essence of the nondirective or neutral approach in therapy. The therapist tries to be present in the client system while taking into account his or her effect on it, and that effect is often that the system balances the therapist's agenda with opposing energy, called resistance. To reduce that opposing, equilibrating energy, the therapist adopts a neutral stance.

Life without disruption is impossible for the seriously disturbed individual to imagine, so she has a choice of feeling that the disruptive forces of chaos and rage are either outside her or inside her. By associating with chaotic and disruptive men, the sexual abuse mother who also happens to be seriously disturbed can find it soothing, relatively speaking, that the abuse is going on outside her body and not inside it. Her psychology becomes like the eye of a hurricane, where her search for peace constellates very powerful and upsetting forces swirling around her. In truly peaceful surroundings, it becomes obvious that the disruption and violence and chaos are within her own psyche, within her own memories, fantasies, and expectations. This makes her want to avoid, or disrupt, true peace.

DAMAGE ASSESSMENT

One treatment for a sexual abuse mother is to place her in the position of a concerned parent. The responsibilities associated with that position interfere with her general stance of ignoring difficulties. Fulfilling these responsibilities also helps remediate the trauma of sexual abuse for her children. The first of these is the need to do a thorough assessment of the damage that was done. The damage assessment is a very powerful step, partly because it counteracts the culture of the family that does not talk about such things. Sexual abuse, of course, almost always depends on secrecy (Madanes, 1990). (Nothing is wrong with family secrets unless, as in sexual abuse families, they occasion bad behavior.) Also, a damage assessment is useful because it seems to be therapeutic for a child to show a concerned parent what hurts.

The parent's commitment to finding out about injuries and to keeping secrets from developing in her family puts her in an active role. She cannot be "asleep in the other room" if she is busy ferreting out information. Of course, the mother typically is merely obeying the will of the therapist as she once obeyed the will of the perpetrator. But nothing is wrong with that. All too often, therapists fail in their efforts to effect great changes when only modest changes are required. Thus, the therapist need not produce a different woman, only one whose passivity is in the service of a better cause, and which cultivates a better constellation of figures.

A good strategy is to encourage the mother to arrange for a trusted outside adult, whether a professional or a relative, to mentor each child. The child visits his or her mentor on a regular basis, disclosing any bad events or bad feelings to the adult, who will then presumably respond appropriately. This technique creates a sense of safety, as any untoward events are likely to be found out quickly and dealt with; it also remediates the mother's position of being a third wheel on the sexual abuse by putting her in the position of being a third wheel on a positive relationship. Flying solo in the child's world may be beyond her; instead, her dissociated stance constellates not a perpetrator and a victim, but an uncle and a niece.

Part of the treatment of sexual abuse mothers is for them to engage in their own therapies to solidify their own stories. If people tend to act in character, then the character in which people act is partly defined by their construction of events, as revealed in their narrative histories. So one goal of individual therapy for sexual abuse mothers is to help them create a narrative understanding of their own lives that makes sense of the fact that sexual abuse happened but which also opens the possibility that it does not need to happen again. The process of constructing such a narrative is in itself therapeutic, since one of the sexual abuse mother's main problems, typically, is the dissociative one of not being able to access her hard drive. She tends to operate on very recent information or on very little information, because information, which in her experience has typically carried bad news, is itself aversive and to be avoided. Constructing her narrative history in therapy forces her to confront and utilize information.

A GOOD APOLOGY

I have already mentioned the need to apologize, but I would like to elaborate on how to make a good apology. Perhaps sexual abuse mothers are too inhibited and too passive to be good at apologizing; they must not get much practice, when so much of their psychology is organized around not doing. A good apology recognizes what I did wrong, why it hurt the person I am apologizing to, how I understand the relationship between what I did and who I am, and how I plan to change so that it will not happen again.

Naturally, the more one acts as a fiduciary to someone else's benefit, the more obligations one incurs, the more chances exist for making a mistake, and the more likely it is that one will eventually have to apologize for something. Thus, as a therapist, I am at my most apologetic, because the relationship is constructed in such a way that there are very few obligations on the part of the patient and so many on the part of the therapist. As a parent, the lopsided distribution of responsibility is also likely to produce a disproportionate number of apologies.

I think an apology is a way of letting the injured party know that I have learned something about the landscape I am operating in, and what it is that I have learned. I may have learned, for example, that in the therapy landscape, pride on my part makes the patient feel like an experimental subject, rather than like a cherished human being. Or I may have learned as a parent that impatience on my part ruins the children's enjoyment of the moment. As in all neurotic confrontations with reality, one would prefer it if one could be proud *and* empathic; or if one could hurry people along and have them savor their experiences at the same time. But that is not the actual nature of the relevant landscape.

A less comprehensive apology merely becomes part of a dysfunctional landscape. A simple "sorry" communicates to the injured party that nothing will change, that the apology is not a precursor to something different but a part of the dysfunctional transaction. "Take what you want and then say you are sorry" is the real lesson many children learn from their parents. Unless the child must also put back what was taken, the apology merely becomes a verbal tic associated with misconduct, whose real meaning is, "You may not express anger at me because I said the magic word."

Unfortunately, many parents try to teach their children how to apologize primarily to themselves, the parents. The problem, as noted, is that the distribution of responsibility between parent and child guarantees that for every age-graded infraction of the child, there will have been dozens by the parent. For every time the parent has a legitimate gripe about the child's tone of voice, there will be ten times when the parent should be trying to figure out what he did wrong to make the child irritated with him. When apologizing is taught in the parent-child context, apology becomes more than ever a sign of submission to the other person's power, rather than an exploration of what went wrong.

A good apology by the sexual abuse mother does not come naturally to her. If she were the type of person to step up and take responsibility for her children's experiences, the sexual abuse might not have happened in the first place. Also impeding her apology is, as noted in Chapter 4, the fact that she has to apologize for something horrible, not for something trivial. The process of bringing her to an apology can be tricky, because of the structural responsibilities associated with the various roles. The therapist must help her learn to take responsibility for the child without taking that responsibility on himself. This misstep can easily happen, especially in court where, under federal law, the state must usually prove that it has made reasonable attempts to help the mother before the children can be adopted. Hearings often put the social worker and the therapist on trial to determine whether they have done enough, rather than the parent. Even short of court action, the therapist must walk a fine line between helping the mother apologize and doing it for her.

Several strategies can help the mother (or even the perpetrator) arrive at an apology. Groundwork for an eventual apology is laid in the prolonged discussion of what happened, what damage was done, and why it hurt (Madanes, 1990). These discussions not only help the parent understand what she is apologizing for, they also help the parent tune in to the child. If the parent is not cognitively too limited, groundwork can also be laid by discussing sexual abuse in the abstract. Often, the mother can see that a mother in a different family should have done something about the sexual abuse, even if she is blind to her own neglect. A third strategy capitalizes on the therapist's dilemma noted previously: if he makes her apologize, then she is not taking responsibility; if he does not make her apologize, it does not happen. In this strategy, the therapist is very clear that his responsibility is to the therapy and the mother's is to the family. The therapist then models good apologies by apologizing for the inevitable departures from perfect technique as they arise, showing the mother that one can take responsibility for one's lapses without falling apart.

Finally, many techniques loosely called hypnotic in the Ericksonian sense (Haley, 1967) can be used. The therapeutic enterprise openly expects an apology, and expects it in a manner that is matter-of-fact and nonblaming. The outlines of such an apology are indirectly conveyed to the mother. For example, the therapist says to the child in the mother's presence, "I'm sure your mom feels terrible about letting that happen under her roof, but I don't want her to say anything about it just yet, because we're still concentrating on getting the whole story." These techniques, which turn the therapist's expectations into parental behavior, may be especially suitable with the sexual abuse victim's mother, who is often quite suggestible to begin with. Dissociation makes people suggestible because the part of the subject that is skeptical is not always available.

The mother's apology is one way for her to help her children not only be safe in the future, but also to feel safe. Adequate safeguards, police involvement, and locks on doors can all make a child be safe, but to feel safe, the child will want some sense that further abuse depends not on the conduct of the perpetrator but on the conduct of her mother. When the mother points out what she could have done to prevent the abuse, and demonstrates that she will behave differently if the circumstance arises again, the child can also feel safe.

Children are also made to feel safe by identifying early warning signs of abuse, so that alarms will go off when these are mishandled, instead of waiting until actual abuse has occurred. For example, a common mistake of sexual abuse mothers is that they did not adequately research people who were to have contact with their children. The mother can describe to the children what she wished she had done instead. This might include running the name of the person by police or DSS personnel; asking about the person in the neighborhood; raising the standards for times when the child may be particularly vulnerable, such as when everyone else is asleep; waiting at least three days between first considering contact with a stranger and allowing it; and waiting at least three months before allowing contact with a complicated person such as a potential romantic partner. Then, if the child finds herself sleeping in the house while the mother is asleep and an unresearched adult or older child is present, an early warning sign has occurred. This event should be handled with great seriousness, because the mother's charge is to ensure not only that further abuse will not occur, but also that it cannot occur. The mother should apologize for her lapse, express remorse for putting her child in a vulnerable position, explore her investment in being naive, and demonstrate an ability to avoid a repetition. A feeling of safety is engendered because there is now a first line of defense. The remedial mechanism will be activated because of a misstep, and does not wait for actual abuse to recur.

Chapter 9

The Sexually Powerful Adolescent Girl

THE NARCISSISTIC FATHER AND THE DEPRESSED MOTHER

The sexually active teenage girl causes trouble in the child welfare system because she is usually not disturbed enough to institutionalize, but the risks of HIV infection, rape, and pregnancy are severe enough to raise serious concerns about keeping her in the community. Her story begins with one of the great patterns in family life, which involves narcissistic men and depressed women. In many families, the father is the source of vitality, while the mother is turned into the functional equivalent of an appliance. The father has a range of interests and activities, while the mother drowns in the quotidian demands of raising children and running a home. The father becomes defined as the planet around whom the other family members revolve. To a large extent, the division between the father's narcissism and the mother's depression follows from the division of roles in the so-called traditional family. The father agrees to be the breadwinner while the mother agrees to run the home. Lurking in this division of roles are the seeds of the mother's depression. Being a homemaker can be extremely gratifying in the long-term existential sense, but it also grinds down a person's vivacity. As Chekhov said, any idiot can handle a crisis; it's day-to-day living that gets you down.

In a more technical analysis of the traditional maternal role, many aspects of a woman's personality inadvertently disrupt her efforts to define herself as a facilitator of other people's development. In creating a space that maximizes the children's chance for self-expression, she dampens her own. When she does show an interest in life, the interest threatens the status quo, and is "punished," either by hostility from the husband or misconduct from the children. The mother comes home from her night out with the girls to find the children still awake and unbathed, and the house in disarray.

SOCIALIZING GIRLS TO BE DEPRESSED

As the so-called traditional mother learns to accommodate her designated role by being depressed, in comparison to her, the husband starts to feel pretty good about himself. At work, he may not make more money or be smarter than everyone else, but at home he is the highest paid person, and also the smartest, in the sense of having an active and stimulated mind. In comparison to her husband's sense of purpose and positive reinforcement by others, the mother begins to see herself more and more in depressive terms, as someone who is incompetent and uninteresting (Zuravin and Fontanella, 1999).

I mean positive reinforcement in the technical sense of overt rewards that come to the father when he fulfills his familial obligations. He is appreciated by the children for spending time with them, and he receives a check at work and status socially. Many of the traditional mother's obligations are reinforced negatively, meaning by the removal of aversive stimuli rather than by the addition of desired stimuli. Thus, housework is negatively reinforced by the absence of dust, dirty dishes, and unmade beds. The traditional father's fulfillment of his obligations seem like accomplishments, while the mother's fulfillment of hers merely avoid embarrassment. A clean house with well-mannered children comes to seem like the norm, with the mother responsible for departures downward and the father responsible for improvements. The father takes pride in owning the new refrigerator; the mother is ashamed if it looks dirty. If the mother seeks positive reinforcement, say, by reminding her husband that she has done the dishes again, she is a whining nag. If the father resists negative reinforcement, say, by resenting it when his weekly paycheck is taken for granted, so that he stops at the bar on the way from work and brings home what he feels like not spending, then he is strong and independent, at least in the eyes of the other guys at the bar.

One way that the traditional family sustains itself as an enduring pattern is to train boys and girls from an early age for their respective roles. This is done primarily by training boys to be narcissistic and girls to be depressed. In one family, a girl stumbled on a toy, and the parents directed her to express anger at the object she had tripped over. They modeled for her how to point at it and say, "Bad train." Many months later, their son had a similar spill. They showed him how to jump over the object. Thus, the girl was taught how to be in-effectively aggressive (the inanimate object being nonresponsive to her anger) while the boy was taught to use his aggression construc-tively and adroitly, and to feel good about himself for doing so. Someday, this girl may marry, and when she is frustrated with her husband, she may recall the futility of expressing anger when frus-trated, and instead sulk depressively and hopelessly. Someday, the boy may marry, and when he is frustrated with his spouse, he may "leap over" her, perhaps by involving himself with other activities or even other women.

It is easy to see how, in such a family, both sons and daughters will depend on their mother but also take her for granted. They are likely to see the father as the more exciting and enchanting figure. The boy can emulate him directly, but the girl's assimilation of the father's en-ergy into her own psychology is more complicated. Her contact with the father is facilitated if the mother has begun to resent the daugh-ter's youth and vitality. As the mother resents the daughter, the daughter may turn to the father for the comfort and warmth that she needs. One theorist describes the essence of the hysterical character, where among other things superficial flirtatiousness is devoid of lust but instead seeks affection, as the psychological equivalent of a girl turning from a rejecting mother and crawling into her father's lap (Wolowitz, 1972). When the behavior of crawling into the lap is translated into interactions with men other than her father, her con-duct is interpreted as sexualized. Of course, in the incest family it is sexualized even at home, but in most families girls can still climb into their daddies' laps without provoking an erotic response.

Thus, there are legions of girls, even in families not characterized by abuse and neglect, who struggle with the temptation to short-circuit the normal acquisition of skills and influence in late adolescence and young adulthood. Instead, they are tempted to transact business with the rest of the world in the currency of sexuality. Every reasonably attractive woman chooses between trading on her looks and her skills. In late adolescence and young adulthood, her looks, at least in the eyes of many, may be at their height, while her skills are just beginning to blossom.

Still, it is a relatively easy choice for millions of women to make, because they resist being defined by their external features and sexual body parts. However, to resist being treated primarily as an object of male lust, the girl must first have obtained from her family a sense of herself as a person. If she has been welcomed in her family of origin, the cherished object of her parents' curious and benign affection, then she will resent being treated as a less of a person in the larger world. On the other hand, if she has been an object of neglect at home, either in the cultural sense of being prepared for a life as a homemaker, or in the pathological sense of being raised with no more curiosity than the parents would have for a houseplant, then far from resenting treatment as an object of male lust, she may find it very pleasant. It will give her, as noted, a sense of power in the world. Beyond that, it will give her a consolidated sense of identity to mask the vague self-definition of the neglected child.

THE CHOICE BETWEEN SEX APPEAL AND SKILLS

One would expect to find, and does in my experience, that the appealing aspects of being treated as a sexual object are exacerbated by a history of sexual abuse. As noted in discussing the sexual abuse mother, the sexually abused girl is likely to have been an object of neglect with respect to being protected. She also is likely to have developed some identity functions that center on her role in the sexual drama. Sexually abused girls also have firsthand, early exposure to the power of sexuality as a form of currency, since they may be accorded privileges and a sense of being special because of their sexual appeal. Most girls do not have to begin choosing between sex appeal and skills until adolescence. The sexually abused girl's choice has been made for her, often before she has developed any alternative identity elements.

Whether she was sexually abused or not, the adolescent girl who capitalizes on her sexual power is very familiar to child welfare professionals. The cast of characters usually includes the wicked stepmother, who is trying to dominate the girl and turn her into Cinderella or Snow White; the energetic man, who makes her feel valuable and will take her away from all this; the parts of the girl's body that draw the attention of men; and a fourth figure, that of Ego, the girl's image of herself. This last figure varies according to the girl's overall identity development, ranging from a self personified as a used condom (a receptacle for disposable male lust) to an intelligent, capable young woman.

One girl, Tiffany, had a Child in Need of Services petition filed on her by her family. These petitions are designed to help children via the intervention of the court system. Sometimes parents are at their wits' end and feel they must do something. But the fact is that every CHINS petition inadvertently exacerbates the problem it strives to address by diminishing the parents' authority over the child, and replacing it with the court's authority.

Tiffany, age fourteen, had a history of truancy, marijuana use, sexual activity, and staying out late. Her father once saw her walk down the street, receive wolf calls from a stranger in a car, and then get in the car with the man. The parents were worried about her potential for self-destructive behavior. Even those few adults comfortable with the idea of adolescent girls having sex must acknowledge life-or-death stakes in the age of HIV. During the family assessment, the state social worker visited the home to obtain background information from the family, which included Tiffany, her parents, and her two little brothers. The conversation was proceeding smoothly until the mother reminded Tiffany that Tiffany had to leave for her part-time job interview. Tiffany exploded, threw an end table across the room, and stormed out.

In the psychological evaluation Tiffany reported a happy early memory of playing Gladys Knight and the Pips with her little brothers, in which Tiffany would lip synch and the brothers would dance behind her. There was no sign of an authority figure in this happy memory. She also reported a memory of being late for elementary school and being told she did not have time for breakfast. Thirsty on the way to school, she saw some ice on a street sign, licked the pole, and got her tongue stuck to it. The male crossing guard helped her extract her tongue from the pole without too much damage by breathing on it to warm up the pole. When her mother was called to school, the mother yelled at her in public for being such a fool. Another memory involved getting into her mother's makeup; for punishment, her mother blew some of it into her face so it would sting her eyes.

The pattern that emerged from Tiffany's clinical material was that the mother's punitive conduct made the child turn a deaf ear to advice coming from maternal authority. Any sound of motherly advice would make the child wheel in anger and lash out rebelliously. From the child's point of view, using the early memory as a guide, the mother's hostility is based on competitive feelings about being a woman (the use of her makeup). Thus, in the family session, when the mother offered apparently innocuous maternal advice, namely, to get ready for her job interview, the child reacted as if she had just had powder blown into her face.

The memory of having her tongue stuck is also illuminating, because it captures the way a quasi-sexual experience with the male crossing guard is not an outgrowth of the child's lust. Instead, it is an incidental consequence of having to obtain from a man compensatory help for problems stemming from being poorly nurtured (not given breakfast). When a thirty-year-old man drives by Tiffany in a car, comments on her looks, and suggests she get in the car with him, it seems likely that some part of this girl tells herself that it is not a very good idea. But as soon she starts to articulate this good advice, she reacts to the internal voice as she reacts to her mother's external voice. She disperses the maternal authority and acts in the opposite direction. The next thing she knows, the man is breathing on her tongue, when all she wanted was something to quench her thirst.

One can see the advantage of understanding the underlying pattern. Although on the surface the girl seems unreasonable in her reaction to the mother's benign suggestion to get ready for her interview, an appreciation of the pattern suggests the necessity of the mother apologizing to the child for her past behavior, and acknowledging the damage that has been done. Otherwise, the child is simplistically expected to behave herself in spite of her conflicted history with her internal parent figure.

Unfortunately, there is no way for the child welfare system to bring pressure to bear on the parent of an adolescent. With younger children, the implied threat exists that the child can be taken from the parent if the parent does not comply with the demands made on her. With the adolescent, with whom the parent may be openly at war, it is hardly a threat to take her off the parent's hands. Thus, in spite of the fact that at some level the mother wants things to be better between her and her daughter, in light of the unlikelihood of improvement, she is organized around the hope that she will seem innocent in the girl's ejection. The more unreasonable the parent can make the child seem to others, the more the problems are blamed on the girl and not on the parent.

Tiffany was sent to a residential treatment facility by an order of the court. (Since then, the Massachusetts Supreme Judicial Court has held that courts cannot always tell DSS what to do with children in DSS custody [*Charrier v. Charrier,* 1993].) The court was apparently responding to the risk Tiffany posed. Judges generally feel better when a high-risk child is placed in an institution, even though there is no reason to think that children are safer in residential facilities than in foster homes (Blatt, 1990; Powers, Mooney, and Nunno, 1990). The incidence of sexual activity, rape, drug use, and death are probably as high in institutions as in foster care. Judges (and newspapers) may think that DSS is not doing all it can for a child unless she is placed in the most expensive and comprehensive program possible, even though these placements are often too artificial to allow the child to apply what is learned in them to postinstitutional life (Curry, 1986).

THE LIMITATIONS OF RESIDENTIAL TREATMENT

The residential facility recapitulates many of the problems from home. Indeed, one report from a residential treatment center diagnosed an adolescent girl as seriously disturbed on the basis of her use of "splitting," a hallmark strategy of a borderline personality organization (see Chapter 4). Splitting refers to the way people who cannot conceive of the same person being both comforting and frustrating split off from their experience of important figures everything that is frustrating or disappointing or overstimulating so they can go on thinking of that person as comforting. This residential report, however, used splitting to mean, "the behavior of pitting one group of adults against another." In other words, the staff were having problems with each other and blamed the patient. (It is intriguing to think of the wasted treatment opportunity, since being blamed for problems in the adult subsystem is likely the same process by which many of the patients in residential treatment got there.) In Tiffany's case, the institution that took her had a long series of rules, each associated with a loss of privileges when broken. This ensured that Tiffany's entire stay there would turn into a power struggle. None of the rules were developed in conversation with Tiffany, and none were adapted to her, the institution being concerned about the difficulty of maintaining order if some children were allowed to do some things forbidden to other children.

The need for a manageable facility can supersede the need to tailor treatment planning to an individual child. Children differ from one another, implying a need for different rules, the application of different reinforcers, and a different overall response orientation depending on the child and situation. However, most facilities standardize their regulations across children. One example is the punishment of swearing either by revoking privileges or by staff rebuke. Making the children speak respectfully to staff members undoubtedly improves staff morale and makes the group seem easier to control, but it is clinically questionable. Punishment of swearing makes sense when the child's alternative is a more mature method of expressing anger, but it is misguided when the child is doing all she can to keep from throwing a punch or running away.

A more subtle example of institutionalizing children by treating them generically rather than tailoring a response to a specific situation involves a girl who repeatedly stepped so close to staff persons that their bodies would touch. Staff decided that this behavior was "inappropriate." A typical banal platitude of clinical diagnosis and treatment planning was used: the child must learn to control her behavior. The staff's only job was to punish the frottage by taking away privileges whenever it occurred. A better approach would have been to develop a plausible hypothesis about whether she was doing it, say, for attention, for sex, for touch, to test the durability of her relationships with staff, or as a method of projective identification of her feelings of being sexually violated. Each of these potential diagnostic hypotheses implies a specific staff response. Indeed, it is better to guess at the meaning of the behavior and take appropriate action than to interpret the behavior vaguely and treat it generically. The first way allows us, even if we are wrong, to keep trying new hypotheses and new interventions until we find one that works. Thus, for example, if she were doing it for attention, sex, or touch, alternative methods of obtaining these gratifications could be arranged (alternatives that cast her in a better light and that do not infringe on the rights of others). If she were testing durability, staff could demonstrate their ability to remain warm and temperate even in the face of the issues that destroyed her family or got her placed in an institution. If the frottage were viewed as a projective identification, the staff person might indicate how embarrassing and violating it felt, showing the girl how to give voice to an experience that she might only be able to express in action.

The role of residential treatment for these girls, if any, should be to hold them still, apart from some of the demands of daily life, while their reactivity issues are vigorously pursued. This agenda is the diametric opposite of the usual agenda, in the sense that the facility typically tries to calm the girls down, whereas I am suggesting that the placement be construed as an opportunity to stir them up.

As an alternative to an institutional placement or a foster home, the victim of sexual abuse, now in adolescence, may want to live with a relative who has a loyalty to the perpetrator and claims that the abuse did not occur. This is a tricky situation. On one hand, the child should be kept in the family. On the other hand, the disbelief is destructive to the child. The child may be wavering in and out of dissociative states either because of the abuse or because of the displacement in her life, so she is never quite sure herself what has happened. The disbelief is also destructive because the stance that it did not happen, assuming there is convincing evidence that it did happen, reinforces the child's tendency to care more about how things look than how they feel. The negative social implications of acknowledging the abuse weigh more heavily than the positive personal implications. In such an environment, the child will forgo her internal motives and needs in favor of superficialities.

Perhaps the best chance of influencing a sexually reactive girl's identity in a more robust direction is through education. A few girls are capable of responding intellectually to ideas, new to them, about how to be a woman. For most, however, the benefit of education is in providing competition for the current identity, which typically bases their self-esteem on their ability to stimulate lust. Learning a way to make a living can provide another source of power and a reliable set of skills, and give them a mode of existence that is outside their sexual drama.

Analysis of the pattern in which the sexually powerful adolescent girl is operating can open avenues for understanding and for intervention. Otherwise, she is merely a containment or a resource problem. When that happens, intervention is designed with no more specificity than deciding between a residential facility, a group home, or foster care.

Chapter 10

The Disruptive Boy

THE INEFFECTIVE DISCIPLINARIAN

The disruptive boy is a placement problem in the child welfare system, because he is not disturbed enough to institutionalize, but foster homes and families do not want him. His drama usually contains three figures: the disruptive boy himself (who may be a girl, of course); the ineffective disciplinarian (Karson, 1973); and the often-invisible other parent who would be effective if only he were available (wait until your father gets home) (Karson and Haupt, 1968). The complex operates, like all complexes, either on the family systems level or on the intrapsychic level. On the family systems level, the role of the ineffective parent is usually played by the mother, while the role of the other parent who could be effective is usually played by the father, but also could be taken by the grandmother, therapist, social worker, school principal, judge, police officer, or residential treatment director. The role of the boy is usually played by a boy, but sometimes by a girl. It can also be played by an impulsive or intoxicated parent or stepparent, with the child cast as the ineffective disciplinarian and the other parent cast as the one who could be effective if only he or she had been home.

INDOCTRINATION INTO THE ABUSIVE ROLE

In accord with systems theory, one can describe the relationships among the figures from any starting point. For example, beginning the punctuation with the boy, a particularly active and aggressive boy will be difficult to control, leading to ineffectiveness on the mother's part. The father may distance himself from the difficulties or resort to physical discipline out of frustration. The physical discipline, like all punishment, remains an effective deterrent only in the presence of the punisher. It makes the father seem effective, because the child behaves when he is around, and makes the mother seem ineffective, because the child misbehaves, now with a vengeance, when the father is not around.

One can begin the punctuation with the father, who derives sex-role satisfaction from being the most effective and accomplished person in the family. This leads to his being away at work a great deal, to his construing child rearing as being within the domestic domain of the mother, and to his Monday-morning-quarterbacking any apparent deficiencies in her performance. Her self-confidence erodes; she perceives herself as ineffective and weak, especially in comparison with males; and the child exploits the mother's sense of ineffectiveness and the father's remoteness by indulging whatever impulses cross his mind. He receives and acts on messages from his parents that as a male, he has higher status than his mother and does not have to obey her. Also, like any child, whose structural role is basically one of self-indulgence, the disruptive boy acts impulsively because he can get away with it.

Beginning the story with the mother, she is a somewhat depressive person with low self-esteem. She does not see herself as having the strength or energy necessary to control an active child. Furthermore, because of her own pent-up, unexpressed aggression, she takes a vicarious pleasure in her child's misconduct. Remember those *MAD Magazine* cartoons depicting people interacting, with their shadows showing what they really would like to do? Oftentimes, the parent acts as she should act and the child acts as she would like to act. Her ambivalence about controlling the child reduces her effectiveness. Or it might be said that every parent is effective, but parents vary in what they are trying to accomplish. The mother's depressive sense of ineffectiveness, or her ambivalence, makes her genuinely unable to control the disruptive boy, whereas the other parent would indeed be more successful, having more skills and energy. The other parent, however, enjoys being superior to the mother, so instead of bolstering the mother with his own energy, he likes to demonstrate how good he is at controlling the child independently of her. The boy then learns that he needs to behave himself in the presence of the other parent (or at school or in therapy) but need not do so in the care of his mother. Minuchin (1974) has said that if a child is bigger than a parent, he must be standing on another parent's shoulders.

The mother's depression creates a further impetus for the child to misbehave, because his disruptive conduct may evoke a tough, disciplinary response in her. This response competes with her depressive feelings. He tries to cure her depression by forcing her to act differently. Similarly, the mother who fears intimacy may become anxious when things run smoothly. She responds much more comfortably and reliably when the child misbehaves. Because she depends on his misconduct to dispel her anxiety when mother and child are close and tender, the intimacy-fearing mother controls him intermittently, so the relationship fluctuates between warmth and disruption. One naive mother exquisitely summarized her investment in her son's misconduct. When I asked her what was her greatest strength as a mother, she replied, "My ability to let him divert my mind from my problems."

The systemic interlinking of the roles in this drama becomes apparent after an abusive father leaves a family and one of the children becomes aggressive. Prior to the father's departure, the father occupies the role of the disruptive boy, mother is the ineffective disciplinarian, and the police are the unavailable but otherwise effective authority figures. After the father leaves, the child's new disruptions have many effects, as in other patterns, that reveal their motivations. These may include the desire to keep family life exciting, to distract the mother from her depression or from her vocational fears and failures, or to reduce everyone's anxiety by putting them in their familiar roles of coping with an angry, unpredictable family member. (Some children keep their parents in familiar, positive roles, as when the doctor's son develops somatic symptoms, when the cop's daughter needs to be arrested, or when the homemaker's daughter gets pregnant and hands over the baby.)

Once, during a home visit, I was able to watch the indoctrination of a newly disruptive boy into the role his stepfather had recently abandoned. The boy, Cody, was eleven. He had a big sister, a younger half-brother, and a baby half-sister. His stepfather had physically abused Cody, his big sister, and his mother, and had left the family about two weeks before I met them. I was talking to Cody's mother and the other children when Cody came home from school with a friend in tow.

Mother immediately told Cody's friend to go home, announcing that Cody had been disrespectful earlier and was not allowed to play after school. Apparently, she was parroting something a therapist had said to her about standing up to men, a group that Mother and possibly the therapist construed to include Cody. Cody was very embarrassed by this exchange in front of his friend, and sulked a bit in the kitchen, self-conscious in my presence. His sister and little brother teased him about the social consequences of disrespecting their mother. Mother did nothing to stop their teasing. Eventually, Cody yelled at his sister to stop. Mother, still operating within a simplistic battering paradigm, told him not to speak to his sister that way, whereupon Cody stormed out of the house shouting words of hatred. His mother, seeking sympathy, told me he was turning out just like the stepfather. The most brilliant psychologists in the world could not have been half so clever as she at devising a strategy for making him into an abusive man.

Children learn to control themselves by being controlled, and then treating themselves as others have treated them. Consider, for example, how children are taught not to run into the street. When a two-year-old dashes toward the street, there are four basic parental responses, which include severe punishment, physical restraint (mild punishment), positive reinforcement if the child stops, and neglect. As noted previously, the main problem with smacking the child, technically, is that the child will thereafter stop at the street only if the parent is nearby. Physical restraint raises similar problems, but because it is such a mild punishment, it does not create a great schism between the child's response tendency when the parent is present and when the parent is not. Furthermore, physical restraint as a disciplinary tool is almost always accompanied by positive reinforcement for stopping.

THE LEGACY OF PUNISHMENT

Positive reinforcement, whether in the form of verbal accolades or more tangible rewards, such as goodies if the child plays for an extended period without going into the street, is the best method for controlling the child's behavior in the long run. Unfortunately, it is not foolproof in the short run, so good parents rely on positive reinforcement plus restraint when the risk of harm is great. One might think that the conditioning effects of positive reinforcement would depend on parental presence, as punishment does, but in fact they do not. Reinforcement affects the internal tendency to emit the response, not just the external manifestation (Skinner, 1953). Children who are reinforced for stopping before they hit the street soon *want* to play safe. Positive reinforcement also eases the process of internalizing the figure of the controlling parent within the child's psyche, since the image to be internalized is benign.

The neglectful or absent parent leaves the child to learn about nature on his own. Nothing in the street, in and of itself, suggests to the child the danger of being there, so he will not learn this lesson. However, even a neglected child will learn not to touch hot things, for example.

The internalization of the disciplinary process sets the stage for the child's individual psychology relative to self-control. The disruptive boy usually has a history of punishment. The second parent in the complex plays the role of the punisher who is effective only when present, while the primary parent is in the position of the neglectful parent, partly because she has taken a back seat to the other parent's punishments. Consider the disruptive boy, sitting in class at school. He has been rebuked by his teacher for not sitting still and now faces the possibility of throwing his pencil at her while her back is turned. The parent on duty within his psyche is not an effective controlling presence any more than his mother is. The off-duty parent, though punitive, would be able to control him if accessed. If the boy stops to think about whether to throw the pencil, he will ipso facto access the influence of the off-duty parent, because the part of him doing the thinking is a viceroy of the parent who can control him. If he stops to think about it, he will not do it. But the boy does not like to think about things, because that viceroy is punitive and makes him feel angry and small.

The child's hostility toward the part of him that thinks is the psychological basis of the cognitive-behavioral technique of teaching disruptive children to think about things before they act (Meichenbaum, 1977). The ten-year-old child is like a ten-year-old jockey riding an energetic horse. To be effective at controlling the horse, the jockey must know something about what the horse wants and must be smarter than the horse. We often find that the disruptive boy on IQ testing has a much higher score on the nonverbal subtests than on the verbal. Verbal intelligence is analogous to the kind of thinking jockeys do, while performance intelligence is more akin to the horse's ability to get around. The impression many disruptive boys give is of a perfectly good horse ridden by a dull jockey. The dullness may be biologically determined, as in hyperactivity, or the result of brain damage, or psychologically motivated by the distaste for thinking about things. When thinking is strong, the "native hue of resolution is sicklied o'er with the pale cast of thought" (Shakespeare, *Hamlet*), and fantasies are less likely to be enacted.

Sometimes the child's disruptiveness is biologically based on an inordinate amount of aggressiveness or on a neurological sluggishness that dulls self-control. They are analogous to a mustang and to a sleepy jockey, respectively. In the latter case, stimulants such as Ritalin and Dexedrine are used because, as it happens, they affect the jockey more than the horse. Stimulants are the treatment of choice for true hyperactivity, i.e., when neurological sluggishness is correctly diagnosed (Barkley, 1998). They have few side effects on the whole and are not considered much riskier than caffeine. On the other hand, the differential diagnosis between activity based on cortical sluggishness and that based on other factors is difficult to make. In this respect, stimulants may be overused in the larger population, where changes in the family system or changes in the school system's accommodations for different kinds of children would be preferable. With children in the child welfare system, however, on balance, if stimulants help a disruptive boy control himself, then the stakes are usually such that it makes sense to administer them. Stimulants can, for these children, make the difference between living at home and living in foster care, and between physical safety and abuse.

Residential treatment is wrong for any child young enough to be controlled physically. One two-year-old girl came into a hospital emergency room after an incident in the bathtub. Her foster mother reported that the child was suicidal and had "tried to drown herself." Not only did the foster mother attribute motives to the toddler that no child her age could possess, but the doctor compounded the problem by conducting a screening interview for suicidality with the baby. The girl acknowledged wanting to kill herself, described her plan ("go under water"), and was unable to "contract for safety" (i.e., promise not to do it). The doctor recommended residential treatment, arguing, as evaluators often do with adolescents and adults, that she required an institutional setting to provide the external structure that she lacked internally. Switching foster homes to one where the child's statements would be interpreted age-appropriately was recommended at DSS. The doctor's concern about the little girl's "despair" was not given much credence. The DSS administrator's counterproposal to residential treatment was to try giving the child a nap.

This is only an extreme example of a relatively common phenomenon by which boys ages seven years and younger, even down to age four, are "strongly recommended" to be sent to group care facilities. The theory is that the "structure" of the facility will contain their disruptiveness and teach them to control themselves. The word "structure" is used almost as much as the word "strongly" in clinical reports. The entire child welfare system could probably be funded by a tax on these words in clinical reports, especially if one added "PTSD" (post-traumatic stress disorder) to the fund. We tax bad conduct, such as smoking and drinking. Why not tax bad language? Call it a syntax, if you like. Technically, "structure" seems to mean scheduled time, so that a structured program is one with little free time (Gunderson, 1978). Generally, though, the word seems to connote an abundance of walls, which are then presumed to provide more physical containment than is possible with a single adult in good health.

Unfortunately, the kind of self-control that children learn in such environments is rarely internalized in the desired form of a cohesive, concerned parent figure. This unnecessarily complicates the ensuing psychology of self-control, which then unfolds not in a dialogue but in relationship to an impersonal institution. There are other advantages to learning discipline in the context of an interpersonal relationship. The discipline itself should be counterbalanced by the affection normally present in the parent-child relationship. Without this balance, the internalized figure to whom the child must account before indulging impulses is one whose opinion of the conduct is not very important to the child.

INTERPERSONAL BASIS OF SELF-CONTROL

Most children learning to control themselves in an interpersonal, versus an institutional, setting are taught self-control in a context that is highly sensitive to cues from the child. Any punishment fits the crime, and plenty of allowance is made for extenuating circumstances. Even the definition of illicit behavior can vary, in a family, from child to child and even from day to day, depending on a host of contingencies. An institution, no matter how much it tries to tailor its rules to the needs of the individual children, must still be concerned about running the institution, sacrificing flexibility in defining what is "illegal" and in meting out punishments.

Residential treatment is wrong for small children also because really effective indoctrinations into self-control require a great deal of time and energy on the part of an adult. Most of the conditioning available in institutions is mediated by underpaid workers with little training. The professional clinical staff may see the child as little as a few hours a week. In fact, a lot of children, especially disruptive ones, would be better off moving directly into preadoptive homes than first being stabilized in interim placements. A preadoptive parent is more likely to summon the time and energy necessary to control a child, since the parent knows that he or she will reap the rewards of success, if any. Unfortunately, many adoptive parents respond primarily to the superficial presentation of prospective adoptees, like buying a used car and not looking under the hood, responding solely to the body work. Spaced-out, traumatized children, who are bound to become explosive in adolescence, are preferred over relatively healthy children who wear their frustration and anger on their sleeves. One preadoptive girl looked so much like Shirley Temple that DSS agreed to withhold her photograph from adoptive recruitment for fear that one look at her would deafen a preadoptive couple to cautions about her internal despair and rage. It has been said that when you have sex with someone, you are having sex with everyone they ever slept with; when you adopt someone, you adopt everything that ever happened to them.

Understanding the pattern behind disruptive behavior can strengthen the rationale for using behavioral principles in its treatment. The main principles of relevance are that punishment only works as long as the punisher is nearby, but otherwise exacerbates misconduct, while genuine self-control derives from positive reinforcement of desirable behavior. The figure of the punisher should not be deferred to simply because he is effective in the short run. The figure of the ineffective parent should be strengthened by training her to control the child with positive reinforcement and mild restraint. Such control is best transmitted via a personal relationship, to ensure that the internalized source of self-control is one the child can turn to comfortably at key moments.

Chapter 11

The Absent Parent Returned

Child welfare professionals are all too familiar with the absent parent returned. The parent has been unavailable to the child, usually because of addiction, incarceration, or, in the case of some fathers, not knowing the child was his. Some parents have drifted away from a child after a divorce, feeling like a fifth wheel on the child's new family. The child has been in the custody of the state for some period of time, and the parent is either released from jail, quits using drugs, or discovers paternity. Then the absent parent presents himself or herself to the child welfare system as a kind of hero, ready to forget the past and forge ahead, rescuing the child from foster care. The problem for the child welfare system is that the parent is not currently unfit, but the child has laid down roots elsewhere.

Obviously, some absent parents return with a different attitude, but that is not the pattern I am discussing. Still, it is worth noting that some parents return to their responsibilities with a humble sense that they have messed up and that it will take a great deal of effort on their part to regain their child's trust. One woman's son was taken away after a series of unjust and bizarre misunderstandings, which included a therapist who thought she understood the father's Spanish but did not, and another odd therapist who reported that mother and son lying naked together had unavoidable incestuous overtones, even though the baby at the time was only a few weeks old. An older son, a toddler, was placed in a middle-class foster home, where he had been happily ensconced for over a year. When the injustices had been discovered and rectified, I asked this mother what it was going to be like for the toddler to return home. She said it would be the worst day of his life. This woman understood not only that the child might prefer the wealthier home, for the natural selfish reasons of childhood, but she also understood the deeper point that the child would blame her for the placement, even though it was genuinely not something she could have prevented.

THE CHILD PUT ON HOLD

More typically, the once-absent parent, who has come to reclaim the child, denies responsibility for putting the child into developmental limbo. The former prisoner claims it was not his fault that he was not available, and he even produces letters showing how he tried to arrange for visits at the jail. He takes no more responsibility for being incarcerated than does another man for having sex with a woman who did not bother to call him, or know how to reach him, when she found out she was pregnant. Psychologically, the parent obliterates the child before using illegal drugs or committing a crime (or attempting suicide, for example). If you really care about your children, you buckle up and fly right. In other words, *the children's* needs and *their* future interests will weigh on the mind of the good parent before an impulse is indulged.

RESPONSIBILITY FOR THE ABSENCE

In the complex I am describing, the parent does not take responsibility for her absence; instead she blames the booze, the warden, or the social service system. Furthermore, the child is expected to be grateful that the parent has returned. The woman who stops using substances can be so organized around living one day at a time and looking to the future and not to the past that she forgets that she has some explaining to do to her own children. She wants the child to be as happy as she is that she is clean and sober. But if she is solidly back on her feet, and if she provides genuine security to the child, the child is bound to feel robbed of his past. He feels this partly because she has now demonstrated her capacity to provide that which he had rationalized as impossible, and it is partly because the current security makes him feel safe enough to ventilate his feelings. In the so-called honeymoon phase after the absent parent returns and regains custody, the child is walking on eggshells, fearful that his disappointment and anger will drive the parent back to drinking or otherwise obliterate him from her consciousness again. Thus, it is a good sign, not a bad sign, when the child starts to misbehave in the parent's custody. Unfortunately, the parent interprets the misconduct as willful, even as an attack on her sobriety. Unfortunately, the professionals also may simplistically equate misconduct with setbacks and depressive quiescence with progress.

With substance abusers, it can be particularly ironic that they are so ill-prepared for their children's remonstrances, because one of the twelve steps is to make amends for the damage done by drinking (Bill W., 1953). Some addicts will apologize to their friends whom they have stolen money from and deceived, to their parents for letting them down, and to their employers for screwing up, but not to their children. Or, having apologized, they let it go at that, as if that constitutes amends. In the child welfare system, one hears, "Yes, but that was when I was drinking." This may be the key element that differentiates the alcoholics in the child welfare system from the alcoholics who avoid it, the latter taking responsibility for the effects of their drinking on their children.

The question of which figure gets drunk when the individual imbibes also affects the likelihood of getting in trouble from alcohol. In some alcoholics, the figure with the best judgment shows the effects the most, and the intoxicated individual acts as lively and impulsive as he ever does, but now without judgment. In other individuals, the impulsive or angry figures may become drowsy, and the individual as a whole is at his most mellow when drinking.

I consulted on one case with an alcoholic mother who was extremely reluctant to acknowledge responsibility for the damage she had done to her children. At first, this reluctance kept her drinking, the alcohol numbing her to her pangs of conscience. Later, the reluctance kept her *from* drinking. As long as she was certain she would never desire alcohol again, she did not need to attend AA meetings. Any impulse to drink on her part would have led her to meetings, and once there, she knew she would have to do a damage assessment and make amends. This was too horrifying for her to contemplate, probably because the ways we hurt our innocent and helpless children are the effects of our misconduct that are most difficult to accept.

Incidentally, the twelve steps book (Bill W., 1953) explicitly warns alcoholics against imposing their amends on their victims, noting that sometimes the other person, having been burdened with the alcoholic's drinking, now does not need to shoulder the burden of his sobriety. Parents sometimes forget that their children have adjusted to a new life in their absence, and foist their sobriety on the children irrespective of the child's needs. These people are justly proud of their sobriety. However, it may be pride itself that led to the addiction, since the bottle is so often a place to drown humiliation. Parents may use their children to soothe their own bruised egos, rather than seeking to find out if there is anything the parent can do for the child.

MAKING AMENDS

With younger children, the parent may act as if the children have been in a state of suspended animation from the time they were left in the care of others. With these children, the dilatory pace of the court system is partly to blame. A crack addict loses custody of her four-month-old baby. A few months in foster care is certainly justified to see if she will stop using quickly enough for her sobriety to be of use to that baby. As the months drag on, though, the potential costs to the child escalate, in terms of losing her chance to lay down roots in important intimate relationships. After a year, DSS decides to give up on reunification and instead plans for adoption. The child may have been placed in a temporary foster home, in which case she faces a potentially devastating disruption whether she goes back home or not. Sometimes, though, farsighted social workers have managed to place the baby in a home with people who are also approved for adoption. Thus, the child can have a relatively normal upbringing if the adoption case is won, normal except for the emotional privations of the preadoptive parents who love this baby but never know if they are going to be able to keep her. However, the case does not come to trial until the child is two years old, by which time the mother has been clean and sober for nine months and has obtained employment. Now she wants her baby back. The legal standard requires that the parent be currently unfit, in other words at the time of the trial, if she is to lose her rights. The upshot is that the baby is growing up in relatively normal conditions, and now she will be ripped out of the situation and given to someone she does not know.

THE CHILD'S POINT OF VIEW

From the child's point of view, what does she care that the natural parents provided her genetic material? From the child's point of view, it is exactly the same as if a baby from an intact family had been ripped away from her parents at two years of age and given to a stranger. Does this have a permanent adverse impact on the child's development? It is impossible to say for certain without conducting an experiment (Kinard, 1994) in which children would be randomly assigned to a condition where they would be yanked from their psychological parents and given to someone else. Of course, no such experiment would be conducted, because it is horrifying to contemplate such an intervention. This feeling of horror suggests that it may not be a good thing for any child, even those in the child welfare system.

The absent parent returned assumes custody not by virtue of her investment of time and energy in the child, and not by virtue of the history of mutual experiences that sustains the feeling of love, and not by virtue of hours upon hours of jiggling the baby's crib to help her sleep or cleaning up her excretions or keeping her environment comfortable and stimulating; she assumes custody solely by virtue of her status as biological parent. Perhaps because the custody is based solely on technical status, or perhaps because these absent parents returned are people who do not know much about genuine intimacy, they expect the kind of respect that children in unbroken homes afford to their own parents. They think, in effect, "She should respect me because I am her mother." This expectation is bound to lead to disappointment.

The expectation of respect, when based on rank, is another problem that is recapitulated in the child welfare system, with feelings on the part of caregivers, from foster parents to professionals, that they should be respected because they are adults. In fact, children do not respect their parents because they are their parents, and they do not respect adults because they are adults. Children respect people who have treated them well—fairly, justly, warmly, with curiosity and joy taken in their safety, happiness, and accomplishments. Parents earn the respect of children, and having earned it, deserve it. Even an officer in the military who actually does have rank and wears its insignia knows she must earn the respect of her troops. But many are the parents, especially among the absent parents returned, who believe they should be afforded the respect of their rank without earning it.

Similarly, parents in the child welfare system get huffy when their children do not tell them the truth. They call their own children liars and manipulators, as do foster parents and professionals, without bothering to ask themselves why children might tell parents the truth. The real reason children tell the truth is that on balance, they find that keeping their parents informed produces just, nurturant, and protective intervention. Parents who do not provide these consequences of truth-telling should expect their children to lie to them. Parents who have misbehaved to the point of mocking the straight and narrow should also expect some lies.

The problem of the absent parent returned brings to focus some issues that are central to all child welfare work. These include, especially, the relatively large structural responsibilities of parents compared to those of children, and the fact that the development of young children cannot be put on hold while parents are engaged elsewhere.

PART IV:
INTERVENTION PATTERNS

Dysfunctional patterns are best changed from within (Selvini Palazzoli et al., 1978). Operating *on* a pattern, instead of *in* a pattern, merely provokes a defensive reaction, as the pattern strives to regain its balance. The pattern's reaction to outside pressure stems from two main sources. One is that a pattern dysfunctional enough to produce child abuse is typically also very rigid. The figures respond to one another systemically, but they respond only to one another. Figures outside the pattern are often ignored or not even perceived in the first place. After all, if the parents in an abuse pattern were capable of responding to a therapeutic or controlling voice, they might have listened to their own better judgment and not abused the children. When intervention from external sources is perceived by the pattern, it mutes the figures, and like muted people, they respond poorly: vociferously, trenchantly, or sullenly. Further, disruption of a pattern from the outside can make the figures feel they are losing their identities, which have been defined in relation to the other figures in the complex. This is especially likely when the figures in a pattern are not robust, that is, when a single problematic pattern defines them. They will respond by asserting their identities in force, by solidifying the pattern that gave them a sense of self.

Besides pattern rigidity, the other major source of resistance to outside change lies in the fact that little in life is simple and clear. As noted in Chapter 8, even a committed pedophile is seen as having his good points by those who know him. Most families, similarly, however dysfunctional, have their good moments. When outsiders press for change, usually by characterizing a figure or pattern as undesirable, the pressure evokes a reasonable attempt to recall a more balanced view. The result is a service system in which the professionals are saying how bad conditions are while the people actually suffering are balancing them by defending the perpetrator or the situation.

Operating from within a pattern requires the social worker or clinician to enter it. On a superficial level, the professional must "join" with the family by demonstrating that she can see the world as they do. It helps if she speaks their native language, and even their lingo, and lives or has lived in their world, but one can also join with a person or family, in my experience, by displaying confidence about similarities (such as how they feel about their children or about being examined by the state) and benign curiosity about differences (such as language or religion). By curiosity, I do not mean wasting too much of the clients' time acquiring knowledge from them, but instead learning the rudiments of their culture beforehand. Professionals who think they are just like the client must take care not to obliterate individual differences; those who think they are very different from the client must take care not to obliterate individual similarities. There must be some way to join cross-culturally, else it would be possible to define a client's culture so narrowly that the only person who could treat him would be himself. Indeed, many therapies enlist the client as a cotherapist for just that reason: only he can translate the symbols in therapy for his unique situation (Freud, 1953a).

The status differential between professional and client must be undercut, not only on the surface, but in the professional's own mind. This is best accomplished by viewing everyone in the encounter, including the professional, in human terms, with a personal background and a particular agenda. When systems theorist Jay Haley presents a videotape at a conference, he describes each family member in the usual way (role, age, work, background) and then uses the same formula for the therapist (say, a twenty-five-year-old Korean-American graduate student who grew up in Los Angeles and was educated in the Northeast, writing her dissertation on such and such, currently single). This helps keep things on an equal footing and facilitates joining on the level of all being human even if all are not culturally identical.

On a more subtle level, joining a pattern requires a clinician to adopt one of its roles. Not to do so is like speaking to the sleeping individual while the dream is running amok; only the characters in the dream can affect it. The part of a girl that is the sexual abuse victim often responds only to the voice of the perpetrator or the voice of the absent parent. If we want her to hear what we have to say, rather than being concerned with how we sound, we have to speak to her in one of these voices. Unfortunately, as in most maltreatment patterns, neither voice is a comfortable one to adopt.

Professionals are only human. We recoil at adopting the guise of the perpetrator or that of the neglectful other parent. We relinquish the opportunity to communicate in exchange for being seen as good people. Sometimes, our understandable interest in being cast as good people backfires completely. We get sucked into a pattern to the point where we are responding as one of the distasteful figures, but we are so convinced that we are good that we do not recognize what we have become (Langs, 1977; Jones, 1991).

We find ourselves punishing the disruptive boy or threatening punishment by someone else. This is not a terrible thing, because at least it means we are in the pattern. It is only terrible if we refuse to recognize what has happened, if we merely reenact the pattern that brought him to us. But if we can recognize the pattern we are reenacting, we can do something about it. We can do what the punitive parent or the threatening parent should have done, and our conduct will not be mere commentary; we will affect the disruptive boy directly. Such recognition can be very difficult for professionals schooled or otherwise inclined to think that they are utterly different from the abusers and perpetrators who have hurt the people they treat. This belief can destroy any hope of effective intervention. Further, it sets the stage for unconsciously reenacting abuse patterns when the professional is blind to the possibility of doing so.

Chapter 12

Dysfunctional Treatment Relationships

As we have seen, patterns replicate themselves in new situations. This can be thought of in terms of identity or in the terms of systems theory. Briefly, in identity terms, the pattern is replicated because the individual behaves in character in such a way that complementary roles are elicited in other people: Desdemona evokes Othello (see Chapter 3 for a synopsis of the early plot). Iago persuades Cassio to go to Desdemona to ask her to intervene on Cassio's behalf with her husband, Othello. Then, Iago plants the idea in Othello's mind that Desdemona is sleeping with Cassio and that she has become his advocate for sexual reasons. Desdemona is so proud of her own devotion to her husband that she considers herself to be above suspicion. Another woman advocating for Cassio might be cautious to distinguish her motives from romance for the sake of her marriage, but Desdemona's perfectionistic pride disdains this caution, and her husband's jealousy goes unchecked. She can see that something is wrong in Othello's troubled expression, but she just cannot bring herself to believe that it could have anything to do with herself. To set his mind at ease would require putting aside her perfectionistic self-appraisal as devoted beyond suspicion. She is so perfectionistically devoted, in fact, that after he strangles her, she uses her last breath to claim she committed suicide, to exonerate him. (It does not work.) Desdemona is so self-righteously devoted that she does not deign to reassure her husband. Her conduct creates the complementary role of jealousy.

Systemic understanding emphasizes the reciprocity in this formulation. Othello, a jealous man, finds his lust awakened when there is another man in the picture. He falls for a woman who must betray her father to be with him; now his lust conjures up other men even when there are none. He is so jealous and angry and proud that no wife of his would ever distinguish her advocacy from romance, because he would find it so insulting to be told not to worry about her fidelity. The systemic formulation also emphasizes the efforts of the system to achieve equilibrium. Thus, one member's character is not just an advertisement for or elicitation of complementary behavior, but complementary behavior arises in the system's effort to equilibrate itself. In systems theory, Othello's jealous feelings and smoldering looks can be seen as efforts on the part of the marital system to rein in Desdemona's unwifely behavior (advocating for another man); Desdemona's persistent, blithe advocacy for Cassio can be seen as efforts on the part of the marital system to rein in Othello's unhusbandly behavior (irrationally suspecting his wife of adultery). The system's effort to equilibrate itself is not always successful; as in *Othello,* a "runaway" occurs when counterbalancing forces inadvertently escalate rather than modulate each other.

The forces that lead patterns to reproduce themselves in new relationships, in new families, and within members of families also operate in the clinical context. Thus, patterns of abuse and neglect are reproduced in therapy, even within the mind of the therapist. This opens the door to the possibility of intervening effectively from within.

THE NEED TO ENTER PATTERNS
TO CHANGE THEM

To intervene with respect to the patient, one needs to adopt the guise of one of the figures in the relevant complex. Otherwise, one is like a modern character wandering ghostlike through a scene in *Othello* trying to communicate with one of the characters in the play. One can speak to Othello only in the voice of one of the other characters, eventually only in the voice of Iago. In this respect, therapy is like that show, *Quantum Leap,* in which the hero inhabits a different character in each episode in order to affect whatever drama that character is involved in. (Assessment is more like Captain Kirk, on *Star Trek,* trying to discern what an uncharted world is all about.)

A family came in with the presenting problem of a twelve-year-old girl, Tracy, not coming home after school. The social worker determined that Tracy waited every day until her father was home from work before she would come home herself, because her stepmother was very strict and would hit Tracy if she were disobedient. The father hit her too, on occasion, but Tracy felt he had a right to hit her, while the stepmother, in her mind, had no such right. The social worker explained to the parents that while hitting Tracy was not technically abuse under the relevant state guidelines (because there were no bruises), still it was not a good idea. The social worker explained that Tracy did not accept the stepmother as an administrator of corporal punishment, so the hitting had a different meaning.

The social worker's understanding of the family issue was fairly sophisticated, but the parents did not respond. The stepmother continued to hit the girl from time to time, and the father continued to support his wife. The family may not have had a way to assimilate into its process the words of the social worker because they were uttered in a way foreign to their mode of interaction. It would be like trying to make a move in a chess match between two other people by rolling dice beside the board: it is an irrelevant move in an irrelevant game. A therapist had some luck with this family by beginning his consultation with them by acknowledging that this was the girl who was causing all the trouble, and then asking the father if the therapist had his permission to slap her if she got out of line during the session. The ensuing discussion of the reasons a stranger would not be allowed to hit her led to a productive conversation about whether the stepmother was more like the therapist or more like the father in terms of her rights to hit Tracy. Admittedly, any surprise the therapist pulled on them might have gotten their attention, but I do think because he was speaking from one of the roles in the drama (that of an adult capable of hitting Tracy), it was easier for them to hear him.

The importance of intervening *within* the client system, as opposed to intervening *on* it, was brought home to me the very first time I was on call for emergencies, while working at a college counseling center. I was awakened at two in the morning and told that I was to go to the infirmary and speak with a young woman who had just been raped on campus. In a panic, I called my supervisor, waking him up, and briefly described the situation on the phone. "What do I do?" I asked. "Don't rape her," he said. It is shocking at first to think that someone as well-intended as I was, without any possibility of even touching this client, could commit the psychological equivalent of rape. But of course that was precisely the risk. If I had tried to meet my own needs, which at the time centered on being seen as an effective therapist, by violating her boundaries in pursuit of clinical material, I would be committing a (mild, legal, forgivable) form of rape. Recognizing my potential to reenact a rape with her, it was then relatively easy to avoid doing so, concentrating our conversation not on the details of what happened to her, but instead on the availability of and mode of accessing her social supports.

One way of looking at the psychoanalytic concept of transference is that the patient, by attributing to the analyst some of the characteristics of a figure in his own drama, thereby gives the therapist a chance to inhabit the relevant role in a manner meaningfully different from the original inhabitant. Thus, a sexual abuse victim who sexualizes her relationship with her therapist allows the therapist to be a different kind of parent from the one who abused her. If she does not sexualize the relationship, the therapist can still be a different kind of parent, but not to the same daughter who was sexually abused. The sexualization of the therapy is based on a kernel of truth, rather than manufactured by the patient from whole cloth. The patient will seize upon some (typically mild, legal, forgivable) breach by the therapist on which to hang her agenda. For example, the therapist may accidentally express a degree of curiosity about the patient's sex life that goes slightly beyond what is called for by the circumstances. When this happens, the therapist is still in a position to behave remedially; now, instead of being a different kind of parent, he can be a different kind of perpetrator. Instead of denying that he was inappropriately curious, he can take responsibility for what he has done, apologize, and take steps to ensure that it will not happen again; in other words, he can do all the things that the original perpetrator should have done.

THE RISK OF REPLICATION

The reenactment of abusive and neglectful patterns in the clinical setting gives the therapist an opportunity to intervene adroitly and effectively. However, sometimes abusive patterns are merely replicated in the child welfare system, rather than manifested and used as an opportunity for intervention. Perhaps the most obvious examples involve blaming treatment failures on patients. This is analogous to blaming family dysfunction on the children. It can become ludicrous, as for example when the therapist is hired to help a girl with truancy, and then reports that the treatment failed because she did not attend the sessions. Surely, implicit in the therapist's taking the case is an agreement to treat nonattendance. More subtle than blaming treatment failure on the presenting problem is blaming it on the patient's personality, but it amounts to the same thing. Other examples of repeating abusive patterns in therapy have already been alluded to. For instance, the therapist who goes too far and asks a sexual abuse victim the details of a date with an age-appropriate partner reenacts the role of a perpetrator.

The role of the mother who is asleep in the other room is reenacted in therapy as well. A sixteen-year-old boy was in residential care for sex offender treatment. He had abused his little brother in their mother's home. Over a year after treatment began, his therapist was asked about progress on his offending, and the therapist replied that it had not come up yet. The therapist was parroting some psychoanalytic ideas, in which the patient's unconscious timing is trusted as to when the patient is ready. However, that psychoanalytic view must be accompanied by an extraordinary sensitivity, which was missing in this case. The analyst who waits for the patient to bring up the material does not wait for it to come up explicitly, but looks for and underscores metaphorical allusions to the experience in the patient's behavior, narratives, and dreams. The therapist who does not detect and interpret this material as metaphorical references to sexual offending is as blind to the offending, relatively speaking, as was the patient's mother. The mother did not notice the younger brother's fear of the patient and did not communicate enough strength to the younger brother to make him feel safe enough to disclose. By the same token, the therapist did not notice her own fears of the patient, and did not communicate enough strength to herself to lead the frightened part of her to "disclose" what was going on in the therapy. If the therapist had listened more carefully, more wakefully, to what it felt like to be in the room with this fellow, she probably would have found plenty of offender material to discuss.

A major reenactment of dysfunctional family patterns occurs in therapy when the clinician treats the child as a need-satisfying object. Abuse and neglect typically boil down to a failure in empathy, a failure on the adult's part to see the child as she really is, a full-fledged separate person. Instead, the adult sees the child as a stage prop in his own drama. When the story is solely about the adult, abuse and neglect can seem justified ("I deserve a day off" or "I'll give you something to whine about"). The professional inadvertently re-creates this position by treating the child as an extension of the professional's own agenda. For example, the professional may need to see himself as the only one who really cares for the child, or as the only one who really knows what is best for her. Usually, the clinician adopts this stance not because he is narcissistically impaired—i.e., not because he is incapable of empathy—but because frustration over the bleak prognosis makes him focus on other professionals as standing in the child's way, instead of focusing on the complexity and hopelessness of the situation. Whatever his motivation, though, he keeps the child in the role of a ping-pong ball if he asserts his special understanding of her, or a conviction that the other professionals are motivated primarily by money, politics, or apathy.

Inadvertent reenactment of an abusive pattern also occurs when a child is made to feel safer in foster care, at home, or in therapy than she really is. Children do develop psychological defenses against the vulnerability to abuse. These include, as noted in Part II, idealization of the parents, avoidance of intimacy, dissociation, and hypervigilance. An important function of these psychological strategies is to protect the child, not necessarily from abuse and neglect, but from being surprised by and being emotionally vulnerable to a recurrence. If the child is again abused or neglected, at least she is not also tricked, betrayed, and disappointed. When professionals offer assurances of safety or permanence that they cannot or do not fulfill, they undermine her defenses. This is especially a concern in therapy. The clinician creates an illusion of protection and safety in his office; the girl relaxes and then has to face an unsafe world. The clinician creates a sense of reliable permanence, and then leaves his job, cannot arrange transportation from a new foster home, or finds he has no control over the insurance coverage and refuses to work pro bono. Or the girl is induced to disclose information that the therapist is legally obliged to report to authorities, and she loses control of her communications and their impact. In these cases, the security of therapy proves to be illusory, and its promise backfires on the patient, hardening her defenses in the future.

ASSUMING DISTASTEFUL ROLES

In families where abuse is severe, aggression gets a bad name. The normally constructive aggressive expressions—ambition, competition, guidance, discipline, assertiveness—all come to seem like variations on abuse. Victims of severe abuse make other people hesitate to correct them on any behavior, to challenge them, or to set limits. However, to avoid being aggressive with such a victim is to replicate the familial pattern, in which all the aggressive energy in the system is housed in the perpetrator. For everybody to treat the victim of abuse sweetly and kindly is no more comforting than was the nonabusing parent's passivity and failure to stand up to the abuse. Again, in choosing up roles in the child's drama, everybody wants to be the kindly, nurturant caregiver—a role that does not even exist—and nobody wants to look like the perpetrator (or the victim).

Avoidance of the aggressive role robs the clinician of the opportunity to employ techniques that might be effective. For example, caregivers rarely attempt to gain control of the reinforcers available, which might enable them to better shape the child's behavior. Yes, this would mean not feeding the child for long enough that she is actually hungry, and caregivers could then use food to strengthen desirable behaviors. One famous therapist (Milton Erickson, in Haley, 1973) induced a mother to literally sit on her disruptive son for an entire day, until they both learned that she was bigger than he was, and until he was hungry enough that he cooperated to get food. If such a technique were employed in the child welfare system today, one would expect to see a lot of hand-wringing, and possibly the clinician brought up on charges.

Aggression in its broadest sense should play a constructive role in professional relationships. The social worker, instead of tiptoeing around issues of concern to the state, should spell them out clearly and straightforwardly. Social workers soon learn from clients that excessive yielding only produces excessive pushing or excessive denial. Frank, respectful clarity is typically rewarded by clients behaving, if not appreciatively, at least without unnecessary suspicion or bullying. In therapy, an absence of aggression takes the form of not adhering to agreed-on boundaries regarding time and fees, or excessive pampering or placating during sessions. Yielding can inadvertently communicate a sense of fragility to abused clients, making them feel they are not strong enough to face difficult issues. Yielding can also inadvertently communicate a sense of fear to abusive clients, making them feel their own aggression is too powerful to be worked with.

The upshot is that clinicians and foster parents may be more committed to the role they are playing than to the child's well-being. Ironically, this is the essence of neurosis itself. It has been said that insanity is when you keep doing the same thing over and over again, expecting different results. To me, neurosis is when people in New York are trying to get to California, but they are committed to the idea of driving north. Driving north makes them feel, say, adventurous, comforted, or self-righteous, as the case may be. The fact that it does not get them any closer to California pales in comparison to the satisfaction they get from driving north. When they finally realize that they are not getting closer to the goal, they blame geography rather than themselves.

Most neurosis, of course, unfolds in a psychological rather than a physical landscape, but the principle is the same. A man who bites his nails at meetings complains that people do not follow his advice. He complains about the human landscape, in which people who bite their nails are not seen as leaders, rather than accepting the landscape as the relevant geography and acting accordingly. One also sees this, for example, in clinicians who argue with parents. These clinicians are more committed to being right than to helping patients. Their arguing produces counterarguments, missed sessions, and passive resistance. But rather than change their argumentative style, such therapists merely reconsider the diagnosis, adding "cognitively limited," "resistant," or "passive" to their conceptualization of the clients. Some antidrug programs also fit this description. The importance of self-righteously denouncing drug use is more important to them than effectively reducing the incidence of drug use. Being nice is appealing to clinicians, but this appeal must be weighed in each case against its effectiveness.

Much child abuse and neglect, like much bad therapy, can be described as the parents choosing a preference for a certain way of doing things over the child's well-being. The great lesson of psychotherapy is generally to learn the features of the landscape in which one is actually operating so that one can take appropriate steps. When therapists do not take the trouble to gear their own steps to the actual clinical landscape, it is unlikely that they will teach patients to gear themselves to the landscapes that give them trouble.

Abusive patterns are reenacted in the child welfare system itself for two main reasons. The first is that professionals who become involved with abusive and neglectful families have no place to stand with respect to some tightly constricted patterns, and assume one of the roles despite themselves. These moments should be recognized and used by the professionals to tweak the patterns they have entered, but this requires acknowledgement that one has not been entirely innocent or adroit. The second major cause of abuse patterns between professionals and families lies in the enormous power differential between them. Abuse thrives on a power differential: it creates opportunities for the abuser and deprives the victim of alternatives. Most child welfare professionals, in my experience, learn in general how easy it is to accidentally exploit the power differential between themselves and clients and take steps not to do so. But any of us is capable, for convenience, speed, money, or a feeling of power, of taking advantage of the fact that we can get away with not explaining ourselves to these clients, with not dotting every "i" and crossing every "t," knowing they are too disenfranchised to lodge an effective complaint. When we do this, we are reenacting the same kind of abuse pattern we have dedicated our professional lives to changing.

Chapter 13

Role Ambiguity
Among Service Providers

STRUCTURAL CLARITY

Problematic patterns from abusive and neglectful families are replicated in the child welfare system in the form of role ambiguity. Health and functionality are indicated when the people of a family or any system know what role they are in and stick to it (Minuchin, 1974). Jimmy Carter was a lovely guy, but carrying his own garment bag off an airplane made headlines and created anxiety in the American public. People needed him to be presidential, not lovely.

Minor departures from role clarity are usually easily remedied by behavior that makes it clear that people know what role they really are in. The family system is put into disarray when the father, because of repeated drinking episodes, has to be put to bed by the children. But if it happened only once, it could be quickly forgotten, and if it happened for some benign reason, such as physical exhaustion, it might merely be funny. Similarly, children are constantly trying on adult roles in play as a form of rehearsal.

Thus, the real problems occur when the roles are genuinely ambiguous. For example, a seven-year-old girl was responsible for baby-sitting for her one-year-old brother. This is definitely pushing the limits of what it is tolerable to expect a seven-year-old to do, but what was especially problematic was that when she became distracted by a TV show and he climbed up the bookcase and fell off and hurt himself, the parents blamed her rather than themselves. She was not merely trying on the role of a baby-sitter; she had become the responsible party. Perhaps it is not surprising that seven years later, she reported that her father had just begun to sexually molest her. She had played the role of mother in the family for such a long time that it seems almost inevitable that the role of wife would follow.

Much of what the structural school of family therapists attempts to do in relating to a family with problems is to reassert the role clarity among the members (Minuchin, 1974). These therapists ask the parent for permission before addressing a child directly, for example, as a way of reminding the family that the parents are in charge of the child and that the child's access to the outside world is supposed to be mediated by the parent.

CLINICIANS AND ATTORNEYS

Clinicians in the child welfare system are quick to spot role ambiguity in families, especially when it involves children behaving as adults and adults behaving as children. They are not so quick at spotting role ambiguity among themselves, but this is an area that deserves careful attention. It is not easy to impart a sense of role clarity to family members when the person imparting that sense is herself in an ambiguous role. Thus, I will examine various conflations of role responsibilities in the remainder of this chapter.

Both the clinician and the attorney are engaged in forms of advocacy, but these unfold in different contexts. The attorney represents the individual and advocates for her legal rights vis-à-vis the world at large. Although the attorney is authorized to offer advice on what direction the advocacy should take, ultimately the direction is determined by the client, and by only one part of the client. The attorney is not entitled to make up her own mind about the client's best interests. Instead, the verbal communications of the client are paramount and, unless the client is mentally incompetent or suggests something illegal or contrary to the initial agreement, these must be heeded (American Bar Association, 1997). Occasionally a child, or even an adult, expresses a goal that is so obviously against self-interest that it must be questioned. Even then, the attorney cannot simply steer the advocacy according to her own assessment, but must typically petition the court for a guardian to be appointed to represent the client's actual needs as opposed to expressed wishes.

The clinician has much more latitude than the attorney in regard to determining the goals of advocacy. Thus, it is perfectly legitimate for parents to consult a therapist for help in controlling their child, and for the therapist to undertake a largely different agenda, for example, to equalize a power imbalance in the marital system that the therapist thinks the child's conduct is designed to divert attention from. The therapist is probably not under an ethical or professional obligation to explain what she is up to, although some schools of therapy may suggest she do so.

Of course, other schools suggest she keep the true agenda to herself, for several reasons. In the typical therapeutic problem, nothing but the clients themselves is stopping them from achieving their stated goal. There must then be hidden reasons why they do not achieve what they say they want to achieve. Making the cost of obtaining their conscious goals explicit might just enhance the family's resistance.

Therapists also dislike disclosing their agenda because conscious advocacy on the therapist's part awakens an equilibrating resistance on clients' parts. The system, in other words, only appears to be out of balance at any time, and it adjusts to the injection of the therapist's agenda with an equal and offsetting force. Therapists schooled in systems theory generally prefer to arrange for the client to work in the desired direction, slowly overcoming the therapist, rather than having the therapist working in the desired direction and trying to overcome the client.

Therapists are also reticent about goals because open discussion of them can lead to endless theoretical debates and arguments about the link between, say, the power management in the marriage and the child's misconduct. The sessions can become psychology courses instead of therapy, with the aim of convincing the clients rather than changing them.

Finally, therapists find that clients have become invested in their symptomatic behavior, and explicit advice about giving up the symptoms leads nowhere. A client is a bit like an unpublished writer who has undertaken to amass the world's largest collection of rejection slips, simply to prove to his friends that he has tried every conceivable publisher and that it is not his fault that his work does not sell. He comes to therapy not for advice on how to get published, but for advice on what to do with all his cherished rejection slips, which have become so numerous that they are interfering with his living arrangements. The therapist will not get very far telling him to just throw them away.

By and large, however, most therapists ally with the client's conscious goal or work toward reframing that goal in collaboration with the client. The couple with the power imbalance will generally become more invested in working on their power differential if they see its connection to their child's misbehavior than if it seems irrelevant (Bordin, 1979). Even when the clinician and the clients are on the same page as to goals, however, the clinician is under no obligation to advocate for the express goals as opposed to the implied or unexpressed goals. Thus, a woman comes in complaining of headaches. She is fed up with being dominated by her husband, but she also feels it is not her place to criticize him. The therapist is under no obligation to provide biofeedback or relaxation exercises to help her with her headaches only. Instead, the therapist is entitled to link the headaches to something such as, say, boredom, and to suggest that the woman obtain gainful employment outside of the home to relieve this boredom. The therapist need not disclose his secret understanding that the employment will either remedy the power imbalance or exacerbate it until it ends. The woman must be fully apprised of likely outcomes only if there is reason to believe the husband's dominance could turn violent. As long as health is defined in reasonable, noncontroversial terms, the therapist can pursue his own vision of the client's health, where the attorney must, if she takes the case, defer to the client's vision of things (as long as the client's agenda is within legal and ethical bounds).

The clinician advocates for one part of a system against other parts. Intrapsychically, the clinician may advocate for what Horney (1950) calls the real self, or for what in pop psychology is called the inner child, vis-à-vis other aspects of the person's psychology. A boy who has been severely neglected presents with a serious depression. The therapist may elect to advocate for the boy's childish needs against the family's need for him to be superficially mature beyond his years, and against his own psychic efforts to keep himself in line. The boy may state, "I want to be better behaved," and the therapist can work with him, legitimately, on not being so rough on himself.

Problems arise when clinicians and attorneys get their roles mixed up. It is beyond the scope of this discussion to consider at length the problems that arise when attorneys act like therapists. Suffice it to say that the client who deserves and tries to employ an effective and zealous advocate for expressed wishes and legal rights loses that advocate when the attorney devotes herself to some other agenda. The problem is compounded because the client not only loses his lawyer, but the position remains filled and the client cannot then get a new lawyer.

Problems also arise, of course, when clinicians act like attorneys. Instead of framing a clinical problem and working on it, clinicians in the child welfare system are sometimes given to framing a legal problem and advocating for a solution. A woman comes to a clinic and begins her first session by saying that the Department of Social Services has her children in foster care. DSS told her that to get them back, she must comply with her service plan. One of the tasks on the service plan is to come for therapy. "I want to get custody of my children" is not a proper goal of therapy, although "I want to be a better mother" is.

Psychotherapeutic work on the mother's parenting skills implies an exploration of her psychological complexes. If the parenting skill in question is not at all a psychological one—if the mother thinks she could be a better mother purely by learning about nutrition, for example—then it is not the therapist's job to teach her nutrition, but to refer her to a nutrition educator or to explore with her what is keeping her from accessing the information.

One of the main influences on clinicians that leads them to choose legal goals instead of psychological goals in working with clients is the role it puts the clinician in. Legal goals tend to cast the clinician in a heroic light—righting a perceived wrong—while psychological goals put the therapist in a challenging or, at best, neutral role. Legal goals create a ready alliance, because legal goals typically imply that the problem is with some external person or institution. Psychological goals tend to create an ambivalent alliance, since they typically imply that the problem is in the client.

The therapist should, it seems to me, see if he can find a goal of mutual interest that is relevant to the mother's desire to regain custody of her children. He should look for psychological reasons why she lost custody, and determine whether a change in that psychology could be effected. For example, a therapeutic agenda relevant to custody might involve the mother's judgment in choosing the men she dates, the mother's ambivalence about expressing modulated aggression to control a child, or the mother's anxiety that arises when things go smoothly, which she alleviates through misconduct.

These kinds of goals are stymied when the clinician does not even take the first step of casting the problem in psychological terms. In fairness, however, many clinicians do attempt to frame a psychological goal, but are thwarted by the mother's statement that, for example, the reason the children are in foster care is that an untrue accusation of child molesting was leveled against her boyfriend. This formulation resists psychologizing. Under these circumstances, the clinician is tempted to stop doing therapy and instead to investigate the accusation. This is not a therapeutic task. There are times, of course, when no therapeutic task can be undertaken until factual issues of who did what to whom are resolved.

CLINICIANS AND SOCIAL WORKERS

Not all overlaps of roles are problematic. There is no reason to limit each function in a system to one and only one figure or member. Thus, for example, older siblings can set limits on and take responsibility for feeding a younger sibling without creating role ambiguity, because these functions are provided primarily by the parents. Similarly, there is a great deal of overlap between the clinician's role and the state social worker's role that is not problematic. Such overlaps include all the aspects of professional conduct designed to improve the parenting skills in the family and the functioning of the system as a whole. The social worker does not trespass on the clinician's exclusive domain when he asks the parent to refrain from an immediate disciplinary response, and to speculate on what reasons the child may have for misbehaving. Conversely, the clinician does not trespass on the social worker's exclusive domain when she suggests a specific after-school program for one of the children in the family. However, there are other areas in which the clinician creates role ambiguity in the provider system by engaging in functions that do lie in the social worker's exclusive domain.

Three aspects of the social worker's job are especially subject to trespass by clinicians. These include the investigation of accusations, making decisions properly made by the child's custodian, and making decisions about case direction. Although all three functions are off-limits to therapists, the three areas themselves overlap, so that once a therapist finds herself operating within one of these forbidden spheres, she often trespasses on the others as well.

It is rare in psychotherapy practice to conduct an independent investigation of the facts presented to the therapist. If the presenting problem is recovery from sexual abuse, for example, the therapist almost always accepts, even if only conditionally, the patient's version of what happened, and works within that version. Sometimes the therapist brings up alternative explanations of what transpired and may even question the accuracy of the patient's recollections, but it is rare that an investigation extrinsic to the therapy is appropriate. This is largely because the therapy relationship arises out of an agreement between the therapist and the patient; it is only the patient who suffers when the facts are not reported accurately in the therapy.

Sometimes, when there is more than one person in the client system, as in family therapy, it makes sense to explore at least to some extent what actually happened. However, here, too, the greatest value clinically is usually derived from working over the conflicting stories and their implications for the parties' relationships to one another, rather than from conducting an investigation into the truth of what occurred. Rare is the instance even in family therapy where the therapist states, in effect, "X is the case; let us proceed." Instead, the therapist is much more likely to suggest to family members that their assertions that X is or is not the case has certain consequences with respect to family functioning that they need to understand and to take into account.

If the daughter says the father molested her and the father says he did not, and if the daughter is still vulnerable to the father because of her age or the living arrangements, then it can be important even in a strictly therapeutic context to determine if she was molested. But the therapist must be extremely cautious in approaching this factual question for several reasons. The therapist is not trained to conduct a factual investigation. The therapist very likely lacks access to all the relevant evidence. And the therapist-as-investigator may lose any chance of maintaining a therapeutic alliance with whichever party is disappointed by the results. The therapy is likely to be better served by an announcement that the therapeutic work cannot go further until the factual question is resolved than if the therapist attempts to resolve the factual question herself.

Even if the therapist determines that abuse did happen, she needs to keep this "fact" contextualized by the therapeutic goals. Thus, the therapist may announce, for example, that given her determination that the abuse did happen, the therapy can go no further until the parent acknowledges it. Alternatively, the therapist may in effect declare that given a determination that no abuse occurred, the therapy will be stalled until the parent stops taking the accusation so personally or until the parent, for example, starts expressing curiosity about the accusation instead of defending himself.

Ambiguity between the clinical function and a social work investigation tends to be most destructive, in my experience, when the therapist is further saddled with ambiguity about whom she is working for. Typically, she has a relationship with a referral source within DSS to protect, either on her own behalf or on behalf of a clinic for which she works. She may be getting paid by Medicaid or some other third party, which may have its own agenda, particularly relative to the length of care. If she identifies her primary client as the parent or as the family, she may be induced to work toward keeping the family together, even if this is ill-advised. If she identifies her client as the child, she may promote an agenda of protecting the child even when a neutral observer would send the child home. Under these circumstances, it is natural for the therapist to pick as the client the party whose choice is most conducive to furthering her personal agenda. It is not hard to diagnose therapists as either genuinely systemic, parent-blaming, child-blaming, or system-blaming.

One therapist wrote of a woman who whipped her son with a belt: "Mother was overwhelmed by the child's uncontrollable behaviors and as a result she was induced to use an extreme means of discipline." In other words, the child made her do it. Another child blamer wrote, "The daughter manipulates the system by refusing to benefit from the mother's extraordinary parenting skills." At the other end of the blame spectrum, one clinician wrote, "The mother projects her own unconscious hostility onto the daughter. For example, after [Peggy] borrowed her mother's jacket without asking permission, the mother accused her of forcibly stealing it." Actually, the mother had reported that Peggy had "ripped off" her jacket, but the clinician did not know this idiom for theft, and thought the mother was concocting a forcible robbery.

System blamers, as noted in Chapter 4, pick on DSS to ventilate their frustration with bleak prognoses. One psychiatrist said that the only thing standing between a particular child and a "healthy adjustment" was DSS's refusal to follow his advice, which amounted to putting her in a mental institution. A lawyer told a homeless woman who had never held a job that the cause of her children's problems was DSS's inability to provide suitable foster care for her children.

In one case, the Department of Social Services referred a family to a therapist, having determined that the mother, Ms. Field, was unfit to raise her son, but also that the child's dependence on his mother was such that an open adoption would be required. (An open adoption is one in which the biological parent retains some rights, usually to visit once or twice a year, to receive information about and pictures of the child, and to exchange presents with the child.) In this case, the trial had not yet been held, so involving the mother and son with a mental health professional ran the risk that the therapist would disagree with the adoption plan and testify for the parent. Thus, the state social worker clearly informed the therapist of the conditions of the work, namely, that the parent's fitness was not open to debate. In the past, Ms. Field would function better after prolonged absences from the son, whereupon the son would be returned to her care, only to be abused again. The therapist agreed to the conditions and also agreed that the goal of the therapy was to facilitate mother and son's transition from one kind of relationship to another. The plan was to obtain the mother's whole-hearted approval of the adoptive plan, in order to reduce loyalty and identity binds that might develop in the new family.

After a few sessions, the therapist determined on her own initiative that Ms. Field was not unfit. This therapist was not merely balking at the idea of getting close to these people and then playing a part in separating them. And she was not the sort of clinician who always supports the mother and almost never recommends adoption, regardless of what may be in the child's best interest. (There are several such therapists in the child welfare system, and quite a few judges as well, in my experience. These therapists should be identified and used only for families that should be reunified. These judges flagrantly ignore the law they have sworn to apply, but little can be done about them.) Neither was this therapist the type who overestimates her clinical acumen, believing that her assessment is superior to the Department's. In this case, the therapist seemed to be making a good-faith effort to resolve a potent ethical dilemma. Observing the mother responding adequately to the child, and observing the mother in a state of relative quiescence with respect to her own psychological problems, the therapist could not blindly continue on a course that depended on the assumption of unfitness. Instead, the therapist began to work on improving the mother's relationship with the son.

Probably a better solution than working on reunification surreptitiously and in opposition to the Department would have been to consult with her client about what direction the therapy should take. The problem, though, was that there was no client to consult with. When a builder sees that the plan does not fit the landscape, she informs the owner/client and lets him decide what course to pursue. But if the house is commissioned by one party, paid for by a second, designed for a third, and occupied by a fourth, it is hard to know whom to call.

This therapist should have convened a meeting either to convince the Department to revisit the issue of fitness, or to be convinced. If neither moved from their positions, she could have resigned from the case. (The normal course of action, to stick with therapy and avoid muddling her role, was not an option in this case, in which the whole point of therapy depended on the adoption plan.) However, to advocate for a change of case direction while in the role of therapist was to create a role ambiguity that was bound to have bad repercussions. For one thing, the unfit mother and the troubled boy now had no one to help them make the prescribed transition. The therapist had increased rather than reduced the boy's confusion about why his mother could not care for him, because the therapist could not understand this either. For another thing, even if Ms. Field were fit, she and her son now had no one to help them resolve their network of mutual misunderstandings, frustrations, and disappointment, since the therapist had now cast herself into a social casework role rather than into a clinical role.

CLINICIANS AND CUSTODIANS

Overlap between the clinical role and that of custodian also occurs quite frequently. Most therapists are able to avoid making parental decisions when the custodian is a natural parent. If you take your child to a therapist to discuss, say, the child's nightmares, it is very unlikely, when you show up an hour later to retrieve your child, that the therapist will tell you that she has decided not to let you see the child because he might find it too upsetting. Nor are you likely to arrive only to be told that the child is not there because the therapist decided to let him spend the night at someone else's house. And yet these kinds of custodial decisions are often made by therapists when the custodian is the state social worker. Again, the major problem that arises from this overlap is that the child loses a therapist and cannot replace her, because the position remains filled even if the functions are not.

Much of what is helpful about most kinds of therapy is that they are conducted in a "play space" in which expressions of emotion, intention, or desire do not lead to immediate action or to untested consequences. A man can explore his philandering fantasies with his therapist without wrecking his marriage or his social status. A child can tell her therapist that she is afraid of her father, and can examine that fear without concern that she will lose her father in actuality as a result. (The exception is when the law, valuing physical protection of the child over the advantages of confidentiality, requires the therapist to trespass on the social worker's functions. These "mandated reporter" laws are a good idea on balance, but they still have some undesirable effects stemming from the role ambiguity they require.) When the therapist starts making custodial decisions, that insulation around the therapy, which makes therapy a good place to work over conflicted emotions and wishes, is destroyed.

Role ambiguity between clinicians and custodians also raises problems with informed consent. Often therapists are unable to, or resent the need to, explain their understanding of the problem and of the treatment to the parents, when they treat the child. In most circumstances, however, the therapist is compelled to provide some sort of rationale for the proposed treatment or else the parent will not agree to it. Our explanations of the potential benefits of treatment, and the reasons for undergoing it, must be especially articulate when the client is paying out of pocket, since the parent then has to agree that the treatment is worth not only the trouble but the expense as well.

When the custodian is a social worker, the therapist is even more disinclined than usual to explain what she is doing. For one thing, the therapist may experience the social worker not as a custodian of the child but as a lower-status professional. Seeking the custodian's informed consent by articulating a rationale for the proposed treatment can undermine the therapist's self-perception as being of higher status in professional circles than the social worker. More often, the therapist is merely responding to the fact that the social worker is the custodian of the child only ex officio. The social worker does not have the kind of emotional investment in the child that a parent would have. From the therapist's point of view, it is as if the role of parent were unfilled. The resulting vacuum creates a temptation for the therapist to fill it herself by making custodial decisions. She does this when she and her colleagues and supervisors make treatment decisions without obtaining approval of the custodian.

In these cases, the two main concerns are the structural ambiguities between the two professionals and a lack of scrutiny over the treatment. The former concern derives from the general understanding that when a child has two parent figures, it is bad for the child if they are in disagreement about important decisions (Goldstein, Freud, and Solnit, 1979). One good parent frequently defers to another, recognizing that it is more important for the child to sense that the parents are a team acting in concert than it is for the child to get the absolutely best decision on any given problem. Thus, divorce court judges wisely resist shared custody except when the parents demonstrate an ability to collaborate, since children are better off with parental clarity than with parental equality.

Usually this kind of disagreement and conflict resolution, for children in state custody, occurs within the child protective service itself. There are several levels of decision makers on any case, and they work to stay on the same page, so that the child does not have to experience a lot of ambivalence within the custodial system. Having achieved this, the last thing they need is for a therapist to come along who acts like a custodian with her own point of view. Further, unlike the father and mother in the traditional family, the therapist has few bonds with the child protective agency, making it even more difficult to resolve conflicts. The solution is to remind the therapist that she is providing a clinical service at the discretion of the custodians, and not at her own discretion. If she does not understand the importance of maintaining role boundaries, how can she help someone else learn to live in a family?

The second concern is that the therapist does not have anyone who must approve of the treatment plan. Any therapist will benefit from having an adult to whom she must explain her treatment decisions. The process of developing the rationale is itself salutary, clarifying the therapist's thinking and raising ideas about alternative courses to pursue. When the therapist is not accountable to anyone for making progress, she will be tempted to redefine whatever has happened as a kind of progress. In most therapies, the patient or, if the patient is a child, his parents, are motivated to question the treatment if progress is not evident. I think every therapist has an obligation either to document progress or to provide a rationale for why things are going so slowly. (When progress is elusive, there are two kinds of therapists: those who blame the patient by upgrading the diagnosis, and those who try something new.) When a child is involved in a therapy for which there is no custodial voice to whom the therapist must be accountable, it is very easy for the therapy to drift. It is said (Minuchin, 1974) that to conduct a successful therapy, you have to involve the person who wants to change, the person who has to change, and the person who can change. If all three are found in one person, then individual therapy can succeed. I would add to the characters necessary for success in therapy some involvement with the person who insists on change.

Chapter 14

The Social Worker and the Family

HOW THE FAMILY ACCOMMODATES THE SOCIAL WORKER

Long-standing or prominent patterns of child maltreatment typically lead to the involvement of the state's child protection authorities. This authority is administered by an agency of various names across the different states, but is ultimately represented in family patterns in the person of a social worker. This chapter will examine the ways the figure of the social worker is accommodated by different family patterns.

The relationship between the parent and the state social worker is extremely complex. Even when handled adroitly, it can produce confusing role ambiguities, especially when the social worker has acted to protect the parent's children. The very involvement is a usurpation of the parental role. Even when required by circumstances, the assumption of the parental functions by the social worker produces the typical effects of role ambiguity. The children sense a fissure in the authority system, and misbehave. Their misbehavior can be construed as an exploitation of that fissure or alternatively as a move on the system's part that demands that the fissure be mended. Indeed, children's misbehavior often leads to adult reconsideration of the authority structure.

STRUCTURAL AMBIGUITY BETWEEN SOCIAL WORKER AND PARENT

Even though the state social worker's presence in the family by definition creates role ambiguities, these can be minimized. Minimizing the sense of usurpation can also soothe a parent's ruffled feelings and reduce the chances of a belligerent or even violent response. Parental violence toward social workers is always a concern. People are more likely to be violent when they are made to feel powerless in an area of their lives that is central to a sense of sex-role adequacy (Wolowitz, 1971). The presence of the social worker in the family is ipso facto a slap in the face to the traditional mother's sense of herself as a good parent and to the traditional father's sense of himself as having dominion over his home.

THE SOCIAL WORKER'S RATIONALE

One way to minimize role ambiguity is to ensure that the social worker is clear and explicit about the rationale for his presence in the family. The rationale for the state's involvement in a family's private matters can be quite slippery, as it becomes conflated with emotional, legal, and moral issues on the part of the family as well as on the part of the state social workers. In spite of considerable on-the-job training and supervision, the social worker's understanding of his involvement in a family may be amorphous, which makes it all the more susceptible to becoming assimilated by the family pattern that occasioned the involvement.

Without a clear rationale justifying the state's involvement with a family, the social worker's own rationale is likely to degenerate into a question of rescuing innocent children from bad people. When the people from whom the child needs to be rescued are obviously not bad, the social worker has no place to stand with respect to the family pattern. The most common examples occur with the parents who for one reason or another are objects of pity: the disabled father with post-traumatic stress disorder following service in Vietnam; the recovering alcoholic man whose drinking got him into an automobile accident that damaged areas of his brain; the schizophrenic woman who was raped by a hospital attendant; or the battered woman who spent most of her time and energy worrying about the next beating. When the actual parents do not fit the social worker's preferred construction, he may accept the pattern's attempt to define him either as the next abuser in a long line of them, or as the next ineffective helper. If he thinks of removing the children, he becomes even in his own mind an unfeeling authoritarian bureaucrat. If he "works with" the family, he feels better about his role, but the months and years slip away while the children deteriorate. Without a clear rationale, then, state social workers (and judges) perpetuate the system by becoming absorbed in the pattern.

A good rationale will emphasize the fact that each child's relationship to our culture is primarily mediated by the parents. But independent of the parents, each child also has a relationship with the government. This relationship is almost invisible unless the parent fails to meet the child's educational or physical needs as defined by the government. The social worker's entry into the family goes more smoothly when there is no pretense that our way of doing things is superior to the family's in an absolute sense; the relativity of our culture's position should be emphasized (Agathonos-Georgopoulou, 1992; Mejiuni, 1991; Collier et al., 1999).

I consulted on a case involving some Cambodian families who participated in the custom of coining, a traditional remedy. I do not pretend to understand much about this practice, except to say that it does leave abrasions on children's arms. I do not think one needs to be apologetic about informing Cambodian families that the practice is not acceptable in the United States. It need not be much different from telling the English that they cannot drive on the left side of the road while they are here. Of course we believe that our cultural rules are better for children and for society than the cultural rules we repudiate. I hope we have not carried our sensitivity to human diversity to the point where we seriously question whether binding girls' feet, for example, is a good idea. However, asserting this belief in the superiority of our own cultural norms only leads to arguments, anger, and defensiveness.

CULTURAL RELATIVISM
AND THE CHILD WELFARE SYSTEM

Adopting a relativistic, nonjudgmental stance enables us to more effectively impose our cultural standards on American families, too. It avoids the question of how many families are required to constitute a culture. For example, there may be a network of related people who regularly engage in father-daughter incest. What makes their claim of engaging in a cultural practice less valid than the claim of Cambodians with coining? Is it duration? I suspect that father-daughter incest is older than coining, even older than coins. Is it breadth? I suspect that father-daughter incest is more widespread than coining. Is it that coining is associated with a geographical center? There are towns in Massachusetts where the incidence of sexual abuse is so high that it could be said to constitute a local custom. The practice can be forbidden independent of its reasons, even though the reasons will be relevant to understanding and changing the practice, and to decisions about the children's welfare.

Thus, our culture can prohibit abrading the flesh of children regardless of the parent's motivation. Motivation is relevant to the decision about whether to remove children from the home because it is relevant to the likelihood of the parent discontinuing the practice, and motivation is even more relevant to assessing the extent to which the entire relationship between parent and child is embedded in a context of sadism. Thus, the American parent who burns his child's arm is extremely likely to be someone who should not be allowed around children. The Cambodian parent who burns his child's arm may well provide healthy parenting, as defined in our culture, outside of this conduct. A converse analogy would involve the parent who cuts off part of his child's penis. If this is done as part of the ritual of circumcision, it is much less likely to reflect on parenting in other situations than if it is done in anger.

The state social worker can approach the family as a kind of cultural cop, whose job it is to ensure that within the wide latitude granted to parents in our culture around decisions about how to raise their children, there are no transgressions into areas deemed unacceptable in our culture. One major study that to my knowledge has never been done, but which would bolster a state's legitimacy in entering people's homes, is to determine what is and what is not culturally acceptable child-rearing practice within each jurisdiction. We do not have good data on how normative many forms of punishment are, nor on how horrified, or blasé, most people are in reaction to various practices. Partly to maintain our legitimacy, and partly to sustain our working alliance with parents, we want to avoid the situation in which the state is self-righteously condemning behavior that is practiced by the majority or by a respectable minority. Professionals at meetings sometimes discuss alcohol use, marijuana use, soft-core pornography, and spankings as if these are entirely foreign to the

American way of life ("I am shocked, shocked to find that gambling is going on in here" [Epstein, Epstein, and Koch, 1942]). If a normative study is ever done, one would also want to exercise caution in distinguishing middle-class norms from poverty norms (Drake and Pandey, 1996). Certainly it seems okay for middle-class people to impose their values on poor people, just as we impose our values on, say, Cambodians. For example, DSS routinely expects even poor parents to transport children to medical appointments, provide suitable nutrition, and arrange for after-school supervision. But it is important to be clear that that is what we are doing, rather than to make poor parents feel unnecessarily defensive. And it is even more important that if we do it, we do it as a conscious decision, and not because we ignore the special stresses and privations of poverty.

The state recapitulates, rather than disrupts, abusive patterns when it adopts a punitive stance toward parents. Children should not be taken from their parents as a punishment for parental misconduct. For one thing, this response grossly misconstrues the parents' reasons for engaging in bad behavior. Even the most evil-seeming parent usually has not made a cynical decision to exploit children. Of course, there may be other good reasons to punish people who treat children badly (not in the child welfare system but in the criminal system). These reasons for criminal sanctions may include isolating the person from contact with children, deterring a vigilante response by other relatives, and venting the outrage of the community.

Another reason not to adopt a punitive stance in the child welfare system, as opposed to the criminal system, is that some parents, even those who have severely abused or neglected their kids, do not seem to inspire punishment. Their children will not be protected by the state if protection is offered only on condition that the parents deserve punishment. The weakest, most piteous parents, though just as incompetent and unfit to raise children as the most wicked parents, may be supported by the courts and the child welfare system simply because they are so helpless. One feels heroic removing children from a family of sadists, but not from a deaf mental patient. I sometimes wonder what will happen if one day the state social worker goes to court and tells the judge that the children were in a home where both parents were found deceased in their bed. Will the judge ask why the state is picking on these people who, through no fault of their own, are merely trying to do the best job they know how? There is no joy in taking away the children of someone who arouses compassion.

The incompetent but piteous parent is a special case of the larger proposition that social workers and judges should evaluate how good a parent the parent is, not how good a client. Some parents become angry at the state's intrusion, even when it was warranted, but especially when it turns out that the report of abuse or neglect was unfounded. These people may be perfectly good parents, but they make lousy clients, because they are irritable and noncompliant. More common are parents whose ability is misjudged, not because they are competent and noncompliant, but because they are compliant and incompetent. Social workers are reluctant to assume custody of children whose parents are pleasant. When I ask what progress has been made by these parents, I am told that the parent has attended every parenting group, has always been home when the social worker expected to meet with her, and has called before cancelling any scheduled visit. This parent is being evaluated on a measure of compliance, not competence (Atkinson and Butler, 1996). If one could program good parenting in a step-by-step manual, as one might program a computer, then compliance and good intentions might be sufficient. But in the complex area of parenting, compliance is not competence. One fears that the worst parent in the world could get her kids back if she would only shower on the day of her court hearing, wear clean clothes, and speak demurely to the judge.

LEVELS OF PARENTAL FITNESS
AND THE SOCIAL WORKER'S APPROACH
TO THE FAMILY

Role ambiguities between social workers and parents are exacerbated by the dual responsibilities of social workers: on one hand, they are supposed to keep families together; on the other, they are supposed to protect children. Since social workers usually get involved with families only when children are not safe at home, these dual responsibilities are often in conflict. The social worker has to switch between being there to help the parents and being there to monitor the parents. Strategically, it can be useful to divide the supportive and protective roles between two DSS staff members. For example, the social worker can work to keep the family together while the supervisor takes responsibility for protecting the children. (This only works, of course, if they do it as a strategy, and not out of sheer disagreement.) Even when the social worker plays both roles, role ambiguities between the social worker and the parents can usually be minimized by clarifying the current level of parental fitness. The issue is whether the family is operating above or below the standard that defines the state's interest in asserting children's rights to care and protection against the parents' rights to control their families privately.

Basically, there are three levels of parental fitness that dictate three different kinds of relationships with state social workers. The highest level is the normal presumption of parental fitness. The lowest level involves a determination by the state, first by the child protective service and then by the court, that the parents are currently unfit to raise their children. The intermediate level involves a sense of overall fitness, but with at least one area of behavior that is problematic enough to justify the state's unwanted intervention. For example, a family on the whole meets the children's needs, but the parents occasionally hit the children and leave bruises. The specific conduct is unacceptable, but the parents are not unfit overall, according to the protective service or to the court.

The highest level can be labeled voluntary cases, in that the family has the right to terminate its involvement with the state whenever it wants, or it became involved with the state only by choice. The second level can be called protective cases, since the justification for the involvement is to protect the children from abuse or neglect. The third level can be referred to as custodial cases, because the state has assumed custody of the children against the parents' will.

When the parents desire to give custody to the state, because of homelessness, say, or because the child exhibits profound psychological or physical problems, the social worker's relationship to the parent is more like the voluntary paradigm than the custodial. The child in question may be at serious risk because of her own behavior, but the posture of the state is not one of protecting her from her own parents. These cases may also involve rebellious adolescents. They are rarely construed as unfitness cases, because the issue is usually that nobody wants the child, and seeing the parents as unfit is pointless.

VOLUNTARY CASES

In voluntary cases, the social worker will find that his work goes more smoothly when he does not trespass on parental prerogatives. His mission in these cases, to improve the family functioning, will be facilitated by his role clarity, because he will avoid putting the parents in a defensive position. Furthermore, enhancing rather than diminishing the authority of the parents over the children will strengthen the parents in the family system. Children's misbehavior is less likely to occur under the auspices of a strong authority. The exception to this general rule is when the parental authority is too strong. Then it becomes like a dictatorship, provoking a rebellious response. However, a strong authority stance, reinforced by the social worker's respectful attitude, usually helps keep the parents sanguine about their role in the family, reducing their need to constantly prove their power over the children and thereby reducing the incidence of rebellious responses. A contented, confident authority structure is also one that emits discipline in a fair and judicious manner, and one that minimizes the children's sense that there are loopholes to exploit.

The social worker's respectful attitude toward parental authority is also likely to help with neglect cases. Often, neglect occurs when parents do not recognize that it is solely up to them to provide the care and protection that their children require. Enhancing their authority within the family does add some risk that they will make occasional bad decisions and not have to answer for them, such as leaving children alone who are too young. This is offset, however, by the enhancement in family functioning that stems from the parents' recognition that they are the last and usually the only line in their children's defense against abuse and neglect.

The social worker communicates respect for parental authority in various ways. He articulates the rationale for his involvement with the family. The articulation is itself beneficial, since it implies a respectful enough attitude to care that the parents understand what is going on. This explanation need not touch on his potential for usurping the parental role, but instead focuses on the extent to which services can be made available to the parents to assist them. With voluntary cases, the social worker becomes a broker of services, whose primary job is to keep the parents informed of their rights and expectations with regard to the mental health, social service, and school systems.

In more detailed ways, the social worker should constantly remain aware of the nature of his supporting role in voluntary cases. Offhand remarks about what the parent should be doing, for example, can corrode the working relationship with the parent in a voluntary case. There is no need for the social worker to set himself up as a kind of superauthority over the parent. The social worker may be in a role analogous to that of a grandparent. He may have better understanding and better skills in the parenting area than the parent herself does, but his job is to enhance the parent's sense of primacy in the child's world rather than to replace her. This is not always easy for social workers or for grandparents to do, because where they should see parents, social workers may see clients, and grandparents may see only their own children. Still, both must make an effort to change their perceptions of the adult, and to respond to her according to her parental role.

One famous formulation of psychological change (Haley, 1973) holds that while hypnosis can be useful, the problem for which people seek change often stems from the fact that the person has already been, in effect, hypnotized. Hypnotists know that waking someone up from hypnosis is not a simple matter of snapping fingers, but involves a whole set of responses including a change in posture, raising the tenor and volume of the voice, turning on lights, and in every way relating to the subject as being in a social encounter and no longer in a hypnotic encounter. Conversely, hypnotizing a subject involves not only waving a pendulum or a light, for example, but a whole host of ancillary behaviors that are designed to put the subject in the role of "hypnotizee" rather than in the social role. Parents involved in the child welfare system are hypnotized, as it were, into believing that they have no power in their families, that their children are uncontrollable, and that nothing they do matters. Both the therapist and the social worker can combat these self-fulfilling perceptions by treating the parents as competent, effective, and caring. The complementary role, which one hopes parents will eventually assume, is projected in the social worker's respectful tone of voice and deferential attitude.

Incidentally, every social worker and therapist involved in the child welfare system must decide how to answer the question of whether he or she has children. I have witnessed some outrageous, if rare, injustices perpetrated on parents in the child welfare system, but on the whole I have seen little that irritates parents more than being told how to raise children by someone who they believe has never tried it. On the other hand, even if one has children of one's own, one does not want to be reduced to speaking from personal experience rather than from a professional point of view. Therefore, there are good reasons for both disclosure and nondisclosure.

My own preference would be to use the nonparent status, if it comes up, to boost the parent's sense of authority and worthiness of respect, and for the professionals who have children to minimize how bad it can make these parents feel to be confronted with somebody who is presumably more successful at raising children than they are. The childless professional can make it clear that he is not there to tell the parents how to raise children, but instead is there to keep the parents apprised of the rules in the state governing child rearing, what the parents need to accomplish to satisfy those rules, and what the consequences are of various actions the parents might take. In other words, he is not there as an expert in parenting but as a guide to the landscape of the child welfare system. I think it is helpful for the professional who happens to have children to adopt pretty much the same role. He might suggest that with his own children he has been fortunate, noting perhaps his advantages in resources, his better neighborhood, and some luck in the children he happened to get. If the professional's own children are not doing well, then his approach on this issue will vary case by case, depending on the reasons they are not doing so well, and depending on the specific family he is serving. The main thing is to learn from his own experiences, rather than merely to impose his concept of his own family onto other families to justify his own parenting.

PROTECTIVE CASES

The role of guide through the child welfare system is central to the relationship between the social worker and the parent in protective cases. Here, the social worker must be careful not to make threats, but must be as clear as possible what outcomes will follow from different behaviors of the parent. The general approach is still to enhance the parent's overall authority with respect to the child. This, beyond any ethical or legal reasons, dictates that the parent should be fully and honestly informed. An ethical dilemma occurs fairly predictably under the following conditions. The social worker, for the good of the child, prolongs the stay in foster care or induces the parent to participate in family therapy, even though the parent could assert her rights in court and avoid the state's agenda. When the parent does not realize the strength of her legal position, the social worker has to choose between keeping her fully informed and inducing her participation in services by playing on the parent's belief that she has no choice. The Department is rarely able to keep a case open against the parent's wishes when the only protective issue has been, for example, minor corporal discipline.

Typically, I would resolve this dilemma by keeping the parent informed in voluntary and most protective cases, while inducing her participation when the child's welfare is at risk enough to put the state on the verge of seeking custody. The child benefits from having an informed, strong parent, but may also benefit from services the parent would refuse. The important thing in weighing risks against benefits is to be sure that one is weighing the child's risks and benefits, and not the social worker's or the parent's.

I think it is best if the social worker is explicit about the role ambiguity created by the report of child abuse or neglect. The social worker can acknowledge that the parental authority has been ruptured, even if only briefly, even if only around a single issue. He can ally with the parent around restoring that parental authority. It may be good in the abstract for the children to have a number they can call to protect themselves from abuse and neglect, but it is almost inevitable that the children will exploit this power vis-à-vis the parents, so that parents are stymied in asserting their authority over their children. The parent sends the child to her room and the child reaches for the phone. Pretending there is no downside to the state's intrusion on the family does not help with this dilemma.

With more hostile clients, the alliance hangs on the mutual goal of getting the Department out of the family. The social worker notes that the family does not want him there and that he does not want to be there. He explains what must happen for them both to get their wish. Depending on the seriousness of the abuse or neglect that got the family involved with the child protective service, the requirements might be as minimal as promising not to strike the child again or to leave the child home alone. They may be as extensive as participating in various evaluations and therapies, or mastering developmental tasks such as empathy and self-control.

CUSTODIAL CASES

In custodial cases, the social worker should be explicit about the fact that the parents have been found, at least temporarily, by the Department and by the appropriate court, to be unfit to provide care and protection for their own children. This fact can be potentially devastating for parents' self-esteem. Nonetheless, it is more destructive in the long run to hide it than to assert it. The difficulty with hiding it is that even though it may make conditions more pleasant in the short run, it promotes role ambiguities, confuses the issues, and deflects the focus from the parents' need to change. If it makes the social worker feel better, he can also tell parents that the finding of unfitness does not mean that they are bad people, but only that they have let their parenting responsibilities slip.

The social worker's attitude should be one of reluctant duty. He should make it clear that in his opinion the best thing would be for the parent to make the changes necessary for a return of the children to her custody, enabling him to stop obscuring the issue of who is in charge of the family. However, his attitude should also be one of fulfilling the obligations that have been imposed on him on behalf of the children. One occasionally sees a parallel between the social worker's not wanting to hurt the parent's feelings in asserting the children's needs on one hand, and on the other, the parent's not having wanted to hurt the boyfriend's feelings in asserting the children's needs. If the social worker cannot be explicit with the parent, how can he expect the parent to be explicit with the boyfriend?

The social worker ideally writes a service plan that, if the parent adheres to it, will ensure reunification. This would allow the parent to know what is expected of her, and would bolster her energy and confidence for changing, since she would know that her effort would be rewarded. Unfortunately, it is not always possible, and almost never easy, to write such a service plan, because it is not possible to program good parenting. Parent-child interactions are too multifaceted, too ambiguous, and too context-dependent to specify beforehand what will be an adequate parental response. This is especially the case once there has been serious neglect or abuse, because, then, merely refraining from further neglect or abuse is often insufficient; the parent, to be adequate, must proactively remediate the effects of her past mistakes or misfortunes. (It is for this reason that a parent can be unfit to raise a child already in foster care, while fit to raise her new baby. The baby does not require the parent to look on her own bad works with equanimity; the baby reflects an image of a good parent, which is much easier for the parent to absorb than the foster child's reflection of a bad parent.)

Still, in general terms, the service plan should say something beyond a requirement to attend various services. It should contain a term that the parent will recognize, anticipate, and meet the child's emotional and developmental needs, that the parent will play with the child, and that the parent will tailor her behavior to signals from the child. Though still vague, these terms at least cast any disagreements between the parent and the state into the right arena. Any arguments will be about whether the parent is empathic, not whether the parent attended therapy.

The parent will complain about the quality of the foster home, bringing up its untidiness, its overcrowded conditions, or the fact that the child keeps getting injured in it. Rather than be defensive, the social worker should acknowledge that the state is not a good custodian of children, who were meant to be raised by parents. The social worker should tie the foster home conditions to the parent's motivation to change, so that he can advocate fully for reunification. A deplorable foster home is the state's way of letting the parent know how little is expected of her; she only has to do better than the foster home. In actuality, a mediocre foster home helps convince the parent that it is best to regain custody. A lovely foster home fills the parent with self-doubt.

The social worker must be careful to reorganize his relationship with the parent once the parent has regained a minimal level of fitness. The parent must once again be empowered to make decisions about the child, especially once the child is physically returned to the parental home. Role ambiguity skyrockets when children are placed with their parents but custody remains with the social worker. Sometimes, the split custody situation is unavoidable, usually because a judge believes that going slowly and giving only some custody is better than giving all. Actually, it is more conservative of our way of life for custody to be fully in the daily caregiver and daily decision maker. Legal custody should follow physical custody. The social worker should explain, once custody is returned to the parent, that custodial decisions are now the parent's. For example, whether a neighbor is an appropriate caretaker after school is again the parent's call. Of course, if the social worker has reason to believe that selecting a particular individual as a baby-sitter will result in renewed state intervention, he should communicate this to the parent. But even then, it is important to make the tone of the communication not an edict, but a question: "Is it a good idea to hire a baby-sitter with a reputation as a child molester?" When the parent appears to be on the verge of making a bad decision, the caution should be similar to what a social worker would say to a new client, namely, that it is up to her, but she should know what his response will be. The social worker here is in the position of the parent of a nineteen-year-old. The child still needs the advice of the older, wiser adult, but the child nonetheless must make her own decisions, and the authority's speech must reflect that acknowledgment.

The same considerations of shifting parental empowerment apply to preadoptive parents. Social workers, therapists, and judges get used to making all sorts of decisions about children. This is fine, as long as custody is in the state, but once custody is in the adoptive parents, it behooves the professionals to reorient themselves dramatically to the parents' new status. Thus, one wants to avoid a situation, say, whether to continue the child's play therapy, in which the adoptive parents are entrusted with the child but not with the decision to terminate treatment. Similarly, deciding the amount of contact with biological parents after adoption should, as much as possible, be entrusted to the adoptive parents and not to judges (*Adoption of Vito,* 1999, and other opinions by judges notwithstanding). Over and over again, the lesson is that, except when parents are unfit, children are better off with strong parents and their occasional wrong decisions than with weak parents and decisions by committee or by judges and social workers (Goldstein, Freud, and Solnit, 1979).

Chapter 15

The State Social Worker in the Role of Parenting Conscience

THE IGNORING PARENT

Parents relate to the state social worker as they relate to their internal parenting conscience, in other words, to the part of themselves that knows better than to abuse or neglect children. The mother who dashed out of the bathroom while her one-year-old was in the tub to answer the phone, for example, had an attitude toward her parenting conscience that might be summarized as, "You're right, but I'm going to do it anyway because the risk seems low." The same woman let her older child, an eight-year-old girl, stay up late on a regular basis. "I know I shouldn't, but." The case came into the child welfare system when a neighbor reported her for letting the older child baby-sit the infant. The mother's attitude toward the part of her that knew better was reflected in her relationship with the social worker. She was pleasant and agreeable at all times, and then ignored the social worker's suggestions.

THE RESIGNED PARENT

A different example involves a parent, Mr. Morton, who felt antagonized and oppressed by his knowledge that he was not living up to his responsibilities as a parent. The inner tension caused him much distress, and he tended to externalize it. When he looked at his children, instead of seeing them for what they were, he saw a silent accusation aimed at his failings as a parent. His reaction was to isolate himself in the basement of the home with his tool bench and his television, where he did not feel so guilty. His eleven-year-old son, Eric, was sexually abused by a cousin. Subsequently, Eric attempted to hang himself, but the light fixture to which he tied his bathrobe belt tore from the ceiling when he jumped off the chair. Mr. Morton reacted to the state social worker the same way he reacted to his internal parenting conscience and to his children: he presented an ashamed, remorseful attitude, while looking forward to being alone again. "Maybe Eric should go into a program, somewhere," he said.

It was not that clear whether Mr. Morton should have known that his nephew was a sexual perpetrator. I think that if it did occur to him—to his parenting conscience—that the nephew was a bit odd, then Mr. Morton's response was one of sad helplessness: "there's nothing I can do about it anyway." When I met him, I was trying to preserve Eric's placement in the family, rather than institutionalize the boy, but I needed some sign from Mr. Morton that he would take responsibility for keeping Eric from killing himself, at least on the weekends while Eric's mother was at work. Mr. Morton gave me the same face he gave the social worker. He should have done better; it is his fault, but what can he do? He cannot watch the child twenty-four hours a day as they could in a program.

I explained that twenty-four-hour supervision is a myth. Even the tightest suicide watches in hospitals check the patient only four or five times an hour. Supervision in residential programs is typically provided by people making close to minimum wage. Instead, I said, trying to involve Eric, one cannot rely on twenty-four-hour supervision, but one can rely on the child's sense of fair play. I did not think it was right to hold Mr. Morton fully accountable for the sex abuse, I said, because he was not aware that there had been anything to prevent. Same with the suicide attempt, I said; at the time, Mr. Morton did not know that Eric was suicidal. Eric did not give his father a fair chance to prevent it, I said.

I suggested playing a game in my office. Eric would try to destroy my Kleenex box, which I placed on the floor near the center of the room, while Mr. Morton would try to keep him from doing so. I was up to a lot of things at once. I was trying to suggest to Eric that future suicide attempts be accompanied by fair warning. I was trying to demonstrate to Mr. Morton that in my role as a parental authority I was not accusing him of anything, to try to change his relationship to his internal parenting conscience. And I was trying to see if Mr. Morton could protect Eric from his destructive impulses. The way they were positioned, it would have been easy for Mr. Morton to get to Eric before Eric got to the Kleenex box. Mr. Morton was a big man who could have stopped Eric with one finger. But just as I was about to start the contest, Mr. Morton said he had a bad back (which was not at all evident from his gait or posture), which would prevent him from protecting the tissue box. I stopped the contest, because I did not want Eric to have to see the Kleenex box being destroyed. I recommended that Eric be placed in a residential program on the weekends. You might think such a placement would be easy enough to arrange, with all the beds empty on the weekends while children are visiting their parents, but in fact, that kind of flexibility was not available, and Eric had to be institutionalized on a full-time basis.

THE REBELLIOUS PARENT

A more successful intervention between parent and parenting conscience was achieved with Ms. Vine. She reacted to her parenting conscience like an explosive teenage girl. She knew perfectly well, for example, that she should not bring men home for the night while her three children were with her, but she did so anyway, in a defiant manner. She would cook and clean usually, but if she realized that she *should* cook or clean, she would refuse. When school personnel tried to talk to her about truancy, she would yell at them, and when the state social worker came by, she threatened him. "If you try and take my kids, I'll kill you."

I saw Ms. Vine and her children in front of the one-way mirror. This is an arrangement that allows a team of cotherapists to observe the sessions, with the clients' permission, of course. From behind the mirror, the team can provide hands-on supervision and consultation, phone in suggestions, and respond creatively to the family system. We had been experimenting at that time with different ways of making clinical use of the arrangement of having two therapeutic figures, the one in the room and the team behind the mirror. We used this structure to reflect the dual goals that most of our families faced with respect to the child welfare system, namely, the goals of child protection and reunification. We found that clients understood these twin goals more easily, as did we, by dividing them between the therapists. The therapist in the room was supportive of the parents and worked toward reunification, while the team behind the mirror was responsible for monitoring the situation for child protective issues. As noted in Chapter 14, the same division of responsibilities is available within the child protective service, if the social worker takes on the supportive role and the supervisor or administrator becomes the skeptical representative of the state interest in protecting children.

With Ms. Vine, we went a step further. We used the relationship between the team and the therapist in the room as a model for the relationship between her parenting conscience and herself. Thus, the overt agenda for the therapy was to discuss with the family the way each member individually and all in collaboration used anger and flight to avoid feelings of sadness. The covert agenda was to demonstrate a different way of resolving tensions between a parenting conscience and a parent. We addressed this covert agenda by having the team call in, over the loudspeaker, to criticize my therapeutic technique on a regular basis. At first, I would respond to these comments as Ms. Vine did to her inner suggestions, in other words, irritably and rebelliously, declaring that I had been doing therapy a long time and did not need the team telling me what to do. Then, I would do the opposite of what the team suggested. For example, at one point, Ms. Vine was reflecting quietly on the way her marriage did not work out as she had thought it would when she was getting married. The team phoned in that it was important to let Ms. Vine continue to reminisce on this sadness in her life. I snarled back at them that she was not ready for this, and changed the subject to the children's truancy and their morning routines.

It is a common family therapy technique to tell clients they are not yet ready for change (Watzlawick, Weakland, and Fisch, 1974; Selvini Palazzoli et al., 1978). The technique, similar to others presented previously, conceptualizes the family therapy as a system itself and not merely an approach to the family's system. Within the therapy system, the therapist's press for change constellates resistance from the rest of the therapy system, i.e., from the family. When the therapist presses for keeping things the same, the desire for change appears in the family. The ideal outcome has the family leaving, changed, feeling they could have done it a lot sooner if not for their sluggish therapist.

These systemic considerations are particularly relevant to the issue of a parenting conscience. When the social worker or the therapist identifies with the parenting conscience, the parent remains in the reciprocal role. A simplified example has the social worker telling the parent, "You should keep better track of your kids." The parent responds by thinking to herself, "But sometimes they are out of control." If the social worker says, on the other hand, "It's hard to keep track of such active children," the parent may respond by thinking, "They should at least let me know where they're going."

Over the course of a few sessions with the Vine family, I "worked out" my relationship with the supervisors behind the mirror. We stuck with this approach partly because my conversations with the squawk box in the room seemed to captivate the attention of Ms. Vine and her three children. Whenever our exchanges began, the family would settle down and watch, as if we were an interesting television show. The team eventually told me on the loudspeaker that they did not think they were better therapists than I, but that they had an advantage being behind the mirror and not so emotionally involved. Ultimately, the team agreed that their good ideas were sometimes presented poorly. They began to apologize if they found themselves giving me a directive, and rewording it as a suggestion. In the first session, for example, the team called in to say, "Michael, ask Sally [one of the children] about the divorce." Later, they called in to say, "Dr. Karson, we're thinking the kids may have something to say on this subject. What do you think?" I stopped addressing Ms. Vine by her first name and started calling her "Mom." Soon, the team merely buzzed me, and we spoke privately on the phone, demonstrating my elevated status.

Meanwhile, in terms of the overt agenda, I was pressing as the main therapeutic goal that every family member should be where they belong when they belong there. With the presenting problems of truancy and breaking curfew, this goal was designed to block the family's reliance on flight to cope with distress. I tried to dissuade the family from paying so much attention to content and suggested attending more to location. If one of the children got in trouble at school, I would compli-

ment her for having been in school at all. At one point, one of the girls
wanted to leave the therapy room to go to the bathroom, so we spent
part of the session discussing whether this was a breach of the location agreement. Ms. Vine was put in charge of this discussion and was
also authorized to make the final decision. She decided that going to
the bathroom was like staying home sick and not like truancy.

A key interaction took place after about a month of treatment. One
of the girls, Sally, told us how much she hated another girl at school.
It turned out that this hatred was based on an embarrassing incident,
in which Sally was left out of a social experience. Sally's brother and
sister began to tease her about this embarrassment. I pointed out that
brother and sister were operating very much in the time-honored family tradition of provoking anger or flight to help family members
avoid sadness. As if on cue, Sally jumped up to run out of the room.
Ms. Vine called out to Sally in a firm, no-nonsense voice to sit down
and finish the conversation. Afterward, with the children out of the
room, the team and I both congratulated Ms. Vine on keeping all the
family members together during a difficult moment. She shrugged
and said that the rule was that nobody leaves the room. Her new attitude toward rules seemed too recent to threaten it by pointing out that
only a month earlier, she herself would have broken any such rule just
on principle. Shortly after this incident, I began to see the family
without the team, largely, I admit, because the team is a costly resource, with several therapists working for a single hourly fee, but
also to model for her the idea that a parent figure can so internalize
the supervisory conscience as to be able to function alone.

There are some other implications of the idea that parents relate to
social workers and clinicians as they relate to their own parenting
consciences. One of these is that the clinician, armed with this proposition, must not rely on it excessively to condemn parents who are antagonistic to state intervention. Good data simply do not exist on how
most people would react if the state intruded on their parental authority and threatened to remove their children. State social workers and
therapists should constantly review their techniques for the possibility of being unnecessarily intrusive or accidentally disrespectful of
clients, rather than being too quick too attribute problems to the client's personality. People in authority have a tendency to misinterpret
misconduct as willful or pathological. This can lead to a misdiagnosis

of annoying conduct, and it can also produce misdiagnosis of quiet, passive, or depressive forms of psychopathology as well-adjusted. In the same way that a residential treatment facility, or even a public school, prefers a depressed kid, who does not make trouble, over an angry kid, who does, state social workers can inadvertently prefer passive, compliant clients who happen to be bad parents over antagonistic clients who happen to be good parents.

Parallels between the state agency and the parenting conscience operate when parents engage in problematic behaviors in front of social workers. This is usually a very clear sign from parents that, even when they are on their guard, alert and conscientious, they are not able to control the behavior in question. A parent who hits her child during a supervised visit has angry impulses that are not cowed by the parenting conscience. The flip side of this inference is that there is usually some hope if the parent is able at least to control his or her conduct in the presence of the state agency. The goal would then be to build on those moments to the point of behaving well even when the professional is not present. Whether good behavior in the social worker's presence constitutes enough hope to warrant maintaining a goal of reunification depends of course on the totality of factors in the case, including the child's age, the degree of psychological involvement with the parent, the egregiousness of the parent's past misconduct, the likelihood of its being repeated, and the assessment of the child's reasonably realistic alternatives.

Chapter 16

When All Else Fails

Ideally, we need not consider what to do when all else fails. Ideally, problems are identified early, sensible treatment plans are developed, and these plans are modified if proved ineffective. But in reality, it is often the case that child welfare professionals must resort to some default option in the event that no available services have helped and the problems have persisted or grown worse.

With respect to parents, if all else fails, if "everything" is tried and nothing works, we decide whether their standard of care and protection is something the state can countenance in its concern for the children. If not, the children are primarily raised elsewhere. As noted in Chapter 14, if the parenting, though bad, is not so deplorable as to warrant permanent removal of the children, then not only should the children be returned, but the child welfare system should reorient itself from a skeptical to a supportive role.

THE MYTH THAT ALL CHILDREN ARE TREATABLE

What outcome is appropriate when all else fails with children? The child welfare system's current bottom line has not been well thought out. In theory, at least as the system would have it, all children can be helped by some program or some therapy currently available. It is not clear that anyone actually believes this, but many feel they must act as if every child can be helped (Graziano and Mills, 1992). In practice, when all else fails, the final option is either residential treatment or running away. The practice derives from the theory, because as long as the judiciary and the legislature insist what every experienced social worker and clinician knows is untrue—namely, that every child is treatable—then children are never let be until they turn eighteen. Untreatable juveniles, unrelentingly subjected to social services, blow out of foster homes and "less restrictive" placements, so that eventually they either run away or they are placed in a residential facility.

Many residential facilities are clean, humane places. Many are staffed with talented and experienced clinicians. But even the best of them provide clinician contact with children only sporadically, and most of the child's time is spent in the company of people making nearly minimum wage, suggesting relatively little training and raising the worrisome possibility that if they are not in this field for the money, sex or power may be motivating them. Further, rhetoric aside, the residential facility is a jail as far as the child is concerned. It is where children who misbehave are sent. Children who behave well do not get sent there. Children leave residential facilities when their conduct conforms to expectations. The more "restrictive" the placement, the more intense its treatment is considered to be. Thus, as untreatable children demonstrate that they are untreatable, they bump down the staircase of restrictiveness—from kinship care to foster care to specialized foster care to group homes to residential facilities. Children could escape from this staircase, but only if it is accepted either that they cannot be treated, or that "restrictiveness" does not equate to intensity of treatment. It is sobering to think that placement in our residential institutions constitutes the harshest toll our society can legally exact from children for noncriminal conduct.

I put "restrictive" in quotes, because like its close relative, the "structured setting," it is hard to tell exactly what it means. A well-run family, most families in fact, are safer and better organized than any residential program. When a girl is raped while in foster care, the social worker is blamed for not putting her in a more structured setting. When she is raped in residential treatment, the social worker is told he did all he could. It is all the same to the girl.

Residential treatment facilities should specialize—no program can be all things to all children. But even once specialized, they need to tailor their behavioral regimens to the needs of the individual child. Any program that has a predetermined system of levels and privileges becomes a Procrustean bed that can suit the particular child only serendipitously if at all. Residential programs should be better integrated with follow-up services. Their goals should never be to address deep psychopathology, but rather to address excessive reactivity and to teach the child how to survive in the community. Still, under current policy, even the best residential facility imaginable would become the last resort for children who do not respond to treatment.

Why should institutionalization be the last resort for children who have committed no crimes, are not dangerous, and are not mentally ill? I would choose instead between two other options for a placement of last resort: either emancipation or residential treatment with teeth. Declaring a child, even a fifteen-year-old, even some fourteen-year-olds, I dare say, but certainly a sixteen-year-old, to be an adult would free the child from a lot of the authority struggles that interfere with his or her adjustment. Emancipation would force the adolescent to bargain for his right to a foster bed or to anything else. I think emancipation would work roughly like expulsion from school— often effective with willful children, ill advised with the severely disabled (*Virginia Department of Education v. Riley,* 1997).

The problem with power struggles with teenagers is that they have so little to lose that, at least with adolescents who have also lost their families and their self-respect, they are fearless in combat and will almost always win. Unless they do something egregious, they cannot be criminally incarcerated, and they have little property to seize. State regulations govern how they are treated in facilities, and prevent them from going hungry or from facing other privations that might otherwise motivate them. Adolescents' combination of having a safety net and little else makes them extremely difficult to coerce into treatment.

DOMINION OVER THE SELF

When adolescents insist on calling their own shots, it is a good idea to acknowledge their power and to treat them as much as possible like adults. For normal children, I sometimes imagine a ceremony when a child reaches eighteen or twenty-two or even twenty-five, in which the privileges of adulthood would be conferred in exchange for relinquishing the right to whine about one's childhood or to use psychological excuses for misbehavior. With children in the child welfare system, parental auspices are absent, and they have to grow up quickly. For DSS children, I imagine a brief ceremony and a firm handshake, while service providers express their condolences that the child never had much of a childhood, but express hope instead that adulthood will be more kind.

Growing up can itself be construed as a process of acquiring dominion over property and over one's own body. In infancy, the person is herself someone's property, for all intents and purposes. Some families never develop beyond that stage, and treat their children very much as if they were pets, houseplants, or, in some cases, dolls. One sees this especially when a child has been living with, say, a preadoptive family for a long time and then an absent parent returns, wanting his property back as if the child were not now a member of a new family. One also sees it when a substance abuser plans, for example, to enter a twelve-month program and wants to put her one-year-old child in foster care for the year, as if the child could be freeze-dried and thawed out when the program ended.

Normally, as children grow, their status changes from that of property to that of owner. The family must balance the parent's interest in the child's well-being against the child's increasing interest in dominion over her body and over her things. Problems occur when the parent misjudges the balance. If the parent overvalues the child's autonomy rights, neglect may ensue, as with the parent who never fed her child vegetables, even as an infant, because she did not seem to like them, and the parent wanted to respect the child's preferences.

Abuse can occur when the parent interprets the child's conduct as if it were coming from an older child, a child the same age as the autonomy rights accorded. One woman hit her son for calling her a bad name, but he was only eighteen months old at the time. Although bad at age grading, this mother was "good" at recognizing her son's independence and autonomy.

When autonomy needs are undervalued, the parents are overprotective. Trouble can develop when the child has to fight to establish her autonomy and privacy rights. One woman, for example, insisted that her son, even at age thirteen, not lock the bathroom door while he bathed or used the toilet. She was worried that he would slip or have some other accident, that he would scream, and that she would not be able to get to him. Naturally, he asserted his privacy rights in other ways, mainly by sustaining such a barrage of hostility toward her that she left him alone as much as she dared.

EMANCIPATION AS A STRATEGY

There is no set timetable for acquisition of ownership of one's own body and possessions, but most people would recognize such milestones as dominion over one's genitals (after about three years, nobody should touch your genitals but you), one's room (after a child is old enough to be left alone, one should knock before entering), and one's money (once in adolescence, the child need not consult with the parent on spending pocket money). Most parents retain some control over the child, even into early adulthood, by imposing conditions on living in the parental home or on financial support. Adolescents in the child welfare system have lost the co-owner and condition imposer who normally reduces their proprietorship over their own bodies and possessions. At their age, they are too close to sole proprietorship to accept a surrogate co-owner. Their resulting independence should be recognized as much as possible, including by the teenager.

It can be useful to make these considerations explicit to the teenager. One can use phrases such as "lost out on childhood" and "being your own woman." A distinction can usually be drawn between acting for one's own sake and acting to have an effect on one's parents. For example, does she really like the way her hair looks or is it primarily to annoy someone else? A true adult acts for herself, not for others. The idea is to make it clear that she is in charge of her own life, within (just like everyone else) the legal parameters.

Genograms (family trees) are useful for summarizing a great deal of information about a family or a child. I would add to the standard format a list of all the people who are concerned about the child. In my experience, in the child welfare system the state social worker and the therapist are typically near the top of the list, while the parent and even the child in question are near the center. My goal as much as possible is to get the teenager herself at the top of the list of people who are worried about her.

To accomplish this, one would require extraordinary support from the child protective service, the courts, and perhaps even the press.

One would have to be able to tell the child, for example, "There is no place for you to stay tonight because of the way you are acting." Because the foster care system is seen as having an obligation to the child, the teenager can carry on like a baby. "Home is the place where, when you have to go there, they have to take you in" (Frost, 1914). For many children, that means DSS. I think it would be better for older children to be confronted with the fact that they have no home than to think DSS is their home. It would be better to lower the age of majority, for discarded children, to sixteen or even fifteen. Is that disadvantaging the very children who most need guidance and support? No, it would be recognizing that they are already disadvantaged, and proceeding from there realistically. It would be emancipation in law for those emancipated in fact.

I think the message to unparentable teens should be, if you want to take responsibility for your life and if you want to make something of it, then the state will give you a relatively clean, relatively safe place to stay while you are doing it. Systemically speaking, I want the concern for the child to be pushed back into the child or her parents, and not to be bottled up in the child welfare system. Otherwise, the system's concern constellates a carefree attitude in the child, which in turn constellates more concern in the child welfare system.

One should work *with* these older children, not work *on* them. As much as possible, they should be included in planning meetings as full participants and, within the parameters set by law and by available resources, as the decision makers. If more than one placement is available, the child should visit them before choosing. If no other choice is realistically available, the child can be informed of the degree of latitude the system can presently afford her, and she can be assured of the maximum amount of autonomy possible, if more choices arise. The social worker can explain the policies and procedures that limit the child's freedom. If their content seems arbitrary to the teenager, the social worker need merely point out that all adults have to comply with arbitrary rules, and that the social worker herself is not taking a stand on the wisdom of the rules. The child should also be told that when adults keep their noses clean, avoid trouble, and pull their weight at school or at work, their autonomy and freedom of choice generally increases.

GAINING CONTROL OVER REINFORCERS

If children are to be locked up without criminal convictions or mental illness, then it should be in an institutional facility that can actually change them, one that does not have its hands tied by misplaced pseudohumanist concerns. Many of the children I see from abusive and neglectful backgrounds simply cannot be changed unless clinicians are allowed to get control over all the relevant reinforcers. Practically speaking, given that even I do not advocate bizarre intrusions on privacy or weird social engineering, this means food and clothes. Suicidal and severely eating-disordered adolescents could not be treated under such conditions, but those children belong in the mental health system anyway, not in the child welfare system. The child's right to three square meals and attractive clothing must be weighed against the child's right to effective treatment.

A behavioral program would have to be designed for each specific child. The energy available for designing such a program, hard work at best, would be greater if the behaviorist had some reason to believe it would be implemented. Hungry children will work for food. At present, however, service providers committed to gaining control over out-of-control children are not permitted to take the necessary steps. I suppose I can offer some consolation to the humanists by noting that such a program would be devoid of punishment; all therapy in it would be based on reinforcing desirable conduct. But the reinforcement would mean something, because it would involve a resource that the child actually wanted. Thus, instead of relying on residential treatment or instead of the child running away when all else fails, I would like to see emancipation or residential treatment empowered to gain control over reinforcers, in spite of the fact that these proposed alternatives, though to my mind more realistic, are not very nice.

I have tried to weave this theme throughout this book and would like to end with it. When service providers cling to benign roles, we are not heard by abusive or neglectful families. In benign roles, we are at best righteous and at worst self-righteous, rather than being organized to create change. When we insist on being the good guys, we evoke a defensive or a balancing response from families, and we are typically ineffective. I agree that the ends do not justify the means, that unnecessarily harsh practices cannot be condoned. That is why I want to gain control of reinforcers rather than to administer punishment, and why I would reserve emancipation for adolescents who are de facto independent, who are unparentable but insulated from the natural consequences of their conduct. But while the ends may not justify the means, neither do the means justify the ends. Bad outcomes should not be applauded merely because they were produced by gentle, optimistic, and humane methods.

References

Adoption of Vito, 47 Mass.App.Ct. 349. (1999).

Agathonos-Georgopoulou, H. (1992). Cross-cultural perspectives in child abuse and neglect. *Child Abuse Review,* 1(2), 80-88.

American Bar Association. (1997). *Model rules of professional conduct.* Westbury, NY: The Foundation Press.

American Psychiatric Association. (1987). *Diagnostic and statistical manual of mental disorders,* Third edition, revised. Washington, DC: American Psychiatric Association.

American Psychiatric Association. (1994). *Diagnostic and statistical manual of mental disorders,* Fourth edition. Washington, DC: American Psychiatric Association.

Atkinson, L. and Butler, S. (1996). Court-ordered assessment: Impact of maternal noncompliance in child maltreatment cases. *Child Abuse and Neglect,* 20(3), 185-190.

Bamber, H. (1999). Interview by Terry Gross. *Fresh Air.* National Public Radio, July 8.

Barkley, R. (1998). *Attention-deficit hyperactivity disorder: A handbook for diagnosis and treatment.* New York: Guilford.

Bateson, G. (1972). *Steps to an ecology of the mind.* New York: Ballantine Books.

Beck, A. (1989). *Depression.* Philadelphia: University of Pennsylvania Press.

Blatt, E. (1990). Staff supervision and the prevention of institutional child abuse and neglect. *Journal of Child and Youth Care,* 4(6), 73-80.

Bordin, E. (1979). The generalizability of the psychoanalytic concept of the working alliance. *Psychotherapy: Theory, Research, and Practice,* 16(3), 252-260.

Bowlby, J. (1969). *Attachment and loss,* Vol. 1: *Attachment.* New York: Basic Books.

Broga, C. (1999). Foster care of adolescents. Training session of Massachusetts Approach to Partnership in Parenting, Amherst, MA.

Charrier v. Charrier, 416 Mass. 105. (1993).

Chuang-tzu (1981). The sorting which evens things out. In A.C. Graham (Ed. and Trans.), *Chuang-tzu: The inner chapters* (pp. 48-61). London: George Allen and Unwin.

Cicchetti, D. and Toth, S. (1995). A developmental psychopathology perspective on child abuse and neglect. *Journal of the American Academy of Child and Adolescent Psychiatry,* 34(5), 541-565.

Collier, A., McClure, F., Collier, J., Otto, C., and Polloi, A. (1999). Culture-specific views of child maltreatment and parenting styles in a Pacific-island community. *Child Abuse and Neglect,* 23(3), 229-244.

Crittenden, P. (1992). Children's strategies for coping with adverse home environments: An interpretation using attachment theory. *Child Abuse and Neglect,* 16(3), 329-343.

Curry, J. (1986). "Outcome studies of psychiatric hospitalization and residential treatment of youth: Conceptual and research implications." Presented at American Psychological Association Convention, Washington, DC, August 26.

Deutsch, H. (1942). Some forms of emotional disturbance and their relationship to schizophrenia. *Psychoanalytic Quarterly,* 11, 301-321.

Dollard, J. and Miller, N. (1950). *Personality and psychotherapy: An analysis in terms of learning, thinking, and culture.* New York: McGraw-Hill.

Drake, B. and Pandey, S. (1996). Understanding the relationship between neighborhood poverty and specific types of child maltreatment. *Child Abuse and Neglect,* 20(11), 1003-1018.

Dukes, R., Ullman, J., and Stein, J. (1996). Three year follow-up of Drug Abuse Resistance Education (D.A.R.E.). *Evaluation Review,* 20(1), 49-66.

Epstein, J., Epstein, P., and Koch, H. (1942). *Casablanca.* Hollywood, CA: Warner Brothers.

Exner, J. (1993). *The Rorschach: A comprehensive system,* Vol. 1, Third edition. New York: Wiley.

Freud, A. (1936). *The ego and the mechanisms of defence.* London: Hogarth.

Freud, S. (1953a). The interpretation of dreams. In J. Strachey (Ed.), *The standard edition of the complete psychological works of Sigmund Freud,* Vol. IV, pp. 1-338 and Vol. V, pp. 339-622. London: Hogarth. (Original work published 1900).

Freud, S. (1953b). The psychopathology of everyday life. In J. Strachey (Ed.), *The standard edition of the complete psychological works of Sigmund Freud,* Vol. VI, pp. 1-310. London: Hogarth. (Original work published 1901).

Frost, R. (1914). The death of the hired man. In *North of Boston.* London: David Nutt.

Goldstein, J., Freud, A., and Solnit, A. (1979). *Beyond the best interests of the child.* New York: The Free Press.

Graziano, A. and Mills, J. (1992). Treatment for abused children: When is a partial solution acceptable? *Child Abuse and Neglect,* 16(2), 217-228.

Gunderson, J. (1978). Defining the therapeutic processes in psychiatric milieus. *Psychiatry,* 41(4), 327-335.

Haley, J. (1967). *Advanced techniques of hypnosis and therapy: Selected papers of Milton H. Erickson, M.D.* New York: Grune and Stratton.

Haley, J. (1973). *Uncommon therapy.* New York: Norton.

Herman, J. (1992). *Trauma and recovery.* New York: Basic Books.

Horney, K. (1950). *Neurosis and human growth.* New York: Norton.

Jacobson, E. (1971). *Depression: Comparative studies of normal, neurotic and psychotic conditions.* New York: International Universities Press.

Janoff-Bulman, R. (1982). Esteem and control bases of blame: Adaptive strategies for victims versus observers. *Journal of Personality,* 50(2), 180-191.

Jenkins, S. and Diamond, B. (1985). Ethnicity and foster care: Census data as predictor of placement variables. *American Journal of Orthopsychiatry,* 55(2), 267-276.

Jones, D. (1991). Professional and clinical challenges to protection of children. *Child Abuse and Neglect,* 15(Suppl 1), 57-66.

Jung, C. (1926). A review of the complex theory. In *Collected Works,* Vol. 8, pp. 92-104. New York: Bolligen-Pantheon.

Jung, C. (1928). Two essays in analytical psychology. In *Collected Works,* Vol. 9, pp. 1-89. New York: Bolligen-Pantheon.

Karson, M., Karson, S., and O'Dell, J. (1997). *16PF interpretation in clinical practice: A guide to the fifth edition.* Champaign, IL: Institute for Personality and Ability Testing.

Karson, S. (1973). Some relations between parental personality factors and childhood symptomatology. *Journal of Personality Assessment,* 37(3), 249-254.

Karson, S. and Haupt, T.D. (1968). Second-order personality factors in parents of child guidance clinic patients. In R. B. Cattell (Ed.), *Progress in clinical psychology through multivariate experimental design,* 97-106. Fort Worth, TX: Society of Multivariate Experimental Psychology.

Karson, S. and O'Dell, J. (1974). Personality makeup of the American air traffic controller. *Aerospace Medicine,* 45(9), 1001-1007.

Karson, S. and O'Dell, J. (1976). *A guide to the clinical use of the 16PF.* Champaign, IL: Institute for Personality and Ability Testing.

Kelly, G. (1955). *The psychology of personal constructs.* New York: Norton.

Kernberg, O. (1975). *Borderline conditions and pathological narcissism.* New York: Jason Aronson.

Kernberg, O. (1984). *Severe personality disorders.* New Haven, CT: Yale University Press.

Kinard, E.M. (1994). Methodological issues and practical problems in conducting research on maltreated children. *Child Abuse and Neglect,* 18(8), 645-656.

Klein, M. (1948). *Contributions to psychoanalysis, 1921-1945.* London: Hogarth.

Köhler, W. (1938). *The place of value in a world of facts.* New York: Liveright.

Langs, R. (1977). *The listening process.* New York: Aronson.

Loftus, E. (1993). The reality of repressed memories. *American Psychologist,* 48(5), 518-537.

Madanes, C. (1981). *Strategic family therapy.* San Francisco: Jossey-Bass.

Madanes, C. (1990). *Sex, love, and violence.* New York: Norton.

Mahler, M., Pine, F., and Bergman, A. (1975). *The psychological birth of the human infant: Symbiosis and individuation.* New York: Basic Books.

Manzano, J., Palacio Espasa, F., and Zilkha, N. (1999). The narcissistic scenarios of parenthood. *International Journal of Psycho-Analysis,* 80(3), 465-476.

Mayman, M. (1968). Early memories and character structure. *Journal of Projective Techniques and Personality Assessment,* 32(4), 303-316.

Mayman, M. (1975). A multi-dimensional view of the Rorschach movement response. Unpublished manuscript.

Megargee, E., Cook, P., and Mendelsohn, G. (1967). The development and validation of an MMPI scale of assaultiveness in overcontrolled individuals. *Journal of Abnormal Psychology,* 72(6), 519-528.

Meichenbaum, D. (1977). *Cognitive-behavior modification: An integrative approach.* New York: Plenum.

Mejiuni, C. (1991). Educating adults against socioculturally induced abuse and neglect of children in Nigeria. *Child Abuse and Neglect,* 15(1-2), 139-145.

Minuchin, S. (1974). *Families and family therapy.* Cambridge, MA: Harvard University Press.

Morton, N. and Browne, K. (1998). Theory and observation of attachment and its relation to child maltreatment: A review. *Child Abuse and Neglect,* 22(11), 1093-1104.

Ogden, T. (1981). *Projective identification and psychotherapeutic technique.* New York: Aronson.

Powers, J., Mooney, A., and Nunno, M. (1990) Institutional abuse: A review of the literature. *Journal of Child and Youth Care,* 4(6), 81-95.

Rapaport, D., Gill, M., and Schafer, R. (1968). *Diagnostic psychological testing.* New York: International Universities Press.

Rosenbaum, D. and Hanson, G. (1998). Assessing the effects of school-based drug education: A six-year multilevel analysis of project D.A.R.E. *Journal of Research in Crime and Delinquency,* 35(4), 381-412.

Schmolling, P. (1984). Human reactions to the Nazi concentration camp: A summing up. *Journal of Human Stress,* 10(3), 108-120.

Selvini Palazzoli, M., Boscolo, L., Cecchin, G., and Prata, G. (1978). *Paradox and counterparadox.* New York: Aronson.

Skinner, B.F. (1953). *Science and human behavior.* New York: The Free Press.

Skinner, B.F. (1971). *Beyond freedom and dignity.* New York: Knopf.

Toth, S., Cicchetti, D., Macfie, J., and Emde, R. (1997). Representations of self and other in the narratives of neglected, physically abused, and sexually abused preschoolers. *Development and Psychopathology,* 9(4), 781-796.

Triumph of the Will (subtitled). International Historic Films, Chicago, 1981. Videocassette.

Twain, M. (1938). *Letters from the earth.* Greenwich, CT: Fawcett.

U.S. v. Carroll Towing Co. (1947). 159 F.2d 169 (2nd Cir.).

Virginia Department of Education v. Riley. (1997). 106 F.3d 559, 577 (4th Cir.).

[W., B.] (1953). *Twelve steps and twelve traditions.* New York: Alcoholics Anonymous Publishing.

Walker, L. (1979). *The battered woman.* New York: Harper and Row.

Watson, P., Little, T., and Biderman, M. (1992). Narcissism and parenting styles. *Psychoanalytic Psychology,* 9(2), 231-244.

Watzlawick, P., Weakland, J., and Fisch, R. (1974). *Change: Principles of problem formation and problem resolution.* New York: Norton.

Weiss, J. (1993). *How psychotherapy works: Process and technique.* New York: Guilford.

Willis, D. (1995). Psychological impact of child abuse and neglect. *Journal of Child Clinical Psychology,* 24(Suppl), 2-4.

Winnicott, D. (1960). The theory of the parent-infant relationship. *Journal of Psycho-Analysis,* 41(6), 585-595.

Wolowitz, H. (1971). Paranoia and power. *Psychiatry,* 34(4), 358-375.

Wolowitz, H. (1972) Hysterical character and feminine identity. In J. Bardwick (Ed.), *Readings on the psychology of women,* 307-313. New York: Harper and Row.

Zagumny, M. and Thompson, M. (1997). Does D.A.R.E. work? An evaluation in rural Tennessee. *Journal of Alcohol and Drug Education,* 42(2), 32-41.

Zuravin, S. and DePanfilis, D. (1997). Factors affecting foster care placement of children receiving child protective services. *Social Work Research,* 21(1), 34-42.

Zuravin, S. and Fontanella, C. (1999). The relationship between child sexual abuse and major depression among low-income women: A function of growing up experiences? *Child Maltreatment,* 4(1), 3-12.

Index

THE HAWORTH MALTREATMENT AND TRAUMA PRESS®
Robert A. Geffner, PhD
Senior Editor

IDENTIFYING CHILD MOLESTERS: PREVENTING CHILD SEXUAL ABUSE BY RECOGNIZING THE PATTERNS OF THE OFFENDERS by Carla van Dam. (2000). "The definitive work on the subject . . . . Provides parents and others with the tools to recognize when and how to intervene." *Roger W. Wolfe, MA, Co-Director, N. W. Treatment Associates, Seattle, Washington*

POLITICAL VIOLENCE AND THE PALESTINIAN FAMILY: IMPLICATIONS FOR MENTAL HEALTH AND WELL-BEING by Vivian Khamis. (2000). "A valuable book . . . a pioneering work that fills a glaring gap in the study of Palestinian society." *Elia Zureik, Professor of Sociology, Queens University, Kingston, Ontario, Canada*

STOPPING THE VIOLENCE: A GROUP MODEL TO CHANGE MEN'S ABUSIVE ATTITUDES AND BEHAVIORS by David J. Decker. (1999). "A concise and thorough manual to assist clinicians in learning the causes and dynamics of domestic violence." *Joanne Kittel, MSW, LICSW, Yachats, Oregon*

STOPPING THE VIOLENCE: A GROUP MODEL TO CHANGE MEN'S ABUSIVE ATTITUDES AND BEHAVIORS, THE CLIENT WORKBOOK by David J. Decker. (1999).

BREAKING THE SILENCE: GROUP THERAPY FOR CHILDHOOD SEXUAL ABUSE, A PRACTITIONER'S MANUAL by Judith A. Margolin. (1999). "This book is an extremely valuable and well-written resource for all therapists working with adult survivors of child sexual abuse." *Esther Deblinger, PhD, Associate Professor of Clinical Psychiatry, University of Medicine and Dentistry of New Jersey School of Osteopathic Medicine*

"I NEVER TOLD ANYONE THIS BEFORE": MANAGING THE INITIAL DISCLOSURE OF SEXUAL ABUSE RE-COLLECTIONS by Janice A. Gasker. (1999). "Discusses the elements needed to create a safe, therapeutic environment and offers the practitioner a number of useful strategies for responding appropriately to client disclosure." *Roberta G. Sands, PhD, Associate Professor, University of Pennsylvania School of Social Work*

FROM SURVIVING TO THRIVING: A THERAPIST'S GUIDE TO STAGE II RECOVERY FOR SURVIVORS OF CHILDHOOD ABUSE by Mary Bratton. (1999). "A must read for all, including survivors. Bratton takes a life-long debilitating disorder and unravels its intricacies in concise, succinct, and understandable language." *Phillip A. Whitner, PhD, Sr. Staff Counselor, University Counseling Center, The University of Toledo, Ohio*

SIBLING ABUSE TRAUMA: ASSESSMENT AND INTERVENTION STRATEGIES FOR CHILDREN, FAMILIES, AND ADULTS by John V. Caffaro and Allison Conn-Caffaro. (1998). "One area that has almost consistently been ignored in the research and writing on child maltreatment is the area of sibling abuse. This book is a welcome and required addition to the developing literature on abuse." *Judith L. Alpert, PhD, Professor of Applied Psychology, New York University*

BEARING WITNESS: VIOLENCE AND COLLECTIVE RESPONSIBILITY by Sandra L. Bloom and Michael Reichert. (1998). "A totally convincing argument. . . . Demands careful study by all elected representatives, the clergy, the mental health and medical professions, representatives of the media, and all those unwittingly involved in this repressive perpetuation and catastrophic global problem." *Harold I. Eist, MD, Past President, American Psychiatric Association*

TREATING CHILDREN WITH SEXUALLY ABUSIVE BEHAVIOR PROBLEMS: GUIDELINES FOR CHILD AND PARENT INTERVENTION by Jan Ellen Burton, Lucinda A. Rasmussen, Julie Bradshaw, Barbara J. Christopherson, and Steven C. Huke. (1998). "An extremely readable book that is well-documented and a mine of valuable 'hands on' information. . . . This is a book that all those who work with sexually abusive children or want to work with them must read." *Sharon K. Araji, PhD, Professor of Sociology, University of Alaska, Anchorage*

THE LEARNING ABOUT MYSELF (LAMS) PROGRAM FOR AT-RISK PARENTS: LEARNING FROM THE PAST—CHANGING THE FUTURE by Verna Rickard. (1998). "This program should be a part of the resource materials of every mental health professional trusted with the responsibility of working with 'at-risk' parents." *Terry King, PhD, Clinical Psychologist, Federal Bureau of Prisons, Catlettsburg, Kentucky*

THE LEARNING ABOUT MYSELF (LAMS) PROGRAM FOR AT-RISK PARENTS: HANDBOOK FOR GROUP PARTICIPANTS by Verna Rickard. (1998). "Not only is the LAMS program designed to be educational and build skills for future use, it is also fun!" *Martha Morrison Dore, PhD, Associate Professor of Social Work, Columbia University, New York, New York*

BRIDGING WORLDS: UNDERSTANDING AND FACILITATING ADOLESCENT RECOVERY FROM THE TRAUMA OF ABUSE by Joycee Kennedy and Carol McCarthy. (1998). "An extraordinary survey of the history of child neglect and abuse in America. . . . A wonderful teaching tool at the university level, but should be required reading in high schools as well." *Florabel Kinsler, PhD, BCD, LCSW, Licensed Clinical Social Worker, Los Angeles, California*

CEDAR HOUSE: A MODEL CHILD ABUSE TREATMENT PROGRAM by Bobbi Kendig with Clara Lowry. (1998). "Kendig and Lowry truly . . . realize the saying that we are our brothers' keepers. Their spirit permeates this volume, and that spirit of caring is what always makes the difference for people in painful situations." *Hershel K. Swinger, PhD, Clinical Director, Children's Institute International, Los Angeles, California*

SEXUAL, PHYSICAL, AND EMOTIONAL ABUSE IN OUT-OF-HOME CARE: PREVENTION SKILLS FOR AT-RISK CHILDREN by Toni Cavanagh Johnson and Associates. (1997). "Professionals who make dispositional decisions or who are related to out-of-home care for children could benefit from reading and following the curriculum of this book with children in placements." *Issues in Child Abuse Accusations*

Order Your Own Copy of
This Important Book for Your Personal Library!

PATTERNS OF CHILD ABUSE
How Dysfunctional Transactions Are Replicated in Individuals, Families, and the Child Welfare System

_____ in hardbound at $49.95 (ISBN: 0-7890-0739-8)

_____ in softbound at $24.95 (ISBN: 0-7890-1588-9)

COST OF BOOKS_____

OUTSIDE USA/CANADA/
MEXICO: ADD 20%_____

POSTAGE & HANDLING_____
_(US: $4.00 for first book & $1.50
for each additional book)
Outside US: $5.00 for first book
& $2.00 for each additional book)_

SUBTOTAL_____

in Canada: add 7% GST_____

STATE TAX____
_(NY, OH & MIN residents, please
add appropriate local sales tax)_

FINAL TOTAL____
_(If paying in Canadian funds,
convert using the current
exchange rate, UNESCO
coupons welcome.)_

❑ **BILL ME LATER:** ($5 service charge will be added)
(Bill-me option is good on US/Canada/Mexico orders only;
not good to jobbers, wholesalers, or subscription agencies.)

❑ Check here if billing address is different from
shipping address and attach purchase order and
billing address information.

Signature_____

❑ **PAYMENT ENCLOSED: $_____**

❑ **PLEASE CHARGE TO MY CREDIT CARD.**

❑ Visa ❑ MasterCard ❑ AmEx ❑ Discover
❑ Diner's Club ❑ Eurocard ❑ JCB

Account # _____

Exp. Date_____

Signature_____

Prices in US dollars and subject to change without notice.

NAME_____

INSTITUTION_____

ADDRESS_____

CITY_____

STATE/ZIP_____

COUNTRY_____ COUNTY (NY residents only)_____

TEL_____ FAX_____

E-MAIL_____

May we use your e-mail address for confirmations and other types of information? ❑ Yes ❑ No
We appreciate receiving your e-mail address and fax number. Haworth would like to e-mail or fax special
discount offers to you, as a preferred customer. **We will never share, rent, or exchange your e-mail address
or fax number.** We regard such actions as an invasion of your privacy.

Order From Your Local Bookstore or Directly From
The Haworth Press, Inc.
10 Alice Street, Binghamton, New York 13904-1580 • USA
TELEPHONE: 1-800-HAWORTH (1-800-429-6784) / Outside US/Canada: (607) 722-5857
FAX: 1-800-895-0582 / Outside US/Canada: (607) 722-6362
E-mail: getinfo@haworthpressinc.com
PLEASE PHOTOCOPY THIS FORM FOR YOUR PERSONAL USE.
www.HaworthPress.com

BOF00